Vasile Băncilă

An ethnic-spiritualist metaphysics banned by the
totalitarian regime

Ion Dur

Technical University of Cluj-Napoca

Preface by
Dan C. Mihăilescu

Series in Philosophy

VERNON PRESS

www.vernonpress.com

In the Americas:
Vernon Press
1000 N West Street, Suite 1200
Wilmington, Delaware, 19801
United States

In the rest of the world:
Vernon Press
C/Sancti Espiritu 17,
Malaga, 29006
Spain

Series in Philosophy

Library of Congress Control Number: 2022940185
ISBN: 978-1-64889-502-9

In eternal memory of my wife,
Doina Marieta

Table of contents

Exordium
Recovering archaeology

If for Horia Stamatu's journalism he needed to use selective archiving, for the metaphysician Vasile Băncilă Ion Dur had to accomplish a work of recuperative archaeology in order to give coherence to a wealth of projects, conspectuses, excerpts, capricious paths and centrifugal impulses. In short, he had to do this in order to bring together as systematically as possible a fragmentism that would otherwise have condemned Băncilă to enrich the string of bio-bibliographical near-misses for which Cioran decreed the curse of the 27th generation to be an achievement in failure, namely the adventures of Bucur Țincu, Petre Țuțea D. C. Amzăr, Cioran himself, Mihail Polihroniade, G. Racoveanu, Ernest Bernea, Sorin Pavel, Petru Manoliu and others.

Thanks to the selflessness of the philosopher's daughter Ileana Băncilă and the efforts of the tireless editor Dora Mezdrea, we have today a substantial series of Vasile Băncilă's Works, published by the Museum of Brăila – Istros Publishing House, as well as by the Museum of Literature Publishing House, where Ion Dur's essay Poste-restante. The "case" of the thinker Vasile Băncilă, the princeps edition of this book, was printed in 2020. After 16 volumes published out of the 32 projected, we can now understand in a well-documented way that Vasile Băncilă, formed in the spirit of the historian Nicolae Iorga and the philosopher C. Rădulescu-Motru, is situated between the metaphysician Nae Ionescu and the sociologist Dimitrie Gusti when seen from the lectern; or between Mircea Vulcănescu, Dumitru Cristian Amzăr and Anton Golopenția, when placed among his generational colleagues.

The first exciting sequence that Ion Dur's exegesis uncovers is Băncilă's undergraduate thesis, dedicated to Schopenhauer and later melted into a possible doctoral thesis on the ethics, sociology and politics of the German philosopher, with many captivating observations about his reception in Maiorescu's and Eminescu's Romania. The thread unravelled here will beneficially wrap round all the rest of this speculative energy devoted to ethno-psychology, the philosophy of culture and militant sociology, with the perspective of the Romanian Idea as a philosophical category in its own right.

Ion Dur's approach is established as a welcome counterpoint to the unfair and tendentious verdict applied in the academic treatise on Romanian philosophy by the Dumitru Ghișe, Nicolae Gogoneață team of researchers;

Vasile Băncilă, who aimed at the sapiential elevation and metaphysical accreditation of the Bărăgan Plain on the level of the undulating Blagian Mioritic space, was seen by them as stuck in the formulas of Thoughtist Orthodoxy. Yet with Wundt, Frobenius, Blaga and Motru's energetism in mind, the young philosopher practised a veritable referential bulimia and worthily studied not only Schopenhauer but also Kant, Bergson, Dilthey and Faguet.

Romanian Existence is the dense chapter that places Băncilă alongside Constantin Rădulescu-Motru, Dumitru Drăghicescu and Mihai Ralea, and the section that deconstructs Transylvania as a "differentiated ethnic psychology" is still highly topical, given that the symbiosis of the Romanian provinces, long dreamed in 1848, 1878 and 1920, is still in the dream stage. Observations on the exceptionalism of the Transylvanian region, the aristocratism of Moldavia and the ambivalence of Dobrogea are well directed inside the ambivalence of destiny, with a section reserved for binomials considered specific to the Romanian space – individualism vs. communitarianism, moralism vs. aestheticism, lyricism vs. intellectualism – but found also elsewhere, either in Europe or on other continents, not to mention on the limes between Catholicism and Protestantism. All these binomials, Ion Dur observes, "make up a spiritual harmonism with complexity, variation and dynamism"; after which he quotes Vasile Băncilă: "The Romanian people never leave the harmonious complex because they are healthy, balanced, classical, because they use culture for life and salvation, and not for show."

Ion Dur's critical discourse aims to identify in some of Vasile Băncilă's finished texts – both published and unpublished – and also in the enormous quantity of thematic worksheets, the unfinished project of a metaphysics that springs from, and rests upon both the ethnic and the spiritual. The exegete runs the risk of asserting that Vasile Băncilă's philosophical performance lies somewhere in the middle; between what the thinker gave and what he could have given, if we extend the potential vectors of his metaphysical syllogisms. Ion Dur's exegesis pleads for the inclusion of Vasile Băncilă among the names that make up the table of values of Romanian philosophy, the strong argument being the existence of a work that cannot be ignored or eluded. Through his ideas, Nae Ionescu's compatriot seems to have ensured for himself an ever contemporary posterity, through – and for – those yet to come.

Vasile Băncilă remains an important private thinker for the Romanian cultural space; an author who, isolated and rejected by the totalitarian ideology, continued to philosophize on his own in the posture of a housebound Anchorite, living and creating in an exemplary communitary solitude.

Dan C. Mihăilescu

The best metaphysics is religion,
and the noblest and ultimate function of philosophy
is to introduce one to religion: the *ancilla* of religion.

Philosophy deals with integral reality
based on the idea of the Absolute

Spirit has existed from eternity both in matter
and beyond it. Analogy with Jesus Christ incarnate;
that is why He could also be perfect as a man. This
is the only solution to the metaphysical problem.

I am not lost in matter, but in God yes. God
is the great and only sufficient reason.

Matter is *densified spirit.*

Vasile BĂNCILĂ

An atypical philosophical diary
– *starting frames* –

Metaphysics is waiting at the *poste-restante*

For history in general and for the disciplines of the human spirit in particular, it is not the future that often seems unpredictable, but the past. The value map of the latter, with its atmosphere and structure, produces surprises that please or displease those concerned with the hermeneutics of values. Since we have been talking about memories of the future, why not accept, with the same conceptual ease, some forecasts about the past!

The intellectual biography and the metaphysical-moral performance of Romanian philosopher Vasile Băncilă (1897–1979) can be best understood through this historical lens focused on the axiological pyramid of Romanian spirituality, a lens turned upon itself, tainted with egoism and envy by the *commodities experts* of Romanian culture before 1989. An occultation operation involving not only Vasile Băncilă, but also other personalities of the Right-wing culture of Greater Romania.

Vasile Băncilă's work is waiting in the *poste-restante* (French: *poste-restante*). I don't know how many people still send letters to the poste-restante today, especially since there are fewer and fewer senders of messages who still use pen, pencil and paper. *E-mail* is, perhaps rightly, the dominant *medium* for a number of reasons – speed, efficiency, convenience, even the discretion that the poste-restante mechanism implies. Except when e-mail doesn't help at all (or merely serves as notification) – i.e., when someone has to send a parcel somewhere.

Changing what needs to be changed, I could say that the relationship between the authentic critic and the author is similar to that between the sender and the recipient in the case of the poste-restante service. However, instead of letters, we have writings, and the recipient – the one who is fit to read them – is unnamed (perhaps known only by reputation), a collective proper noun that refers to those critics able to use axiological-aesthetic criteria in order to decipher the meanings and significances of a text. *The more, the better* for the possible polysemy of a writing. From the average of critically applied angles and variously drawn conclusions the reasonable moral and aesthetic truth (even the *metaphorical* truth, as Paul Ricoeur would say) of a work or – generically speaking – of a type of discourse finally emerges.

I took this explanatory detour in order to suggest that the writings of a Romanian thinker, the philosopher Vasile Băncilă, attempted to reach their readers/critics using a poste-restante address; these were texts that awaited a favourable critical meteorology, after the fall of the totalitarian regime. After decades of freedom of expression, his work is not the only one which falls into the category of *backlog* of contemporary Romanian culture; there are restitutions or recoveries that need to be attempted in a balanced way, without prejudice, as far away as possible from the temperature radiated by the magma of politics or political correctness; received, so to speak, *sine ira et studio*, and not *cum ira et cum studio*.

*

Whoever opens the second volume of the Treatise on the history of Romanian philosophy, in the section "Thoughtist Orthodoxy", learns who Vasile Băncilă was and what he thought, from three lines to which is added a footnote visibly biased towards the totalitarian ideological context. It is said of Thoughtist metaphysics that "it was mainly represented by *Vasile Băncilă* and *Petru P. Ionescu* (who succeeded the former, after the latter stopped collaborating with *Thought* magazine) and, to a certain extent, by *Stelian Mateescu*" (Ghișe–Gogoneață, 1980, p. 682).

And in the bibliographical reference, in addition to brief information on the writings and publications to which he collaborated, it is mentioned that Băncilă broke away from the Thoughtist circle in 1938–1939, "noting that the national doctrine is being transformed into a form of 'chauvinistic imperialism', used as an instrument for various 'competitions in domestic and international politics'" (Ghișe–Gogoneață, 1980, p. 411).

It is also stated that he isolated himself from the publication *Thought*, although he was: "the main 'metaphysician' of the group" and that he "set out, in extensive attempts, to philosophically found Orthodoxy, to develop a spiritualist-theistic philosophy that would assimilate the 'attitudinal' data of the ethnic" (Ghișe–Gogoneață, 1980, p. 682).

The paragraph "Attempts to establish a spiritualist-Orthodox metaphysics" (Ghișe–Gogoneață, 1980, see pp. 704–706) of the same Treatise, where the subject of metaphysics is addressed, also invokes some of Vasile Băncilă's ideas, quoting in particular from the essay "The Spirit of Celebration" (*Thought*, no. 4, April 1936) and from the exegesis on the philosopher Lucian Blaga (*Blaga, Romanian Energy*, 1938).

In Băncilă's project of metaphysics based on the transcendent, on divinity (through the concept of *cosmism*), the following are invoked: the overabundant use of metaphors and less of concepts with heuristic force, an overemphasis on the metaphysical meaning of celebration (it is a "*summum bonum* in the world of values"), the transformation of ethnicity into the foundation of philosophy, the reduction of the role of "systematic philosophy to the updating, clarification, completion and sublimation of the 'latent and diffuse philosophy' that the people would possess, the 'intuitions and lines of peasant spirituality', of the 'peasant philosophy'".

A fundamental flaw was allegedly detected in the fact that Vasile Băncilă linked "the ethnic, some elements of the popular worldview to a religious conception", seeking to "exploit the peasantry, popular culture in favour of Orthodoxy (...), misinterpreting them [!]"

To these would be added the relation between the cosmic world of the peasant and the idea of God as the ultimate essence, both dogmatic and divine; and the perception of the peasantry as something undifferentiated, static, "outside real historical evolution".

Perhaps much more has been said about Vasile Băncilă, in different times, by Lucrețiu Pătrășcanu[1] or Dumitru Micu,[2] even if a few "biased truths" were also included.

*

Anyway, I harbour only good thoughts about this raccourci from the Treatise on the history of Romanian philosophy! For the intentions of the exegete, who thought he had formulated his ideas *à rebours*, in the "official" code of the totalitarian era, appear to us today, fortunately, as value judgments fully appropriate to Vasile Băncilă's thought. The indictments of that time are today, paradoxically, a more than politically correct plea for the truths in which the ethnic-spiritualist and personalist philosopher had always truly believed.

This represents a favourable hermeneutic turning point favoured by the installation, after 1989, of a different value climate in Romania, with different evaluation criteria and a different measure of transparency in the management of its historical and cultural past. It has thus been possible to exploit an immense archive that contains the "tremor of nerves" (Eminescu) of a "housebound Anchorite" such as Vasile Băncilă – who "belonged to the city of Brăila more than any member of Brăila's elite" (Popa, 2006, p. 7); Nae Ionescu,[3] Petre Andrei,[4] Ernest Bernea,[5] Sorin Pavel,[6] Anton Dumitriu,[7] Mihail Sebastian,[8] all imbued with the aura of a tragic destiny.

The recovery of Vasile Băncilă's philosophical-literary legacy has, above all, the support and encouragement of his daughter, Ileana Băncilă (who justifies a form of posterity in which the author believed, posterity through one's children); to this was added to this the effort of a skilful and seemingly tireless researcher – editor Dora Mezdrea, together with the understanding and help extended by the "Carol I" Museum of Brăila, the Istros Publishing House and, in equal measure, the Museum of Romanian Literature.

Some essays, perhaps the best known and most consistent,[9] were thus re-introduced into the public circuit, and printing of the *Works* began in 2003; it is estimated to comprise no less than 32 volumes (I will refer to some of them later in our analyses). With such a massive legacy, with such a deep imprint, Vasile Băncilă is unquestionably a *case in point* in our culture as a whole, and in Romanian philosophy in particular (Vlăduțescu, 2002, see pp. 110–115).

This is a special case, firstly, because of all the material written over time and through the *construction site* that opens under the eyes of the archive researcher; secondly, because of the *ideas* and *virtualities* inherent in a partially known work, one that is ambitious in its encyclopaedic tendency, but above all in its intention to build its own personally original system of philosophy.

In fact, most of the manuscript pages left by Vasile Băncilă to posterity constitute a veritable and atypical *philosophical diary* of dense opinions, judgments and syllogisms reflected in ideas and attitudes. A diary that constitutes the meta-physical testimony of a Christian thinker who finds in the Spirit, in the Great One, in God the Archimedic point and the constellation of his life-long reflections.

The philosopher Blaga[10] saw Vasile Băncilă as a threat to the spirits of high Romanian culture, N. Bagdasar[11] considered him "the most prolific creator" of his generation, and Nichifor Crainic[12] appreciated his "intellectual honesty".

Avatars of a biography

Vasile Băncilă's biological biography was extremely tense, if his not at all agreeable confessions are to be believed. He had various troubles because of his wife's "family of origin" (Băncilă–Blaga, 2001, p. 72) which is why he wanted to move to Transylvania, and he was also tempted to go abroad for about five years. Wounded by a gun in his left arm (July 1917) after voluntarily joining the battle front, he never made a complete recovery. The "serene and dreamy" young man had suddenly become a man "dominated by physical suffering", so that, after repeated surgeries and six or seven months in hospital he was left "practically an invalid", without ever asking for a reward for "what had been his faith and his duty" (Băncilă, 2000a, p. 78).

In his correspondence with Lucian Blaga[13], Vasile Băncilă accuses, more than once, along with moral revolt, a nervous weariness close to a kind of

Sartrian nausea (he even uses the term "scorn") towards various familial and social constraints. He seems to be constantly harassed by life; his job as a teacher is very demanding; at one point he commutes between Brăila, Bucharest and Sinaia, where he had been appointed professor of Philosophy to the class in which King Michael studied; he loves Brăila, the Bărăgan and the Danube, but will eventually move to Bucharest.

However, it is not for all these that Vasile Băncilă becomes *a case*, but rather for his intellectual biography (the philosopher and historian of philosophy Gh. Vlăduțescu classifies him as belonging to the "new spirituality"): the various lectures and conferences he held, some of which became texts in their own right; the essays and studies published in the press of the time; and – above all – the huge piles of annotated files and notes regarding his supreme goal: the elaboration of a system of philosophy.

In the same exchange of letters with Blaga, he does not hesitate to say, on the one hand, that he does not exclude the possibility of only the former (*id est*: conferences, printed essays) surviving him; and on the other hand, that he will probably be judged *not after what he offered*, but *after what he could have offered*. The latter seems to be the code applied to the huge archipelago of thematic files designed by this *housebound Anchorite* during the totalitarian regime. Posterity was not, therefore, eluded by his work, even if Băncilă, as he tells Blaga, valued more – perhaps only rhetorically – the posterity one obtains through having children.

If I were to compare him with anyone, the closest example would be Nae Ionescu. The shorthand lectures or notes taken by the Professor's former students are a kind of the equivalent of Vasile Băncilă's immense documentary fund, huge numbers of unprocessed files that, because of their lack of interpretation, remain unassembled and unprepared for publication in a final form.

For both thinkers, *oral style* and the *occasionality* of creation are essential determinants of their *scriptural* being. In the case of Băncilă, one can also add the summary character his files often have, the continuous approximation from various angles of an obsessively pursued theme. Hence the difficulty of the exegete approaching the unfolding act of his thought, a process intermittent on the surface and continuous in its deep layers, a panorama of fragmentary meditation yet not a tautological datum, the figure of tautology being an arduous repetition of cardinal, elementary i.e., fundamental ideas. All this frequently and involuntarily imprints upon the hermeneutics of Vasile Băncilă's texts the characteristics of an interpretive archipelago, a fragmentism of commentary despite his desire for exegetical organicity.

The continual reworking of ideas is, I believe, something other than "an itinerancy of the spirit, driven by its own all-knowing vocation" (Băncilă, 2008, p. 58). It constitutes not exactly a retroactive hermeneutics, but an implicit form of correcting or straightening what has already been said. I am forced to take into account those added nuances, which – willingly or unwillingly – change the overall picture. They are rectifications by added meaning, implied by new entries springing from the "author's mood, disciplinary perspective, a sudden revelation, another cognitive angle, a recent reading or the immediate reality, pure and simple", as editor Dora Mezdrea rightly says.

Might it be the case that the philosopher does not aim to complete his work, but rather his cognitive journey, without falling into contradiction and sophistication! I would say that such a judgment is partly true. The compilation of *ad-hoc* files or notes is the first stage of research, of whose important pedagogy Băncilă was fully aware.

But then, where does this *unending continuum* of a possible whole that only cares about parts but not about their assembly into a unitary structure, come from! One gets the feeling that he deliberately left this last operation, the assembly, to posterity; which will probably decide to evaluate him, as the philosopher wrote to Blaga, not after what *he offered*, but after what *he could have offered*. Otherwise, I could suspect him of hesitation – and not of helplessness – in front of a construction site where the craftsmen and construction materials needed to erect a building are all present, but the beginning of the work and the tying of all the parts into one are relegated *ad calendas graecas*.

*

There is no doubt that the most fertile period of Vasile Băncilă's creation remains the interwar period, especially the third decade of the last century; beyond the projects completed during this period, the intellectual exercise developed after 1950 (tens of thousands of written sheets) amplified the fecundity of his elaborations. The Second World War discouraged him, his public appearances became fewer or non-existent, his collaborations with magazines also entered a shadow zone; Blaga's repeated invitation to send him something for the *Saeculum* magazine received no response from the man he considered when he was designing the publication, to be his "main collaborator".

Vasile Băncilă took "early retirement" from his teaching position at the age of 51 (1948); as if by a miracle he escaped the prison experience, lived modestly and avoided visibility in that "obsessive decade" of culture strangled by political and ideological revisions. Along with other personalities, his name was also put in parentheses and omitted from the value hierarchy of Romanian culture.

It is a period in which, in his "housebound Anchorite" room (I like the phrase!), he sketches projects, reads and writes enormously, file after file, in the hope of times more favourable to the affirmation and publication of his creations.

After the partial contextual *ideological thaw* that began in 1965 (without the phenomenon being the exclusive merit of any political figure at the top of the decision-making pyramid), Vasile Băncilă began to emerge, timidly, in the cultural agora (see "The case of Vasile Băncilă in Romanian philosophy": Popa, 2006, pp. 9–20). He was invited to speak about Iorga[14] at the Romanian Radio Broadcasting Conference (October 4, 1968); the magazine *Tribune* (Cluj) asked for his collaboration ("Memories and reflections" on Blaga; no. 25, June 19, 1968).

Later, at the beginning of the eighth decade, his signature appeared in *The Star, The Morning Star, The XXth Century*. Almost a decade after his death, in 1987, an Opus consisting mainly of his unpublished essays, *Portraits and Meanings*, will be printed with a preface by Zoe Dumitrescu-Buşulenga ("Unicorn" collection of the *Journal of Literary History and Theory*, G. Călinescu Institute, Bucharest). And also, in the ninth decade of the twentieth century, an exegete like Paul P. Drogeanu made the most of Băncilă's meditations on the idea of celebration in his book of cultural anthropology, *The Practice of Happiness. Fragments about celebration* (Eminescu Publishing House, 1985); while Ion Oprişan (from the same G. Călinescu Institute) included a long interview with Vasile Băncilă about Blaga in his volume *Lucian Blaga among his contemporaries. Annotated dialogues* (Minerva Publishing House, 1987).

Notes

[1] Pătrăşcanu, L. (1900–1954). Romanian sociologist, jurist, Marxist philosopher and politician; for my approach, see "Three students of Nae Ionescu", in *Currents and trends in Romanian philosophy* (1946). Bucharest: Socec Publishing House, pp. 120 et seq; other works: *Basic problems of Romania* (1944), *Under three dictatorships* (1944).

[2] Micu, D. (1928–2018). Romanian historian and literary critic; see *"Thought" and Thoughtism* (1975). Bucharest: Minerva Publishing House, pp. 168–176; other works: *History of Romanian literature: from popular creation to postmodernism* (2000), *Tudor Arghezi* (1940, 2004).

[3] Ionescu, N. (1890–1940). Interwar Romanian logician, pedagogue and philosopher, a Balkan Socrates, mentor of Mircea Eliade's generation; with the exception of one volume, his work was published posthumously, after 1990.

[4] Andrei, P. (1891–1940). Romanian sociologist, politician and philosopher; among his writings are *Philosophy of Value* (1945), *Sociological Works* (1983).

[5] Bernea, E. (1905–1990). Romanian sociologist, ethnographer and philosopher, follower of the ideology of the Legionary Movement; specialized studies of Marcel Mauss and Martin Heidegger; among his writings: *Christ and the human condition, Christian anthropology* (1932), *Invitation to simplicity. Confessions for a New Man* (1939), *Frameworks of Romanian Popular Thought* (1985).

[6] Pavel, S. (1888–1941). Nonconformist interwar Roman intellectual, one of those who promoted the "White Lily Manifesto" (1928); among his writings: *National Revolution* (1935), *Krinonis or Steps of Loneliness* (2001).

[7] Dumitriu, A. (1905–1992). Romanian philosopher, logician and mathematician of Greek origin; among his writings: The *Metaphysical Value of Reason* (1933), *East and West* (1943), *History of Logic* (1969), *Alétheia* (1984).

[8] Sebastian, M. (1907–1945. Real name: Iosif Mendel Hechter, Romanian intellectual of Jewish origin with Right-wing ideological views, novelist, playwright, literary critic; among his writings: *For two Thousand Years. Texts, Facts, People* (1935), *The Holiday Game* (1939), *The Star Without a Name* (1942).

[9] See Băncilă, V.: *Portraits and meanings,* prefaced by Dumitrescu-Bușulenga, Z., edited by Băncilă, I. (1987). Bucharest: Supplement of the Journal of Literary History and Theory; *Aphorisms and para-aphorisms,* vol. I, edited by Ileana Băncilă (1993). Timișoara: Marineasa Publishing House; *Lucian Blaga, Romanian energy,* edited by Ileana Băncilă, (1995). Timișoara: Marineasa Publisihing House; *The religious initiation of the child* (1996), Anastasia Publishing House; *Philosophy of ages,* edited by Ileana Băncilă (1997). Bucharest: Anastasia Publishing House; *Correspondence Vasile Băncilă – Basil Munteanu,* edited by Zamfir Bălan (1997). Brăila Museum, Istros Publishing House; *Constantin Rădulescu-Motru,* edited by Ileana Băncilă (1997). Constanța: ExPonto Publishing House; *Manuscriptum,* Băncilă, Vasile, special issue, year XXIX, no. 3–4 (112–113), 1998; *The religion of love and Pestalozzi,* edited by Dora Mezdrea (1998). Constanța: Ex Ponto Publishing House; *Small testaments,* vol. I–II, edition, notes, indices by Dora Mezdrea (1999). Bucharest: Eminescu Publishing House; *The space of the Bărăgan Plains,* edited by Dora Mezdrea (2000). Bucharest: Museum of Romanian Literature Publishing House, Museum of Brăila – Istros Publishing House; *Correspondence Vasile Băncilă – Lucian Blaga,* edited by Dora Mezdrea (2001). Bucharest: Museum of Romanian Literature Publishing House; Brăila Museum – Istros Publishing House; *Art and knowledge,* edited by Dora Mezdrea (2002). Bucharest: Museum of Romanian Literature Publishing House, Museum of Brăila-Istros Publishing House.

[10] Blaga, L. (1891–1961). Poet, playwright, translator, the most valuable Romanian philosopher of the last century; among his works: *Poems* (1942), *Dramatic Works* (1942), *Trilogy of Knowledge* (1943), *Trilogy of Culture* (1944), *Trilogy of Values* (1946).

[11] Bagdasar, N. (1896–1971). Romanian philosopher; among his works: *Contemporary Philosophy of History* (1930), *David Hume. Research on the Human Intellect* (1936), *Theory of Knowledge* (1941).

[12] Crainic, N. (1889–1972. Pseudonym of Ion Dobre, Romanian poet, theologian and philosopher with Far-Right ideological views; among his works: *Orthodoxy and Ethnocracy* (1938), *Nostalgia for Paradise* (1939), *Germany and Italy* (1943).

[13] See Băncilă, V. – Blaga, L. (2001). *Correspondence.* Museum of Romanian Literature, Museum of Brăila: Istros Publishing House.

[14] Iorga, N. (1871–1940). Romanian University Professor, historian, writer, politician. He founded and edited several newspapers and magazines. He wrote and published extensively on Romanian and world history.

Introduction

This essay is a recovery and resignification of the thought of Vasile Băncilă, a Romanian philosopher banned by Nicolae Ceaușescu's totalitarian regime. In the notes left by the author to posterity, we find harsh judgments against Romanian national Communism. In particular, he sanctions the tragedy that it brought about on a human level in Romania, a country that had become a desert of the soul under the dictatorship. A kind of Sahara that changed even the meaning of his meditation, as he says in a confession made in 1962, somewhat at the beginning of the totalitarian hell: "my philosophy fights against the decline of the spirit: today, the values in which I believe, the classical values of man, are in decline, in danger of death; so my philosophy *today* is an *agonistic* philosophy: it fights with death". Then, a decade and a half later (in 1976), he spoke of the birth of that "new man, the demiurge of the laboratory and the planet, the human termite armed with 'science'", the "original" product of a miserable *industrial and political romanticism*.

*

It is estimated that Vasile Băncilă's work will comprise 32 volumes, of which about 17 have been printed so far. The recovery of this philosophical-literary heritage has the support and encouragement of the author's daughter, Ileana Băncilă; to this must be added the efforts of a skilful and tireless research done by the editor Dora Mezdrea, together with the Museum of Brăila "Carol I" – the Istros Publishing House and the Romanian Literature Museum Publishing House.

  With such a deep tracing, Vasile Băncilă constitutes, indisputably, a *case* in Romanian culture today, especially in philosophy. He is a special case because of the material he produced over more than five decades and because of the vistas he opens up before the eyes of the archival researcher. On the contrary, we do not elude the ideas and virtualities inherent in a partially known work, which is ambitious by its encyclopaedic tendency and especially by the intention of building its own original system of philosophy. The philosopher Lucian Blaga saw the essayist Vasile Băncilă as a threat to the spirit of Romanian culture, the historian of philosophy N. Bagdasar considered him "the most fruitful creator" of his generation, and the philosopher and theologian Nichifor Crainic appreciated his "intellectual honesty".

*

The essay has three parts and several chapters. In the first part, I was interested in the author's early writings. The reflections on the role of philosophy in life, including the role of this discipline in the education of high school students, are very important. The young Vasile Băncilă writes dense pages about the relationship between irony and education, about the thoughts of one of the greatest Romanian poets, Mihai Eminescu. The philosopher's syllogisms on the fringes of Descartes' and Schopenhauer's philosophy, from which he tries to detach himself through a slightly passionate criticism, are also notable.

*

In the second part of the essay, I explore the writings of Vasile Băncilă who tries to put together a possible system of philosophy, more precisely: an *ethnic-spiritualist metaphysics* which, when it was elaborated and even afterwards was in clear contradiction with the official ideology of the totalitarian regime. I analyse, step by step, the relations between part and whole (*pars pro toto*), but also between existence and metaphysics. Then, as a consequence, I am interested in the philosopher's judgments about a kind of metaphysical *curriculum vitae* of Romanian existence.

*

The philosopher Vasile Băncilă starts from the bottom, from metaphysical reality, to reach the top, the Absolute, the Great One, God. It is a philosophy of one who has a spiritual sense for what extends beyond the immediate. Or, which seems to be the same thing, the thinker has a philosophical vocation manifested by a sense of the transcendent, in the general sense of the word.

Vasile Băncilă meditates on wisdom in two registers: either he speaks of philosophy, or he has the philosopher by his side. There are also instances in which he expresses himself impersonally. His notes detail, in an original way, the ideational and problematic load of the great chapters of the disciplinary understanding of philosophy: ontology, gnoseology, axiology, praxeology; or the 11 sections that comprise his own system of philosophy.

Towards the same chapters point philosophy and the philosopher, philosophy ultimately. One thing must be said, however: through Băncilă's literary aptitude, his reflections often have the gift of plasticising ideas through the wording and examples given, sometimes reducing the degree of conceptual combustion by ambiguities of meaning. He is very interested in the *intensity of expression*, he is attracted by memorable forms and formulas, as concentrated (militant, as he says somewhere) and creative forms of aesthetic and, perhaps, metaphysical emotions.

*

I received the metaphysician Vasile Băncilă *sine ira et studio*. But I did not hide the shortcomings and shadows of his reflections, just as he himself did not treat one thinker or another lightly. I have not eluded the rancour of his opinions towards various authors, his xenophobic accents towards Jews and, in part, towards some Gypsies.

Receiving a philosophical system, Vasile Băncilă says at one point that "you occasionally get to places where the argumentation becomes worryingly sparse and you see the author instinctively resort to paralogisms or, in the rarer case, when he is aware of what is happening, sophisms". It's a judgment that can also be, unfortunately, self-referential, which is why we've also used it.

*

The Romanian version of this book: *Post-restant. The "Case" of Vasile Băncilă* (2020, Bucharest: Museum of Romanian Literature Publishing House) has had an excellent reception from specialized critics. I will limit myself here to quoting a small fragment of what the critic and literary historian Dan C. Mihăilescu said, in a text that appeared in the cultural magazine *Horizon* (2020, no. 10), a review that became the *Preface to* the present volume:

> Ion Dur's critical discourse aims to identify in Vasile Băncilă's finished texts – published and unpublished – but also in the enormous quantity of thematic worksheets the unfinished project of a metaphysics that springs from, and rests on both the *ethnic* and the *spiritual*. The exegete runs the risk of asserting that Vasile Băncilă's philosophical performance lies somewhere in the middle between *what the thinker gave* and *what he could have given*, if we extend the potential vectors of his metaphysical syllogisms. Ion Dur's exegesis pleads for the inclusion of Vasile Băncilă among the names that make up the table of values of Romanian philosophy, the strong argument being the existence of a *work* that cannot be ignored or eluded.

Vasile Băncilă remains an important *private thinker* for the Romanian cultural space, an author who, isolated and rejected by the totalitarian ideology, continued to philosophize in his own spheres in the posture of *a housebound Anchorite*, living and creating in an exemplary community solitude.

Give me some room! – so would sound the command of the metaphysician, ethicist and moralist Vasile Băncilă, a command not at all pathetic or indulgent, but uttered in a clamorous tone; and as an argument for such an imperative, coming from the best of all possible worlds, he points to his published and unpublished essays in print, along with the dozens of piles of manuscripts.

The hundreds and thousands of Vasile Băncilă's worksheets are, basically, the pages of an interesting *atypical metaphysical diary*, certainly one of ideas, in which the author expounds concepts, his own syllogisms, or enters fragmentarily into a dialogue on various topics with philosophers of all calibres and from all times, including philosophers considered "anonymous".

Part I.
Writings from youth

Chapter 1

To philosophize in order to live

1.1 "A huge number of worksheets"

After 1990, as I already mentioned, Vasile Băncilă's work began to be (re)published, thanks mainly to his daughter, Ileana Băncilă, and the researcher Dora Mezdrea. Under the care of the latter, the first two volumes of the *Works*, which include original writings from his youth, appeared in 2003 and 2004 (I: 1920–1923; II: 1923–1926). From the "Note on the edition", we learn that Vasile Băncilă's archive, preserved *tale quale* since the death of the philosopher until the beginning of the third millennium, includes, "in an undifferentiated way, finished texts and preliminary sheets, plans of works, studies and editions, some newspaper excerpts, reading sheets, bibliographies and a huge number of worksheets" (Băncilă, 2003, p. 5).

These chronologically arranged notes outline the way in which the young Vasile Băncilă was formed, showing the factual and virtual intentions which structured his intellectual becoming. He became a student of the Faculty of Philosophy and Letters of the University of Bucharest starting with the autumn of 1918, supported by his family with about 300 lei per month; not long after, he was able to become financially independent with the money he received for teaching classes at an Evangelical school (see Popa, 2006, pp. 29–34).

He was privileged to have some of the best teachers: C. Rădulescu-Motru, Vasile Pârvan, Nae Ionescu, N. Iorga, C. Dumitrescu Iași, D. Gusti, G. Murnu, M. Dragomirescu, R. Ortiz, D. Onciul, I. Rădulescu-Pogoneanu, O. Densușianu, S. Mehedinți, G. C. Antonescu, D. Russo, Ch. Drouhet. Of all these, the first three will enrich him in a special way through their erudition and intellectual depth, by their ideational and moral synchronization with the Western academic environment.

He will graduate from the faculty in October 1922, with dual BA exams: in the History of Philosophy he will sustain the thesis "On *The World as Will and Representation*" (included in a study: "Schopenhauer's practical philosophy", as this was an author he considered as a possible topic for his doctorate); in Pedagogy he will present the paper: "Herbert Spencer's Pedagogy". In the meantime, before graduation, he makes his debut in the magazine *Student Life* (July 1921), his first article being on "The Congress in Cluj and the

Congress in Chernovtsy. Background and perspectives". Around the same time, he marries Felicia Rădulescu, a student of French language and literature, and soon after, their first child, Ioan, is born. The family was and always remained Vasile Băncilă's number one priority, so many intellectual projects (including the doctorate) will be partially put on hold.

Vasile Băncilă was not a leisured author, who wrote only on Sundays – and I will try to avoid somehow harming the intrinsic meaning of this day (see, among others, Noica, 1992, pp. 22–25). He spoke as a teacher, but also in the public arena, and he always wrote, even after the fateful year 1944 when he was forbidden to publish. Essay, studies, aphorisms and para-aphorisms, portraits and memoirs, journals, correspondence – these are the registers in which Vasile Băncilă tried his hand at writing.

*

The two volumes of Notes from his youth are not organized systematically, but chronologically, so they can be read randomly, especially as the themes of the texts are extremely varied. Our readings are, of course, unfaithful, and because Vasile Băncilă's texts are not widely circulated, I will favour the quotation while rationalizing the paraphrase.

Knowing what the author's obsessive preoccupations were over time, our attention is inevitably directed in a selective way. I am thus interested, above all, in what the student and, later, recent graduate thought about philosophy, a discipline in which he had tried his hand most of his life. For example, in his fourth year at university, he drafted a "Plan for an Ethnic Philosophy" (October 1921), and another on what "Philosophy" (December 1921) and "Nation" represented (Băncilă, 2003, see pp. 98–105, 110–118).

I don't know if these sketches were seminar assignments or if they represented an initiative unrelated to his curriculum in any subject. But one thing is certain: after the Great Union (1918), the national idea was the backbone of Romanian culture, and the most sensitive field for the national character of creation was represented by philosophical reflection, the *ethnicity* of Romanian metaphysics being intensely debated in the interwar period. And it is also certain that Băncilă's intentions as founder of a philosophical system were formulated a little later: in the outline of the *Philosophical framework* (Băncilă, 2007, pp. 492–500) published in the *Flowerbud* magazine of the "Michael the Brave" High School in Bucharest.[1]

1.2 A philosophical framework

Let us first consider what features the young student Vasile Băncilă claims for the sphere of philosophy. His notes are placed at the beginning of the third decade of the last century, against the strong and dominant background of positivism. He attended, one assumes curiously and with tense attention, Nae Ionescu's metaphysics course in the academic year 1920–1921. It is, perhaps, the ferment that generated the (unpublished) text "Philosophy (*Philosophare...*)", some 13 pages about: "I. What is philosophy; II. The relations between philosophy and disciplines of the same level (religion, art, morality); III. Philosophy and its biological and social role" (Băncilă, 2003, pp. 110–118).

He aims to relate the definitions or merely the opinions of various authors – such as Kant, Schopenhauer, Wundt, Spencer, James, Bergson, Schinz, the ancients and others – to a series of questions he formulates in the preamble to his notes. There are about nine interrogations – elementary and naïve, one would say today – regarding the essence of philosophy: whether philosophy encompasses somehow the totality of the moral sciences or just those supplemented by the natural sciences; whether philosophy can only be a theory of knowledge or just the systematization of natural sciences; whether philosophy can be identified, in fact, with the history of philosophy; whether philosophy is the discipline that formulates questions about the totality of existence (although it cannot solve them itself); whether philosophy has as its object of study the capture and rendering of the metaphysical; finally, whether philosophy can be an overall intuition or a total belief, formed according to personal subjectivity (in the latter, he expressly quotes James and Nae Ionescu).

It is just a work plan, with juvenile and simplifying probing, and Băncilă does not venture to foray into the works of certain philosophers, quoted or not, leaving this approach for a later date. It seems important, for the time being, to offer an implicit methodical answer to *what philosophy is*.

The opinions of the young Băncilă, which will become dominant in the hundreds of work files kept decades later, seem today to verge on banality, but let us not elude the moment and the context in which they were sketched. In fact, he sets some milestones for a long reflexive ulterior journey.[2]

It starts by asking what a discipline is. It needs to have an exclusive object and also its own method. The first, the object, is logical in nature (otherwise "neither sociology nor philosophy would have an object"); without telling us what he means by logical, he merely states that it should not be perceived as "the same object to be investigated from a different point of view", as Emmanuel de Martonne did (the appeal to a geographer and pedagogue, even if prestigious at the time, is not among the most pertinent of his ideas).[3] As for the method, it cannot be lacking (otherwise it remains only a theoretical possibility of science) and is not inevitably original.

More interesting are the notations, also juvenile, about *common sense*, which do not seem reminiscent of Aristotle's commonplaces, but rather of observations made from the collective mind. He sees in common sense a phase of the knowledge of the self, devoid of critical spirit (with only a "very rudimentary semi-conscious criticism") and method. Common sense (different from what is understood today by *common sense*) has three characteristics: first, it is "a reaction of *the whole* to *the total*. The whole soul is placed directly in front of the total Cosmos: the product of their endosmosis is common sense" (Băncilă, 2003, p. 111); secondly, the same common sense represents a "hypnotic state of consciousness" devoid of the I/non-I distinction, as in the primitive mentality, where the individual has no identity but constitutes an amorphous whole together with the community (this is similar to what Lucien Lévy-Bruhl said, at the time, in *La mentalité primitive*, 1922); a third meaning of common sense lies in the fact that all the results of knowledge obtained in this way are immediate (as in Bergson), given by intuition, by semi-conscious and non-extended reasoning, by experience.

The conclusions drawn from such an approach: knowledge will thus be integral (not *unified*, not systematic, but a kind of conglomerate), with many prejudices, with a *bazaar of beliefs* at the level of the individual; a naive realism (a phrase taken, I believe, from Motru),[4] pragmatic, with limited experience ("it will not be able to see the volcanoes of the moon"), full of contradictions (see popular proverbs).

Finally, common sense is a kind of skeleton key, because it has a convenient answer for almost everything, and for those finding themselves in such a phase it is the only "way to satisfy the human soul." Synthetically put, common sense is "the solution to all problems of the spirit, thematic and practical, through immediate (intuitive, rational, experimental), uncritical and semi-conscious notification" (Băncilă, 2003, p. 112).

In order to investigate common sense somewhat more completely and picturesquely, Vasile Băncilă proposed to study folklore. It can thus be seen that the milestones of his path were intended to distinguish *popular* philosophy from *disciplinary* philosophy ("Either common sense or philosophy").

The next segment – in a plan that set the necessary steps for unravelling what philosophy is – was that of science, within which critical sense is installed and the non-self appears almost entirely human, with specific methods of research and verification. But one question remained, namely, how did the spirit pass through such a phase; and whether or not philosophy and science were born at the same time (should one doubt the syncretism of the foundations!). For the latter puzzlement, he offers variants: "Perhaps because of the pain in the world; perhaps because it has reached the limits of the non-self; perhaps because it saw certain illusions of the spirit; perhaps through its own intellectual maturity, etc." (Băncilă, 2003, p. 112)

It is important that philosophy does not remain at a scientific stage (science being, for the young Băncilă, not an attitude towards life, but at most one similar to common sense), because it is not autonomous like the scientific spirit, but presupposes something personal: "*an objectification of temperament*" (emphasis added). Just as philosophy has not remained at the level of common sense and cannot be confused with it, so too does its link to science, the latter not being able to replace either.

And with this we arrive, through a seemingly Hegelian triad, at the third form of the human spirit, at the *possibility of philosophy*, whose origin is the same as that of epistemology: the critical attitude will be actualized not only in relation to the non-ego, but also to itself. The spirit interrogates reality (the reality studied by the sciences) and returns to its starting point.

*

What would, in the end, constitute the specific characteristics of philosophy? It tries to be an ultimate and integral knowledge, even if, gnoseologically speaking, it is the knowledge of a particular thinker, which was preceded by a question that targeted the whole of reality (it will be the somewhat Kantian answer to the question: what can one know?). Philosophy is also, through its object of study, systematic, simultaneously concerned with the quantitative and the qualitative, with necessity and freedom, with principles rather than laws.

Therefore, the philosophical spirit is the one that "tries to know reality as such, in its function, conscious of the return upon its knowledge" (Băncilă, 2003, p. 114). A product of this spirit, philosophy is not to be confused with it. While the philosophical spirit is something positive, philosophy can also take a negative form, as happens in the case of scepticism. Kant, for example, says Băncilă, seems to have been imbued with the highest philosophical spirit, but his philosophy was surpassed by other systems of thinking (which lacked the same philosophical spirit).

Here the influence of the thinker Nae Ionescu is clear: "*philosophy is integral knowing* (not knowledge; philosophy is something already objectified, something produced, inert) *carried out on the basis of the perception of a reality or factor considered ultimate, through the self-critical function of the mind*" (Băncilă, 2003, p. 114; a self-criticism different from that of morality, science or poetry, which stop at the phenomenal).

Inevitably, philosophy is *systemic*, a unitary system on the one hand and an ultimate reality on the other. Băncilă admits the view according to which the object of philosophy would be "an attitude of philosophizing, a method"; it is philosophizing in itself, as some understand it; not something "fixed, inert, objectified," but something fluid, in the making, "the exercise of the philosophical spirit".

And he details this exercise:

> There is a confusion here: the river flows, but the flow, as a phenomenon, is something static, inert. Philosophizing is continuous, but the object of philosophizing, which is philosophy, is something inert, eternal. Without this eternity, philosophy could be either anything or nothing, unless it has something permanent (every essence has an existence). Hence, the same illusion as with free will: *because you can do what you want, you think you want it* (Schopenhauer); because you philosophize continuously without ever reaching some fixed conclusion, you believe that the object of philosophy is non-fixity, relativism. In fact, the object of philosophy, however relativistic its points of view, is absolute (Băncilă, 2003, p. 114, emphasis added).

The example he uses is that of pragmatism, a follower of truths confirmed by the criterion of "useful consistency"; this criterion, according to thinkers who philosophize in this way, being something absolute. Therefore, "truths exist only because there is an absolute truth". As in the case of sceptics, who claim that nothing is true except *this* truth (which is thus absolute).

1.3 The perception of metaphysical reality

If this is the case with the object of philosophy, then how can it ever be studied, Băncilă wondered. First of all, the thesis that understands philosophy as a kind of "encyclopaedia, an ideal 'Larousse'" (Băncilă, 2003, p. 115) based on logical or alphabetic criteria is far from being universally accepted. Most philosophers have achieved the unification of the world, of the whole of reality by postulating a hypothesis that has become the core of their thinking (in Schopenhauer's case – the will, in Bergson's – the vital impetus; I will limit the analysis to the commentary on Băncilă's text). Or by the formulation of a hypothesis, but considered from an extra-human angle (which is equivalent to a principle), for example: the law of universal attraction (but here one talks about science, not philosophy, as suggested by the example invoked: Poincaré).

The most appropriate alternative for the foundations of philosophy is "*the perception of metaphysical reality*," which implies that we are dealing with an ultimate reality, with a thing in itself that we can know. Otherwise, philosophy has no object, therefore, it does not exist ("The thing itself either is not, or it is and you cannot know it, therefore philosophy does not exist ...").

But things are not so categorical and irreversible: "First, that a thing in itself must be: it is either Kant's *noumenon*, or *the reality of naive realism*" (Băncilă, 2003, p. 115).[5] Those who deny the existence of a thing in itself turn everything into appearances, being even less realistic than the philosopher Kant. A reality in itself (by which everything can be explained unitarily) exists even for absolute idealism: *the self*. And for the thing itself, when it cannot be perceived, on the one hand, it is enough that "one has thought about it"; and on the other hand, in the case of the impossibility of knowing it, philosophy exists through the very philosophical discourse that points to such an inability.

The two requirements are now invoked: the explanation of integral reality and its objectification through an adequate discourse. And if the second explanation is not possible, an attitude similar to that of the nineteenth-century positivists or Italian pragmatists, those who banished philosophy and generated an "amusing caricature of the serious caricature of philosophy" is not appropriate.

Vasile Băncilă's idea had the appearance of a rather sophisticated axiom: "Explaining the inability to explain is philosophy. As soon as there is a tendency in us to philosophize (and there is!), there is also philosophy, even if it would not lead to explanation as to the explanation of non-explanation. *Any complete intellectual formulation of the philosophical spirit* – which is a reality – *is philosophy*" (Băncilă, 2003, p. 116).

And with the Kantian philosophy of the thing in itself, as well as with the possible relation between *potency* and *act*, we could enter into a dispute which, for connoisseurs and non-connoisseurs alike, has no place and purpose here. What is certain is that the student Vasile Băncilă was a motivated and inquisitive mind which was not satisfied with instantaneous semi-preparedness, a spirit interested in the fundamental problems of philosophical discourse, whose existence consisted in a subjective, and not objective, reason, a philosophy which was *composited*, imprinted, as we shall see, with the *ethnic* factor.

*

Băncilă's plan – whose objective was represented by: what is philosophy – then advanced, in point VI, towards an important conjunction: metaphysics and philosophy. It was not a question of the categorial distinction between metaphysics and philosophy which Blaga and even Băncilă would later discern, but of the meta-physical rethinking of the world; otherwise formulated, metaphysics is now understood to mean not only the tendency to philosophize, but also the explanation of ultimate reality, the founding reality, through *essences*.

For Băncilă, to philosophize seriously presupposed "to have metaphysical needs, whether of a logical or biological nature, in addition to a mind turned on itself" (Băncilă, 2003, p. 116). The metaphysical need, the student was keen to point out, is not to be confused with "the spirit of research, which can be common sense (in the latter the biological reason predominates and there is very little logical need), or the philosophical one: in the first case, it leads to cosmogonies, religions; in the second, to hypotheses and philosophy".

This is not the place for a justificatory dialogue either. It is certain, however, that the young Băncilă was attempting an atypical understanding of philosophy, one that did not synchronize with the canon of the day, an intellectual drift that he could probably only have encountered in the courses held by Nae Ionescu. Metaphysics was, for him, "a generic colour that enters into philosophy," or "one of the elements of the philosophical" which can also be found in other combinations (for example, in religion). A little later, he would write a stack of worksheets on his conception of metaphysics, which now he only approximated in an Aesopian way.

Therefore, objective meta-physical (my hyphen, I.D.) reality is studied by philosophy, and the meta-physical *necessity* makes of the philosophical spirit nothing but philosophy. Metaphysical necessity thus represents "the exhortation and, moreover, the *matter*", and intelligence – its instrument, so that "philosophical truth is created by the philosophical intelligence from the matter given by necessity".

To create philosophy, therefore, requires a strong *metaphysical temperament*. Intelligence alone – sometimes greater than that of the authors of systems, but in the absence of deep metaphysical necessity – is not enough, serving only to criticise, or to compile histories of philosophy.

Through the grid of a creator's psychology, Vasile Băncilă placed a special emphasis on metaphysical necessity and on the metaphysical temperament

with which the understanding of the world as a unitary whole was objectified
– that is: the *expression* it acquired.

Empty intelligence was of no use in the empirical sphere or even in the
exercise of the philosophical spirit: "Frivolous intelligent philosophisers and
scholarly philosophers are people who have philosophical intelligence, but
no metaphysical needs" (Băncilă, 2003, p. 116).

1.4 Philosophy is abstract religion

Next in the outline of the study sketch of young Vasile Băncilă comes point
VII, that is disciplines analogous to philosophy. The explanation here is
negative, it indicates those disciplines that *do not* replace philosophy, and
therefore cannot constitute philosophy alone. For example, the natural
sciences. A different status is given to sciences *of the apparent* (not included
in those mentioned above), which constitute a second threshold of such
sciences and which, being solidary with philosophy, belong to it; they are, as
far as we understand, the *noological sciences*, disciplines which, for various
practical reasons, do not have the power to refer to philosophy and, precisely
for this reason, are studied elsewhere.

After this excursion, intended to be structurally enlightening for the
definition of philosophy, follows a natural corollary. First of all, philosophy, in
order to be what it is, requires either a hypothesis, or a principle considered
hypothetical but taken as truth, or the grasp of metaphysics (which, says
Băncilă, did not occur then). Secondly, philosophical intelligence draws its
fertile sap from temperament and virtual beliefs, which means that
"*philosophy cannot exist without faith*: it insinuates itself even in critics (see
Kant) and sceptics" (Băncilă, 2003, p. 118). Philosophy and religion are the
disciplines most in need of faith which, however, is not to be confused with
logical faith. "Religion is concrete philosophy; philosophy is abstract religion.
After that comes common sense as a whole, then science."

It is clear to us now, even from this final sentence, where Vasile Băncilă's faith
was hidden: in his metaphysical need, in his metaphysical temperament, in the
ontology (with its underlying metaphysics) that he conceived starting with the
sapiential accreditation of *another space* (that of the Bărăgan Plains), next to
Blaga's *Mioritic* space, and continuing with a specific gnoseology, one in which
art is the seminal fluid, the seed of metaphysical meditation.

These are the two great caryatids that, since the interwar period, have
supported Vasile Băncilă's projected *system of philosophy*. And it is also here

that the first approximations or projections announcing the horizon of a spiritualist metaphysics appear, one that has as its germ the ethnic factor.

*

The text I comment on continues with Part II, 10–15 lines about the relationship between philosophy and disciplines of the same rank (religion, art, morality); finally, in Part III, Băncilă explains in a few sentences the biological and social role of philosophy, intelligently commenting on the old Latin adage to which he alludes, but without explicitly mentioning it: "*Primum vivere, deinde philosophari.*" In the first part, the satisfaction that the human spirit gives to fundamental needs: truth, morality, beauty, religion, is emphasised; reiterating the endosmosis between philosophy and religious need, which is as complete as that between the latter and common sense ("patriarchalism has made society happy – but modernism?"). Religion – says Nae Ionescu's former student – probably "should not even be based on religious experience, because that is the domain of science (it would be stepping on the wrong foot), but on considerations of other reasons" (not specifying what these might be).

In conclusion, he overturns the meaning of the proverb: "I have not written for those who first want to live and then to philosophize, but rather for those who first want to philosophize and then to live; or, rather, for those who live in order to philosophize, or, even more truly, for those who philosophize in order to be able to live" (Băncilă, 2003, p. 118).

Notes

[1] On the first page of the text, in the footnotes, there is the following note: "This article was supposed to be printed in 1938, when it was written following a specific invitation to that effect. At that time, it bore the following note: *These pages are a very concise outline of the spiritual ideas and positions we have held so far and, at the same time, a framework or ideational structure for those we shall hold from now on.* However, we stopped printing it at that time, because we hoped to develop at least some parts of it soon and thus provide a more complete summary of the attitudinal perspectives that guide us. Circumstances, however, did not allow us to do so" – see *Works*, vol. V, quoted edition, p. 555.

[2] The full meaning of *philosophy* or *ethnic philosophy*, as well as the intrinsic *relationship* between philosophy and *metaphysics* can be found after leafing through the huge volume of *worksheets* written in several decades (between 1936–1979); for the *definition* of philosophy – see Băncilă, V. (2007). *Works*, vol. VI, quoted edition; for the meaning of metaphysics – see Băncilă, V. (2009). *Works*, vol. VII, quoted edition, System

of philosophy. 2. Metaphysics, edited by Dora Mezdrea, Brăila Museum: Istros Publishing House; for reflections on *being* – a fundamental problem for philosophy – see Băncilă, V. (2015). *Works,* vol. X, quoted edition, System of Philosophy. 5. Communities of existence: A. The ontological community: Existence as a being. B. Romanian Existence, edited by Dora Mezdrea. "Carol I" Museum of Brăila: Istros Publishing House.

[3] T. Martonne, French pedagogue and geographer, known in the interwar period for his contributions to tracing the borders of Greater Romania and his research into some Romanian geographical areas (he called the Făgăraş mountains "a kind of Transylvanian Alps").

[4] Rădulescu-Motru, C. (1868–1957). Romanian University Professor, philosopher, psychologist, playwright. Among his writings: *F.W. Nietzsche. Life and Philosophy* (1897), *Problems of Psychology* (1898), *Romanian Culture and Politicianism* (1904), *The Power of the Soul. Psychology of Parvenitism* (1908), *Romanianism. The Catechism of a New Spirituality* (1936), *Psychology of the Romanian People* (1937), *Time and Destiny* (1940), *Romanian Ethnicity. Community of origin, language and destiny* (1942).

[5] In 1912, Rădulescu-Motru, C. published *Elements of metaphysics based on Kantian philosophy,* where, in the first part, he explores "Mirror-consciousness. The critique of naive realism" – see, selectively, (1984), *Energetic personalism and other writings,* Study, anthology and notes by Gh. Al. Cazan, text established by Gheorghe Pienescu. Bucharest: Eminescu Publishing House. Băncilă was of course familiar with the works of his teacher.

Chapter 2

Ethnic philosophy

2.1 What is the nation?

Starting frames

In 1918, when Vasile Băncilă became a student, Marin Ştefănescu[1] was still in Bucharest working as a university assistant in Motru's department; in 1919, he became a full Professor of Logic and History of Philosophy at the University of Cluj. It is possible that Băncilă attended seminars held by Ştefănescu and was inspired and stimulated by the ideas of this scholar who would try, through *Romanian Philosophy* (the first history of its kind, 1922), to apply the grid of a *harmonic spiritualism* in order to decipher the foundations and destiny of native metaphysical reflection.

The idea of an ethnic philosophy – that is: Romanian, or, even more literally, philosophy *in the Romanian language*, even if the notions do not interfere and are not identical, just as they do not overlap with the popular vocabulary – permeates interwar thought and was an apple of discord (or concord) during the totalitarian regime. Let us remember Mircea Vulcănescu[2] with *The Romanian Dimension of Existence* (1943), who seems to have been inspired by Băncilă himself (as Noica[3] in his turn, was inspired in his philosophical utterances by Mircea Vulcănescu), a similar subject being partially dealt with by C. Rădulescu-Motru in *Romanian Culture and Politicianism* (1904), where he is interested in the dissolution of the individuality of the Romanian people under the harmful influence of politicianism, and, above all, in *Romanianism. Catechism of a New Spirituality* (1936).[4] I cannot fail to mention: Nae Ionescu, with his *Course on the history of metaphysics* (university year 1930–1931)[5] and his gazetteering in *The Word*; Mircea Florian with his studies "Philosophy and nationality", "The sense of a Romanian philosophy" and "Romanian philosophy";[6] Constantin Noica, with *Pages about the Romanian soul* (1944) or other essays whose essential feature is *Romanianness* or *Romanianism*; Ion Petrovici, [7] "La nationalité en philosophie" (1932); to which we will add the sociological answer of Henri H. Stahl, "Philosophizing on the philosophy of the Romanian people".[8]

We know Cioran's astute reply to Noica, in a letter sent after the latter wrote *The Romanian Sense of Being* (1978): "Your last book is excellent, except that it might as well have been called *The Paraguayan Sense of Being*. If I were you, I'd go back to *Logic*: where, if not there, can one rave better?" (Cioran, 1995, p. 310)

But it is not the Cioranian irony, which may as well be an ethereal form of comradely jealousy-cum-banter, that interests us; it is the fact that philosophy has always had at its core the *problem of being*. *What is being* and, alongside such a fundamental question, the other registers of sapiential meditation: *knowledge* and *valorisation*, to mention the most important ones, all remain the determinations that make up the matrix of philosophical reflection.

Ethnicity as will and representation

In October 1921, when he was in his last year at university, Vasile Băncilă conceived an ambitious "Plan for an Ethnic Philosophy" (Băncilă, 2003, pp. 98–101), an idea taken up by the author in his later notes (Băncilă, 2008, *passim*). It is a maximally summary sketch, a manuscript of about five pages, written in pencil on both sides of the paper. A simple and precise composition in three parts: the first – a historical introduction; the second – about the definition of a nation; while the last one is entitled *towards humanity*, indicating only the number of chapters, but not their names.

What follows deals laconically with *the nation*, perhaps as a subject providing the *ethnic code* for philosophical meditation. There are two other fragments dealing with the same subject of the nation (Băncilă, 2003, pp. 33–34, 102–105); the first was written on March 24, 1921 (subtitled "*Sur la nature de la volonté ethnique*"), thus predating the plan for ethnic philosophy; and some November 1921 sheets, written a month after the conception of the same plan.

In retrospect, I will read chronologically what the young Băncilă writes about the nation. He was concerned, above all, with understanding the nature of *ethnic will*, an important *metaphysical category* even for the pure sciences. Here, too, there is a plan stretching over 11 chapters, beginning with the necessary history of the problem under discussion. No bibliographical source is given, however, apart from references to various cultural-philosophical spaces.

What did the young Băncilă find essential in his approach to studying the metaphysical category called ethnic will? First of all, it was a *sine qua non condition* of any nation. At the same time, the ethnic metaphysical category was also an ethical one, a binomial that he proposed to approach psychologically through the prism of connections between intuitions, ideas and will (the vital impulse and intuition were concepts already imposed by French philosophy), with energy or ethical intuitions prevailing among them (here there is a glimpse of the same lectures by C. Rădulescu-Motru; noting that *the philosophical atmosphere* was marked by the work of Henri Bergson).

*

I open a parenthesis I believe necessary in order to specify that the nation has become, today, a plurivocal notion, a controversial reality.[9] Since Mihail Kogălniceanu[10] (who defined the idea of nation in a complex way), the concept of nation has been often invoked and challenged in the public space, the national idea being, after the Great Union (1918), an obsession of the public discourse which claimed it for both the political and cultural spheres. I do not think that an exclusive distinction was being made at the time. At least in the Romanian context, *ethnicity* or *ethnicism* (from the Greek *ethnos* – human group with common traits) referred to a group of people, a community that could ultimately constitute a people – a concept sometimes synonymous with ethnicity or nation.

But the latter two are distinguished, especially today, by the fact that ethnicity, unlike nation, does not acquire political expression. The modern political nation is, on the one hand, based on the will of the people (e.g., the French or American nations), and, on the other hand, it identifies nations formed on the basis of ethnic and linguistic criteria (e.g., the German nation). The tendency is to overcome historical and ideological opposition and to propose a sociological concept of the modern nation, against a background of politically integrating different populations through a common political project.

*

But let's return to Vasile Băncilă's notes on the nation. In his lecture on *What is a nation*: *Qu'est-ce qu'une nation?* given at the Sorbonne (11 March 1882), Ernest Renan reveals a feature that might help us better understand the mindset of the student Băncilă who, in his fourth year, was probably also intensively reading Schopenhauer for his degree theses.

The present essay could be subtitled *ethnicity as will and representation*. A nation must be desired, Schopenhauer said, and to desire something, it is necessary to activate one's volitional resources, that is to say: the will. The individual will if we are talking about an individual, or the collective will if we are talking about a group, a community. At the beginning of the third decade of the last century, when Băncilă put his thoughts on paper, it was precisely the ethnic will that was spreading in the Romanians' national being *like yeast in dough*, to borrow a comparison from Blaga.

Ethnic will is therefore a dual metaphysical category, ethnic and ethical in equal measure, with intuition as its content. Hence a series of conclusions that the young Băncilă formulated concerning the ethnicity of the individuals who make up the nation. He states, theistically, that not all individuals are ethnic, indeed no single individual is completely ethnic, or only ethnic. He also takes into account the nature of individuals (they are a bio-psycho-social expression) and, correlatively, the nature of the nation as such, which constitutes *only something spiritual.*

Things are beginning, in a way, to clear up, despite the arborescence of the various clarifications that the student Băncilă makes in a *brief* even *telegraphic* style. The nation therefore appears to him as an abstraction and as something that is exclusively related to the spiritual side of society; it is pure creation and it represents, after all, the culture of a society. Moreover, the nation is not only the product of the latter, but also its ideal. He rejects the notion that the nation is a biological expression, an appearance which stems from the fact that the nation was and is, in such cases, united with society.

In point V of the sketch, alongside the factors and the way in which the metaphysical category is produced (aspects that have only been formulated), Vasile Băncilă specifies who the nation's representatives are: the people of culture and the peasants ("from this we can see how the peasant is an admirable ethnic construction, without being nationalistic; indeed, he may even be anti-nationalistic, although in national forms": Băncilă, 2003, p. 33).

He does not exclude from his approach – one of cultural anthropology, with insertions of political philosophy concerning the collective (unconscious) mind – a certain taxonomy of ethnic complexes according to "the unity, cohesion, consciousness and motricity of metaphysical categories", without forgetting the contribution of race (at the time, the concept of race was overvalued by political and biological factors). The focus here is on the English space characterised by *objective individualism,* where social initiative and cohesion are at their highest; which is not the case with the *psychic collectivism* of the Germans or the egoistic *subjective individualism* of the Latins and Orientals.

At the same time, the student Băncilă is interested in those factors that can substitute for metaphysical matter. For example, in a subject people or nation, such a translation takes place as religion comes to have ethnic value. Examples are close at hand: for the Romanians of Transylvania or those of the Principalities, the law that works is that of ancestral life. It seems, however, that the Balkan Peninsula had a different story: either the ethnic sense was not sufficiently developed, or, as in the case of the Greeks, religion took on an ethnic form.

A very important thing for the ethnic will, i.e., for the nation, is what Băncilă calls the *small homeland*, whose reality subsists even in the absence of a form of the nation. A profound structure fills this small homeland, identified in childhood, with meaning which "alone *absolutely legitimises* the meaning of life"; the determinations of childhood are essential to the feeling of a nation: memory (which reveals the lost paradise), the ethnic soul, the metaphysics of the soul that is formed then: "*Whoever does not have an ethnically rich childhood can hardly understand his nation.* I even think that after 15–20 years you can't become ethnic anymore." (Băncilă, 2003, p. 34)

Hence the need for appropriate education, one that offers the child "not a didactic nationalist catechism, but concrete intuitive elements of ethnic metaphysics: landscapes, history, a rich small homeland". This is why, in order to feel deeply and religiously the homeland (a term which, says Mihai Eminescu, comes in the Romanian language from the Latin *patres*, i.e., from parents), it is necessary to remember childhood. In this chapter, which deals with the metaphysical category and religion of memories, the foundations of national feeling are already condensed.

Finally, what Vasile Băncilă called the valorisation of the individual is needed for ethnic will: through society, naturally and organically linked to the individual (for "in other countries *you mean nothing*"); and through ambition for your nation, "even if you are not an ethnic construction" (Eminescu, whenever he met his friends, had a specific greeting: they would say "Long live the nation!", to which the poet would reply: "Up with it!").

About the nation, on five pages...

Before observing what the student Băncilă kept and what he added about the nation in his plan for an "ethnic philosophy" (Băncilă, 2003, pp. 98–101), I will specify a series of conjunctions that outline the nine chapters of Part II of this plan, entitled "What is the Nation". Here, as in the previous sections, the personal readings and information provided by the courses Vasile Băncilă attended at university are apparent.

In the first chapter of the section, he wanted to be original and exclusive, trying to explain what the nation is ("after me"). He then proposed to write about: some metaphysical-ethnic categories (English, French, Germans, Russians, Jews); the origin and evolution of the nation in comparison with its previous phases and the highest stage it has reached; the organisation of the nation; the relationship between nation and personalities, or between art and nation; the relationship between nation and social class; the creative factors of a nation; finally, in chapter IX, he specified the corollaries which should be deduced from the way he defined the nation. All this was followed by part III of the plan: towards humanity, or, as he rephrased it, humanity, comprising four chapters.

The summary that follows in the text, not at all revised or stylized, is not systematic and follows only sporadically the sequence of the announced chapters. Being a "complete and original complex of tendencies", concentrated in a "suitable cultural expression", the nation, like the individual (the one who mediates the reform of the nation), has a personality, this personality being examined from various angles by the student Băncilă.

Balancing between the abstract and the concrete (the latter being the moral dimension), the nation is, in a complete and adequate definition, subjective objective: "*a unitary character*", on the one hand, and a "*metaphysical category*" ("anything that refers to the attitude towards life is metaphysical": Băncilă, 2003, p. 98), on the other; between the two, there is a complete agreement.

Culture is the continuous product of a nation, just as the nation is the generator of what Fouillée called ideas-force, national ideas with a dynamic character. And the last and greatest instrument of ethnic creation is the state (Băncilă refers us here to Wundt, about whom he had surely learned from Constantin Rădulescu-Motru's lectures).

In this sense, the tendencies manifested inside ethnicities are converted into culturalised forces. We cannot discover, at the level of the nation's personality, a disjunction between its will and its intelligence; on the contrary, these form a kind of ethnic imperialism, which is nothing other than cultural.

By mirroring the individual and the nation (not by chance, since the nation works on the individual), by detecting in the latter traits similar to the former, Băncilă spoke of a certain congruence between personalities and the nation, considering that those personalities that do not take into account the national character are –"after a work of identification" – either totally or partially admitted to, removed from or seceded into those cultural spaces with which they are related. It is no secret that in universal culture, nations seek out those works or ideas that suit them.

And so the young Vasile Băncilă arrived at an unusual mode of universal circulation of values, unilaterally oriented. For "a nation becomes richer when the strength and breadth with which it attracts cultural products from as many nations as possible becomes greater". It must, however, respect certain conditions: it must preserve its original character, its unity and "the capacity to admit and include into its character the most varied accidental personalities" (Băncilă, 2003, p. 99). In the light of the first condition in particular, the nation represents, says Băncilă, "*the development and cultural realisation of a prime inspiration of a metaphysical nature*".

The preservation of its original, primary character is essential, however, because once it has been changed (by various historical accidents, with internal or external causes), we are dealing with another nation ("like a song that has turned into another, by forgetting the original inspiration"). Therefore, the major tendency (ignored by some) of nations is to become one with humanity, to integrate the culture of humanity into their content, even if nations are somehow akin to closed seas.

Finally, we also learn what ethnics or ethnic philosophy is: it is "the essence of the social" (Băncilă, 2003, p. 100). An essence, we have seen, with a double nature: metaphysical and moral, dimensions by whose depth and breadth a nation is assessed.

Vasile Băncilă's sketch refers, I will emphasize once again, to the nation-culture, the nation-artefact (English, *artefact*) culturally original and originary, which retains a primary inspiration of a metaphysical nature. By developing the individual's personality as much as possible, such a structure does not prevent originality, if it manifests itself. The environment influences it directly and by a "contrary logic: it may be precisely in the midst of a nation that the man who supports its cultural antipode appears" (Băncilă, 2003, p. 100; see Schopenhauer, an author who was always on Băncilă's desk). Moreover, personalities interpret and enrich the ethnic character, so that through each work of culture we discover a new face of the identity of the ethnic soul.

The five pages, written in pencil on both sides of the paper, ended with those more futuristic lines on humanity (Băncilă, 2003, pp. 100–101), for which he proposed a four-chapter approach. Chapter one contained only one sentence: humanity "will be a natural product". Period. The second chapter followed, in a somewhat Kantian key: the *condition of the putty of humanity*, which would sum up the "theoretical identity (actual and virtual)" of the individual as such, seen through the prism of its logical construction, but also through the possible existence of a culture in which a congruence of ethnic characters would function (a relatively utopian condition).

Such a futurological perspective also presupposed the ideal concordance of interests (which the third chapter of the outline would have given an account of) once the nation had already been achieved. Culture would thus be the factor that would facilitate "ideal concord", "by removing false ethnic points of view, by finding larger formulas inside which ethnic nuances would agree" (there was a lot of ethnic enthusiasm on Băncilă's part in the autumn of 1921, but also a lot of epistemological naivety).

Finally, he also speaks of an elusive form of material concordance: "a powerful means for humanity, though not exactly pure and profound" – he invokes the currency depreciation in some countries because of which the whole of Europe is suffering, the economic interdependence of Europe, and quotes Keynes and Cadmus.

But the economy of humanity also includes self-love, which the student Băncilă did not elude. In the future, small collectivities such as the family and the nation will remain, "those with great self-love will worship humanity", and "warlike self-love is not needed". Also in the future, it is possible for the individual, the city and humanity to play a larger role – all people will come to know the fundamental ethnic nuances and will speak the same language, so that nationality will become a matter of personal conscience, even if it will be a more complicated process than in the case of religion, the ethnic preceding the latter and remaining after it.

In the last chapter, the fourth, Băncilă posed the problem of the individual means necessary to achieve humanity: "universal morality of feeling"; "power of abstraction"; "multiple perception", necessary to grasp "all the nuances, all the ethnic truths"; "cosmic egalitarianism" (there is a solidarity of people who represent for the universe "a nothingness"). These are ideas that are merely stated, without any cognitive support.

Four more pages about the nation...

A month later, in November 1921, the student Vasile Băncilă is again concerned with the nation and compiles some sheets on about four pages, devising a five-part plan: what the nation is and conclusions arising from the given definition; the genesis of the nation; the duties of the individual; and "towards something supranational" (Băncilă, 2003, pp. 102–105).

In the opening part, he repeats, slightly differently formulated, things he said in relation to the individual-nation binomial, with two clarifications that I wish to emphasise: first, individuals can enrich the nation with new qualities, for example, the English – with practicality, with empiricist metaphysics; second, it is not the economic that is the indispensable element of a nation (a good departure from Marxist determinism), but the soul (C. Rădulescu-Motru had already written about the power of the soul and the psychology of parvenitism, in 1908).

Nor were the conclusions drawn from the definition of the nation offering any novelty. Perhaps just some semantic overtones, such as the fact that the nation implies fundamental interests (which it satisfies within itself, without appeal to foreigners, even if it is obliged to exchange "currents of culture" with them), interests that give stability and duration; or the autonomy of the nation and its relationship with the family.

Here he quotes Marin Ştefănescu, who had already moved to Cluj in 1919 and who considered the family as the origin of the nation. It is true, says Vasile Băncilă, that the two are similar; only the family is not so complex, and is not autonomous. Then he adds: "The patriarchal family still works, because it is *large*, but it is almost something ethnic" (Băncilă, 2003, p. 103).

Also from Motru's courses came what Băncilă called a formative factor in the genesis of the nation, namely, that of "the *common* experience of the *soul, in a long historical interval*". Or the duties of the individual, the one who works so that his own society becomes a nation and he a personality, through the creation of culture, through the introduction of democracy, through social difference, through harmony, through international justice. And nationalist morality makes the ethnic consistent with the humanitarian, and the individual – with the social.

The supranational, which he mentions in the last part, is practically a kind of synonym for the humanity that Băncilă wrote about earlier. It will come "in a natural way, and not through the superordination of a nation, from one day to another". He proposed to address questions of cosmopolitanism, internationalism (economic internationalism is old), humanitarianism.

Vasile Băncilă's *ideo-logical* attitude also accepts small oscillations. He changes his mind, for example, about the role of the economy which he sees, this time, as one of the means of achieving nationhood. He cites as arguments: the situation of Switzerland (which is suffering and "no longer has transit"); the depreciation of currency in small countries, a phenomenon which also affects the rich ones; the fall of Russia, which is thus preventing the recovery of Europe by a shortage of raw materials (the case of Germany, whose machines are lacking in Russia, the situation of Poland, France and certain cities in England, all of which imported raw materials from Canada); to which he adds the example of Romania: on 17 November 1921, the setting of the maximum price for Romanian grain caused financial disaster because of foreign currency.

In these notes, he also restated something, implying he had said something new: whether nationality could ever become a matter of personal conscience (this time, Vasile Pârvan was quoted),[11] like religion. At the same time, the question also extended to the ethnic, and to something measurable such as its impact on the person; can it represent something particular, being "the *common historical experience, in its actual condensation*" (Băncilă, 2003, p. 104), i.e., can it be something historical and, at the same time, suprapersonal?

And he ventures again into futurological assumptions. If man is the same everywhere, if in the future there will be only a few worldwide human types which will represent fundamental theoretical variants and will be completely individualized in just a few forms, then nations, which are not individualized by original notes, will disappear – and there will remain a few general types, not called national anymore, but "empirical, transcendental, lively, massive, etc.".

The similarity can be made with the regional forms of a nation, which the man of culture (also a product of the nation) knows and can choose from. With one difference, however, for such an analogy: "The region only gives something picturesque, or a certain style, and not a *complete metaphysics*, as *the complete ethnic* gives. But then it won't be something national, the nation – it will be *philosophy*. As I today have philosophized as a matter of conscience, so then will the nation: it will be a system of personal philosophy or a philosophical school, alongside other schools, on the same level" (Băncilă, 2003, p. 105).

However, Băncilă immediately formulated a question, still valid today for the process of globalisation (or *glocalisation*): will the regions survive in the face of the national spirit? Will the individuals of a nation be able to escape "the local historical experience, so that all the individuals in a given zone do not take on a general local form"?

Vasile Băncilă did not outline an answer but stopped at the approximation that nations "will become a matter of conscience, not so much personal as regional", that they will reach an ethnic solidarity, just as "strong common memories bind two or more people, all their lives" (in Băncilă's writing, now and especially later, comparisons and metaphors, deeply suggestive and with impact on the receiver, abound).

Sociology of the nation – the draft of a reply

Young Băncilă will return to the concept and analysis of the nation after graduation, as can be seen from the text entitled "Theory of the Nation" (Băncilă, 2004, pp. 213–280), dated January 10, 1923.[12] It is a more extensive work, with a plan conceived in a couple of months (March 2, 1923), where no less than 14 chapters were planned to make up a book: *Sociology* or the *Problem of the Nation* (it is a title mentioned in parentheses).[13]

As it was constructed, Băncilă's approach was neither philosophy nor metaphysics, even if some chapters referred to a problematic area. Important, for example, in order of sequence, are chapter V, on ethnic reality, or chapter VI, on the means by which the metaphysical category is achieved, where he quotes the Italian Mancini (with his "ideal nation"), but also "people such as Gusti" (with his "gross error"), "spoiled by the *political* conception of the nation, as it was at the time of the French revolution".

Here too, Vasile Băncilă has conclusions drawn from the definition of the nation (in fact, it is not a definition given by using the grid of logic, a discipline to which the author often refers, but rather an analysis or a description). It invokes fatality, the notion of ethnic freedom; but it also invokes the evolution of ethnicity, with a "punch: the poetry of patriotism", chapter IX – with "an analysis of the national sentiment".

The other chapters also arouse interest: on the selfish elements in ethnic cohesion; on ethnic morality, where he states that it "leads to democracy, to sacrifice, to the recognition of other nations; the imperialism of the people against the nation" (Băncilă, 2004, p. 215). Or the section in which he aims to capture "the present moral phase of mankind and the nation" ("For the present moral state of man, ethnicity is the highest that it can be, a benevolence."), and to propose a chapter title at the end: "Towards internationalism".

It must be said that, in Băncilă's text, the chapters are not clearly delimited. The sociological perspective of the problem of the nation, the metaphysical and moral weight of the construction projected around the ethnic is evident, as are interstices of philosophical anthropology or incursions into the collective mind (see the paragraphs "Discovering the nation", or "The causes of German chauvinism": Băncilă, 2004, pp. 216–220).

"Theory of the Nation" seems to be a construction with the ambition to *replicate* similar enterprises of the time (C. Rădulescu-Motru, Nae Ionescu, D. Gusti, S. Mehedinți,[14] Pascal Mancini), but it may also pass as an unfinished edifice, with many virtual spaces. Some aspects of the sketches I have analysed above are present, expanded now; others emerge in a novel and somehow integrating structure.

Vasile Băncilă always seems to be reconciling with himself, an agreement that also takes on a form of quasi-retouching, sometimes made in a rhetorical key. For example, when he meditates on the definition of the nation, he tells us that he had some doubts after giving it the meaning of a *metaphysical category*, only to return "with determination to the first definition", believing nevertheless that a paragraph should be added to show the dual character of metaphysics: both theoretical and practical (he often gives himself themes for studying, too many of these being left in the phase of accounting and suggestion: "to show...", "to insist on...", "to investigate...", "to do...", "to solve once and for all...", "to study..."). An endless travail of re-construction and exploration; these are, among others, the cognitive vectors of the endless *notes* written by the young essayist from Brăila.

He emphasizes the fact that the nation is: "collective metaphysical attitude", "collective attitude to life", "metaphysical mass" (in strictly geographical terms), or "metaphysically massive", being fond of the latter, finding in it a definition that is "technical, suggestive, correct, brief, implies the idea of something virtual, dynamic, latent"; as the nation is "an absolute – that is, a cosmic and collective one", a "common *atmosphere* – you feel that you are entering another atmosphere; the earth is divided into ethnic zones", but it is also the society that "*satisfies man completely, really or virtually* (virtually, if the people are subjugated and tend to emancipate themselves)" (Băncilă, 2004, p. 224).

Attentive to specific differences, he engages in a long digression on the relations between ethnicity and religion, ethnicity and culture, the psychology of peoples (suggesting some "frighteningly subtle and flavourful" chapters). He cannot get past the very weak metaphysical quotient of religion, it being rather a *biological association*. But it is not a question of "the metaphysical ideas of religion and the fact that religion satisfies the metaphysical instinct of the people, but the way in which each people takes these ideas and satisfies itself with the occasion or element given by religion" (Băncilă, 2004, p. 221).

Émile Faguet, whom he quotes, says that *religion is cosmopolitan, but churches are national*; churches are not national, adds Băncilă, but the religious beliefs of a people are. He sets out to argue with others, including Schopenhauer, on the subject: religion is the metaphysics of a people. Thus he returns to the ethnic, considering it without any reservation "*primordial – the first day* of creation" (Băncilă, 2004, p. 221), religion itself being a creation of the ethnic, despite the fact that the earliest societies were religious in nature, religious consciousness thus preceding the ethnic.

Should Vasile Băncilă contradict himself in this way? No, and this is because he does not see religious consciousness as a generative principle, but as a result (namely: of ethnicity), not to mention the fact that religion is very accessible to the many, while ethnicity is more difficult for the people to understand, even if they live it and have an ethnic instinct (they are *its most faithful repository*). History *versus the* logic of history, a binomial that also explains the phenomenon whereby culture, in turn, also comes from ethnicity.

For Vasile Băncilă, the nation is in fact a multifaceted metaphysical category. This explains the many distinctions formulated to define it (in the text to which I refer, he specifies some 31), or to circumscribe it. Always speaking of metaphysics, he always defines its determinations (but not as often as he will do much later). The metaphysical is "a reaction to the phenomenon of life as such"; a reaction, however, unconfirmed by experience (even if "the material of expression is taken from it"), but an *aprioric* one. Through these, it is always in search of the essence of the nation, the result being an essentialism that is both cultural and spiritual. And also an organic vision under which everything appears structured.

As he himself says, Vasile Băncilă was looking for "an explanation of the nation; if not a true one, at least one that would clarify a number of problems better than those explanations we have today". The essence of the nation was deduced by applying several methods: mainly concordance, alongside which – for verification – he used experimental methods: the method of difference and the method of concomitant variations. And because "everything depends on the point of view you take" (as one critic put it), it remains to be seen *what that point of view* is: is it true, good, correct, useful, theoretical or practical?[15]

It does, however, add some kind of research rules: if you want "to make science, you have to depragmatize yourself, to castrate the practical, to keep it only as an object of study or a condition of understanding. *Is truth dangerous from a practical point of view? Don't tell the crowd!* This is the usefulness of technical language!" (Băncilă, 2004, p. 238; my emphasis).

A privilege that a sociologist like Dimitrie Gusti did not have. Eclecticism should be completely eliminated, as it is not the norm, but rather "opportunism or incapacity". And, avoiding any inappropriate association, he declares frankly: "After all, I am a Poincaré-ist."

*

At the time, the way in which the problem of the nation was approached was rather poor. What, according to Băncilă, were the causes of insufficient, inadequate analyses of the nation? The fact that "historians, geographers, revolutionaries, statesmen, lawyers, scholars or erudites" wrote about it, and not "race sociologists and metaphysicians. *Every subtle problem demands its metaphysician*; because it is a problem of sociology; and the difficulties of this discipline are known" (Băncilă, 2004, p. 241).

On another level and a little differently, I will reiterate a significant line: Vasile Băncilă reproduces the same words that a professor who came to the Philosophy department after Vasile Pârvan would have said: "So far you've wasted your time, let's start again!"

In his ethnic élan, the young Băncilă, professor of philosophy, seems to exaggerate with his own logical-rational deductions, even when they take a rhetorical turn. Speaking, for example, of pseudo-ethnicities, communities that cannot have a complete metaphysics or are indistinguishable in any way from other ethnicities, invoking the existence of small peoples that can confuse larger ones, he ends up somehow giving grist to the mill of imperialist tendencies: "And isn't it better to enlarge the large ones, to serve as ethnographic material, as the Germans wanted? Isn't it true that the bigger the people, the more they give, in terms of complexity and power? And then, isn't it better to keep the large peoples? In any case, should ethnic aborigines be absent?" (Băncilă, 2004, p. 242).

But he does not stop here with the cascade of questions around the edges of such a *burning issue*. True, he says, if we are convinced that a community "is not and will never be *anything* under the aspect of ethnic metaphysics, then it is better to melt into a neighbouring nation"; only we cannot know this, "except in the very rare cases of fragments of old peoples, which, however, we respect as such"; beyond some peoples which remain thousands of years in the same state (he does not give examples) and manifest *ethnic pessimism* (this is the meaning of the Romanian *doina)*, it is "impossible for a collective mass, *put in good conditions*, not to emerge from a collective metaphysical personality" (Băncilă, 2004, p. 242; emphasis added).

But Vasile Băncilă sometimes has categorical errors, let's call them that. He disputes, for example, the existence as nations of certain known spaces: Switzerland, Belgium, which "could never be", and the USA – "if it weren't for the English language and the Yankees, what would it be? They are the barbarians of the United States", "a nation in the making", "damned if they will be; with the virtualities of creating a metaphysics both strong and complex", especially *"the metaphysics of the economic ideal* (and the metaphysics of imperialist pride?)" (Băncilă, 2004, p. 248, on the psychology of the Americans and their difference from the English; he summarises here some essential features). As he offers, symmetrically, partial but good approximations of a possible future: "Russia, the United States, and Japan will in the future have the most powerful metaphysics [!]; and as they happen to be side by side, it will not be surprising if the centre moves to them, and they start dictating to the world" (Băncilă, 2004, p. 250).

*

There are important phases in the evolution of the ethnic: when it has reached the threshold of the nation and when it becomes conscious, first in the educated or ruling class, then in the whole ethnic mass, so that in the third phase, the nation reaches the "scientific consciousness of the metaphysical ethnic category" (the situation of France or England at that time). And then there is the phase when a nation takes into account not only its own right, but also that of the other nations (no single nation had reached this point of evolution, although the Romanians, as a people, are "well endowed" from the perspective of the fourth point of view, having a real cultural superiority).

Vasile Băncilă compares the phases of evolution of the nation with those of the individual and wonders whether it is possible to change the metaphysical category of an ethnic group, which would be equivalent to changing the character of an individual. An analogy with similarities and differences that cannot be crossed. For an individual's character can change with age; but if the same thing happens to a nation, which thus changes its metaphysical category, then we are dealing with a different nation. "Well," says Băncilă, "that's easy to say, but difficult to apply", because how do we know *when* that nation became another! It is true that in evolution the essence changes so many times, and in this case, *the national essence* is precisely the metaphysical category we are talking about. So what? It is a hypothesis that "cannot be useful".

Professor Vasile Băncilă's current discourse is always interrogative, even if he is not satisfied by the solutions of successive, unexpected and numerous *approximations* (there is here a personal code that the author seems to have preserved in his discursive being). In the background of the ethnic, however, there remain the figure and the metamorphoses of the individual, as instances of analogy or comparison. An *organicism* in which he finds similarities, but also radical differences, even antipodal situations. This is what he does when he speaks, more practically than scientifically, about the death of nations or their morality, about ethnic cohesion, about the psychology of the people, about patriotism or nationalism, about the relationship between ethnicity and social classes (noting that this was the beginning of the third decade of the twentieth century).

But it is not only the individual that is taken as a reference system: "Between humanity and the nation there is not, there cannot *be* the same relationship as between the nation and individuals". In many of the answers given to various questions, he uses comparisons and analogies. And this is out of a desire to find a *definition* as appropriate as possible for the *essence of* the nation: "Finally, let me give a grammatical summary definition of the nation based on the enumeration of the main definitions above, followed by a brief, militant definition, which will remain as an ultimate conclusion in the mind of the reader" (Băncilă, 2004, p. 265).

In this sense, Vasile Băncilă makes, at one point, a curtain call with many of the characters of the ethnic group that has reached the stage of the nation: *fatality, complexity, freedom, unity, durability, soul autonomy, the most creative culture, conscience, social classes, democracy, respect for another nation.*

Ethnicity, Băncilă adds, is a subject that lends itself to bias. What is repugnant to us in some nations: vanity, selfishness, hypocrisy are not products of ethnicity, they do not belong to its essence, for they are fatal to any society. And ethnic idealism is represented by people of culture, not by politicians, who are either inherently selfish or are forced to manifest themselves in this way, and this because they defend the interests of the "common people".

Towards the end of the manuscript on the theory of the nation, as he did in previous texts, Băncilă emphasized: ethnic temperament (for example: the reaction of the Hungarians when they were separated from Transylvania and some other territories: "Never, but never!"); the ethnic category (a German monk would not have done something identical to Louis XIV "when he renounced the horrors in the Low Countries"); the nation, which is not only a metaphysical category, but also something real (although there are good arguments even for something abstract); the homogeneity and solidarity of ethnicity (examples and exceptions); the philosophical school and religion can change, but not the nation (ethnicity is "a latent metaphysical complex"); the exceptional value of music in rendering the nature of a people, of ethnicity.

2.2 Profile of Romanian Philosophy

A flawed taxonomy

Volume VI of Vasile Băncilă's works (2008) also contains some notes on the identity of our national philosophy. In November 1940, he systematically set out some eight directions in which it would be affirmed. First, there was philological philosophy (Tocilescu, P. P. Negulescu,[16] M. Florian, N. Bagdasar, P. Andrei, Bîrsănescu, D. Gusti), which oscillated between critical sense and massive philologism. In some of these, for example, in Gusti ("genius manager in science"), the attitude is *administrative*, by organizing the ideas of philosophers.

There followed a period of Romanian structural positivism (not Comtiste), manifested by attachment to the phenomenon (Parhon, again P. P. Negulescu, C. Rădulescu-Motru), after which mysticism was established (a little in Motru and, paradoxically, in Şt. Zeletin),[17] with the specification that, in a Romanian context, there are no pure mystics; so that immediately, perhaps naturally, a philosophy of Orthodoxy or Orthodoxism was established (Nae Ionescu, Nichifor Crainic).

The formation of modern Romanian culture favoured other orientations of thought, such as rhetorical philosophy (T. Maiorescu,[18] Coco-Iaşi, I. Petrovici), but also rhetorical and conversational philosophy (Coco-Iaşi,[19] Alice Voinescu);[20] and the philosophy of historians (N. Iorga, V. Pârvan), when history facilitated cultural assimilation. The penultimate direction would have been that of frivolous philosophy (sectarianism?), which includes philosophical minorism and *Salon atheism* (M. Ralea,[21] D. Suchianu).[22] Finally, integralism, both rational and mystical, represented by Blaga; beyond which there seems to be an aestheticizing philosophical direction of literary critics, or perhaps a critical one, illustrated in some aspects by Nae Ionescu and Constantin Noica.

It is easy to see, with an unbiased eye, that several names are missing from Vasile Băncilă's quotations made in 1940. For that time, it is surprising (I am talking about his national attachment to the values of Romanian thought) to note the absence of Dimitrie Cantemir,[23] the Transylvanian School, Ion Eliade Rădulescu,[24] Eufrosin Poteca, Simion Bărnuţiu,[25] Vasile Conta,[26] Mihail Kogălniceanu, Ion Zalomit,[27] Mihai Eminescu,[28] Bogdan Petriceicu Haşdeu,[29] Alexandru D. Xenopol,[30] Marxist philosophy (Constantin Dobrogeanu-Gherea),[31] but also of authors from the interwar period: the philosopher Constantin Antoniade,[32] a historian of philosophy such as Iosif Brucăr,[33] Dumitru D. Roşca,[34] Dumitru Stăniloae,[35] Emil Cioran, Mircea Eliade, Camil Petrescu,[36] Petre P. Ionescu (concerned with the *metaphysics of thought*, like Băncilă, whom he followed as a collaborator of the journal *Thought*), Stelian Mateescu[37] (the list is incomplete; in a later entry, he will recalibrate his judgment).

Beyond these absences, a question looms on the margins of the systematization of directions in Romanian philosophy: which of the *national* authors cited are *also European*? It is a question for which Vasile Băncilă does not attempt any answering approximation, especially since, among his projects, there was also a *history of European philosophy* in some nine volumes (see Băncilă, 2008, June 1947, p. 32).

Elusive justifications

It is true that, without further justification, he stated a couple of decades later – around July 1971 – that modern Romanian philosophy had the misfortune of being formed in the second half of the nineteenth century, a period "when the Western philosophical atmosphere was vitiated by empiricism". After that, it took its revenge through Iorga and Pârvan,[38] "partly through C. Rădulescu-Motru, and very profoundly through Nae Ionescu and Lucian Blaga – but then came the second impropriety: Communism" (Băncilă, 2008, p. 116). Băncilă's conclusion was that, between 1918 and 1940, Romanian philosophy had begun to develop in a very promising way.

But what came before modern Romanian philosophy? Didn't Băncilă retain anything from the first philosophical synthesis operated in *traditional Romanian culture*? He who claimed to be part of the patriarchal Romanian community, of the traditional Romanian village, of the Orthodox faith of the Romanian peasant!

An explanation could perhaps be found in a note from August 1973, where he said: "The most authentic philosophical thought in the three Romanian countries has been represented, until recently, by historians (and theologians). The most *organic*, in any case" (Băncilă, 2008, p. 123). By "recently" I mean up to Vasile Conta, or especially up to C. Rădulescu-Motru, Nae Ionescu and Blaga. A generic historical Chronicler is now quoted, followed by Cantemir, the Predoslovii, the Ivireni chroniclers, Bălcescu, Kogălniceanu, Xenopol ("a historian and a philosophical intelligence"), Hașdeu, Iorga ("historian, great writer with fundamental philosophical intuitions"), Pârvan ("historian, philosopher and poet"), Kico (i.e., the historian P.P. Panaitescu). He thought it would be interesting to study "*the archaeology of the* formation of a philosophical discipline in Romania".

And now the next thought just occurred to him: "What to say of folklore: philosophy par excellence; all folklore has a philosophical structure". With a philosophical vision that differs from one people to another, folklore represents, for nations, the most organic way of seeing the world (*Weltanschauung*), but also their psychology (he refers to Liviu Rusu's book – a secondary doctoral thesis).[39]

Beyond the space of the worksheets, from the two relatively completed essays dated March 1965 ("The Genesis and Evolution of Philosophy") and September 11, 1965 ("The Value of Philosophy"), the latter also quotes Romanians two or three times: Bălcescu, Eminescu, Maiorescu, Hașdeu, Pârvan, I. Petrovici, Nae Ionescu, Blaga (see Băncilă, 2008, p. 188), all illustrating a concept of philosophy seen as the *embellishment of life*, in the paragraph on philosophy and pragmatic efficiency, Stephen the Great is mentioned together with Napoleon, Pericles, Caesar, Charles the Great, personalities who rarely appear in history (see Băncilă, 2008, p. 189). Brătescu-Voinești is also mentioned; after the First World War, he constructed an improper, disastrous ideology based on a kind of *homo angelicus (a* similar gesture was made by J.M. Guyau in the field of morality), in contrast to those who exaggerated the identity of *homo oeconomicus,* including the ideology of Marxist Communism.

Notes

[1] Ştefănescu, M. (1880–1945). Romanian Christian philosopher, historian of philosophy, logician. Among his writings: *Essay on the relationship between dualism and Kant's theism* (1915), *Romanian Philosophy* (1922), *The Problem of Method* (1938), *Christian Philosophy: Contributions to the Understanding of Philosophy* (1943).

[2] Vulcănescu, M. (1904–1952). Romanian philosopher, philologist, politician, sociologist. Among his writings: *The two Romanias (*1932), *The peasant household and cooperation* (1933), & als, *D. Gusti and the Bucharest sociological school* (1937), *The war for Greater Romania* (1938), *The Romanian dimension of existence* (1943), *Our daily Good Lord: studies in religion* (posthumous, 2004).

[3] Noica, C. (1909–1987). Romanian philosopher, logician and publicist, the greatest thinker after Lucian Blaga; in his youth he had a Right-wing ideological orientation; the ontological operator of his philosophy is the concept of "in" (a term which is originally a preposition); among his works: *Mathesis or the simple joys* (1934), *Pages about the Romanian soul* (1944), *Romanian philosophical discourse* (1970), *The Romanian sense of being* (1978), *Six maladies of the contemporary spirit (*1978), *Being and becoming* (1981), *Letters about the logic of Hermes* (1986).

[4] See Rădulescu-Motru, C. (1980). *Personalism and other writings.*

[5] See Ionescu, N. (1996). *Course on the history of metaphysics.* Bucharest: Anastasia Publishing House, *passim.*

[6] Florian, M. (1888–1960). Romanian philosopher with doctorate in Germany: *Concept of Time in Henri Bergson* (1914); for the present reference, see *Experience as a Principle of Philosophical Reconstruction,* Bucharest, Gramar Publishing House, 2002, pp. 141–151, 166–186; other writings: *Metaphysics and Art: the Fate of Metaphysics* (1946), *Logic and Epistemology* (1946), *Recessivity as Structure of the World* (posthumous, 1983).

[7] Petrovici, I. (1882–1972). Romanian philosopher, memorialist and politician; among his writings: *Philosophical research* (1907), *Logic problems* (1911), *Introduction to metaphysics* (1924), *Titu Maiorescu, 1840–1917 (*1931), *Kant's life and work* (1936), *Schopenhauer* (1937), *The philosophy of compromise* (1937).

[8] Stahl, H. H. (1901–1991). Romanian anthropologist, ethnographer and sociologist, important representative of the *monographic school* of Bucharest; among his writings: *Technique of the sociological monograph* (1934), *Sociology of the Romanian Devalmaș village* (1946), *Theory and practice of social investigations* (2 vols., 1975), *Dimitrie Gusti. Critical studies* (1986); for the present reference, see *Romanian Sociology* magazine, no. 11–12/1927, 1–3, 4–6/1938.

[9] Basically, there are two great theories of the nation that have become classics: the French one (one state, one nation), and the German one (which accepts the existence of parts of the nation beyond its geopolitical borders). In 1913, I. V. Stalin had spoken of "the national question and social democracy", meanings which then found their way into dictionaries. Today, to simplify, we speak of two views of the nation: one which considers the nation to have a real existence, the other which identifies it as a *cultural artefact*, a virtual invented community which therefore does not belong to any social group. There are nation states, such as Romania, but there is also talk of *civic nations* (Belgium, France, Poland, Slovakia), the civic nation designating a contract between citizen and city, between citizen and state; multi-ethnic states are also possible, as is the distinction between nation and people, many states referring to the latter in their definition (Austria, Germany, Switzerland, Finland, Portugal, Czech Republic); or neither nation nor people (Denmark, Norway, Netherlands, Luxembourg, Serbia, Montenegro, Liechtenstein, Republic of Macedonia, Cyprus).

[10] Kogălniceanu, M. (1817–1891). Romanian liberal politician, lawyer, historian and publicist; among his writings: "*The History of Wallachia, Moldavia and the Transdanubian Wallachians" (1837),* "*The Despoiling of the Gypsies, the Abolition of Bohemian Privileges, the Emancipation of the Peasants"* (1837; both works, printed in French, were signed Michel de Kogalnitchan), "The Demands of the National Party of Moldavia" (February 1848).

[11] Pârvan, V. (1882–1927). Romanian historian, archaeologist, essayist; among his writings: *Nationality of Merchants in the Roman Empire* (1908), doctoral thesis in German), *Historical Ideas and Forms* (1920), *Memorials* (1923), *Getica. A Protohistory of Dacia* (1926).

[12] It is a manuscript of 46 pages, written on both sides. Subsequent quoations are from the volume, with the page number in brackets.

[13] To see the place of this approach in interwar sociological discourse, see Dungaciu, D. (2011). *The Interwar Elite. Romanian Sociology in the European Context* (Contributions to a Sociology of Sociology). Bucharest: Small Wallachia Publishing House.

[14] Mehedinți, S. (1868–1962). Romanian geographer and geopolitician. Among his writings: *Problems of Contemporary Geography as a Science of the Cosmos* (1900), *Introduction to the Study of Geography* (1904), *To the New Generation* (1912), *The Political Man* (1915), *The Statesman's Characteristics* (1919).

[15] Speaking of Gusti's mistakes or superficiality, he says: "From a political or legal point of view, of course, Gusti's definition may be good, but from a scientific point of view, it is not."

[16] Negulescu, P. P. (1872–1951). Romanian philosopher and politician. Among his writings: *Philosophy of the Renaissance* (2 vols., 1910–1914), *Genesis of the Forms of Culture* (1934), *Destiny of Mankind* (4 vols., 1938–1944), *History of Contemporary Philosophy* (5 vols., 1941–1971).

[17] Zeletin, Ș. (1882–1934). Romanian philosopher, economist and sociologist. Among his writings: *Metaphysics of the Back* (1912, unfinished), *From the Land of Donkeys. Writings* (1916), *Romanian bourgeoisie, its origins and historical role* (1925), *Neoliberalism* (1927), *Thoughts about the world and life* (1928).

[18] Maiorescu, T. (1840–1917). Lawyer, philosopher, politician, aesthetician and the first Romanian professional critic. Among his writings: *Daily notes* (1851–1917, 42 notebooks), *Philosophical considerations for everybody* (1861), *About Romanian poetry* (1867), *Against the contemporary direction in Romanian Culture* (1868), *Mr. Caragiale's comedies* (1885), *Eminescu and his poetry* (1889), *Aphorisms about wisdom in life* by Arthur Schopenhauer (1890, translation), *Critique* (3 vol., 1892), *Parliamentary Discourses* (5 vols., 1895–1915).

[19] It is a name that, unfortunately, the history of Romanian philosophy has not remembered.

[20] Voinescu, A. (1885–1961). Romanian writer, essayist, theatre critic and translator. Among her writings: *Interpretation of Kant's doctrine by the Marburg School. Study on Critical Idealism* (1913), *Montaigne. Man and Work* (1936), *Aspects of Contemporary Theatre* (1941), *Diary* (posthumously, 1997).

[21] Ralea, M. (1896–1964). Romanian philosopher, psychologist, sociologist, diplomat; his father was Bulgarian and his mother - Jewish. Among his writings: *Interpretations* (1927), *Attitudes* (1931), *Explaining Man* (1944–1945), *In the Extreme West* (1955).

[22] Nor is the philosophical performance of this name recorded by Romanian philosophy.

[23] Cantemir, D. (1674–1723). Romanian ruler of Moldavia, encyclopaedic spirit, philosopher, historian, geographer, musicologist, composer. Among his writings: *Divan or The Wise Man's Dialogue with the World* (1698), *The Unfinished Icon of Sacred Science* (1700), *Hieroglyphic History* (1703–1705), *History of the Rise and Fall of the Ottoman Empire* (1714–1716).

[24] Heliade-Rădulescu, I. (1802–1872). Romanian philosopher, writer, politician. Among his writings: *Romanian Grammar* (1828), *Philosophy. Closure of aforementioned sayings* (1840–1842), *Equilibrium between antitheses or spirit and matter* (1859–1869), *A quick glance upon the origin and language of the Romanians* (1836).

[25] Bărnuțiu, S. (1808–1864). Romanian university professor, philosopher, historian and politician. Among his writings: *Public Law of Romanians* (1867), *Private Natural Law* (1868), *Public Natural Law* (1870), *Encyclopaedia of Theoretical Philosophy, Metaphysics*.

[26] Conta, V. (1845–1882). Romanian philosopher, writer, politician. Among his writings: *Theory of Fatalism* (1875–1876), *Theory of Universal Ripple* (1876–1877), *Attempts at Metaphysics* (1879), *Basics of Metaphysics* (1890).

[27] Zalomit, I. (1810–1885). Romanian professor of philosophy. Among his writings: *Principles and Merits of Kant's Philosophy* (1848), *The State of Public Instruction in Romania* (1862).

[28] Eminescu, M. (1850–1889). Publicist, metaphysical thinker, prose writer, the greatest Romanian poet. In critical editions, his work is printed in 16 A4 volumes.

[29] Petriceicu Haşdeu, B. (1838–1907). Romanian encyclopaedic spirit, writer, historian and politician. Among his writings: *The historical archive of Romania* (1865-1867), *Critical history* (1873-1874), *Words from the ancestors* (1878–1879), *Etymologicum Magnum Romaniae* (4 vols., 1887–1898, unfinished work).

[30] Xenopol, A. D. (1847–1920). Philosopher of history, historian, economist, Romanian writer. Among his writings: *Röesler's Theory. Study on the stagnation of the Romanians in Thracian Dacia* (1884), *A historical enigma. Romanians in the Middle Ages* (1885), *History of the Romanians of Thracian Dacia* (6 vols., 1888–1893), *Fundamental Principles of History* (1900).

[31] Dobrogeanu-Gherea, C. (1855–1920). Romanian writer, socialist thinker of Jewish origin. Among his writings: *Neo-serfdom* (Economic and sociological study of our agrarian problem) (1910), *Critical studies* (1923), *On metaphysical and scientific criticism, On metaphysical and scientific aesthetics*.

[32] Antoniade, C. (1880–1954). Romanian writer, historian, philosopher and diplomat. Among his writings: *The Realism Illusion. Essay on Philosophical Criticism* (1907), The *Philosophy of Henri Bergson* (1908), *Imperialism of German Culture* (1915), *Three Figures of the Renaissance: Pierre Arétin, Guichardin, Benvenuto Cellini* (1938), *Figures of the Cinquecento: Princesses, Courtiers and Courtesans* (1939),

[33] Brucăr, I. (1888–1960). Historian of Romanian philosophy. Among his writings: *Essays and Studies* (1919), *Philosophy of Spinoza* (1930), *Philosophers and Systems* (1933), *Bergson* (1935).

[34] Roşca, D. D. (1895–1980). Translator of Hegel into Romanian, Romanian philosopher. Among his writings: *Taine's Influence on Hegel* (1928), *Tragic Existence* (1934), *History of Philosophy* (1964), *Lectures on Aesthetics* (1966), *Lectures on the Philosophy of History* (1969), *People and Climate* (1971).

[35] Stăniloae, D. (1903–1993). Romanian priest, theologian, university professor, publicist. Among his writings: *Catholicism after the war* (1933), *Orthodoxy and Romanianism* (1939), *Lucian Blaga's position on Christianity and Orthodoxy* (1942), *The Life and Teachings of St. Gregory Palamas* (1938), *Jesus Christ or the Restoration of Man* (1943), *Dogmatic and Symbolic Theology* (2 vols., handbook in collaboration, 1958).

[36] Petrescu, C. (1894–1957). Romanian novelist, playwright, philosopher. Among his writings: *Last Night of Love, First Night of War* (1930), *The Bed of Procrustes* (1933), *Theses and Antitheses* (1937), *The Aesthetic Modality of Theatre* (1938), *The Doctrine of Substance* (1940, 1988).

[37] Mateescu, S. (1903–1976). Romanian writer, philosopher. Among his writings: *Dialectics of the Absolute* (1933).

[38] Pârvan, V. (1882–1927). Romanian historian, archaeologist and writer. Among his writings: *Relations of Stephen the Great with Hungary* (1905), *M. Aurelius Verus Caesar and L. Aurelius Commodus* (1909), *Historical Ideas and Forms* (1920), *Memorials* (1923), *Getica. A Protohistory of Dacia* (1926).

[39] Rusu, L. (1901–1985). Romanian psychologist, literary historian, aesthetician. Among his writings: *Goethe, a few aspects* (1932), *Max Dessoir, aesthetician and philosopher* (1933), *Essay on artistic creation. Contribution to a Dynamic Aesthetics* (1935), *Logic of*

Beauty (1946), *From Eminescu to Lucian Blaga and Other Literary and Aesthetic Studies* (1971), *Writings on Titu Maiorescu* (1979).

Chapter 3

Philosophy and high school

3.1 Notes for an ephebology

There is a conjunction that interested the young Vasile Băncilă, perhaps to the highest degree. He was disturbed by the deviant role of philosophy at that historical moment, more precisely "The Role of Philosophy in High School" (Băncilă, 2004, pp. 89–143), about which he wrote at the end of 1922. It is a manuscript of about 112 pages, partly typed and conceived, I believe, as a *reformist reaction* to the frustrating reality that the newly appointed philosophy teacher (with *magna cum laude* in his Bachelor's degree) perceived. His teaching activity began, in the fourth year of his studies, at the Evangelic High School in Bucharest, where he taught until the school year 1922–1923. From the autumn of that year, he worked as a teacher for the subjects of philosophy and logic at the Normal School for Boys in Brăila, and between 1925–1927 and 1929–1930 he specialized in Paris, as a member of the Romanian School of Fontenay-aux-Roses – Iorga's school.

"The role of philosophy in high school" is a predominantly pedagogical approach, comprising three parts. In the first of these, an attempt is made to approximate the notion of philosophy; a precise and correct formulation was impossible in the evolutionary stage of this discipline at that time, designed to satisfy the human being's instinct for knowledge, *the metaphysical instinct*, the strongest of the spiritual instincts. The young professor Băncilă perceived the non-unitary object of philosophy (in a *transitional* phase), its relationship with the positive sciences, its property of arriving not at truth but at hypotheses and probabilities; philosophy offers, says Băncilă, "an infinite vegetation of possibilities of truths – a vast equatorial forest in the field of thought".

*

Pedagogically speaking, philosophy develops the formative culture of the individual, starting from a synthesis of the forces of the soul and arriving at a form of synthesis, one which contributes to the formation of *the ideal* (see Băncilă, 2004, pp. 287–290) and which also leads to wisdom (or to some form of wisdom), even if it does not reach it. It is at this point that Băncilă invokes the question of age (see Băncilă, 1997), which is extremely important for the pedagogical spirit and for the psychology of the child (he quotes Locke, Kant,

Pestalozzi, Rousseau, Comenius, Claparède). He thus attempts approximations for what he calls an *ephebology* (from *ephebus*, lat.), a term he invented ad hoc; his discourse on the metaphysical function in childhood and adolescence – but not youth – also acquires *gender* overtones in this segment.

After a long presentation about the needs of adolescent learners, about the directions and the extent to which philosophy can be made available to everyone, the teacher proceeds to draw some pragmatic conclusions. The philosophical systematisation of knowledge, the need for unity of knowledge, synthetic curiosity, the voluptuousness of creation, the – instinctive – relationship between the subjective absolute and existence itself are some of them. But the vectors that guide the philosophy-adolescence binomial are then nominated, pedagogically, in five directions: the *question of the unity of the objects of education, science and religion, formal culture, the ideal and the physiological substratum of education.*

It starts with the so-called cheetah of pedagogy (and education), namely: the correlation of the objects of education, noting a lack of this feature in the specific process of education in Romania, a disease hundreds and thousands of years old; here is a valuable guideline for today's teachers, not only those who teach philosophy but also those who instruct students in science and religion, teachers who must not suffer from pedagogical laziness or use improvisation; as it is also an important document that should be appropriately assimilated and applied by the Minister who coordinates national education.

The conclusions that can guide the formal culture of the adolescent are also actual, going beyond the simplistic pedagogical trilogy of intellectual, moral and physical education, by insisting on the culture of forces in adolescence (for which he specifies about six directions). Here, too, Vasile Băncilă makes full use of his pedagogical training from one of his Bachelor's theses, an area in which – as he would later tell Blaga – he was unduly late.

The pedagogue in him, though without much experience, was precisely oriented towards secondary education, which he would later coordinate as director in the Ministry in charge. He considered the sociological and metaphysical formation of a collective critical understanding, on the one hand, and historical and geographical understanding, on the other, to be important for adolescence. He also saw the moral understanding and mystical background that emerge at this age as important; all of these, together, feed the formation of the definitive soul value of the *ethnic instinct.*

3.2 Childhood or the small homeland

Vasile Băncilă pays a lot of attention to the great stages of life. Childhood, or *the small homeland*, is considered the period of an individual's life when the logical, metaphysical and biological basis of ethnic strength is built, using sources with a considerable contribution to the formation of the adolescent's personality that will give strength to ethnic attachment. And one more thing worth mentioning: the importance given to the development of the spirit of grammar (let us remember, from Ion Creangă,[1] what havoc such an attitude caused at the school of church singers in Fălticeni),[2] the same grammar that I. L. Caragiale[3] recommended, for journalists, in conjunction with honesty ("Honour and grammar!"), while Aristotle saw in said grammar an exclusive ontic condition for the quality of being human.

The absolute priority, however, was represented by philosophy classes (characterized by courtesy, simplicity and life), classes of "a baroque and guilty insufficiency", surpassed in number by those of agronomy and zootechnics; philosophy, says Băncilă, should no longer constitute a kind of ironic garnish for the school curriculum, but should be introduced – with at least one hour a week – starting from the fourth and fifth grades, and gradually increasing its weight in the curriculum. All the more so as the essential motivation of Băncilă's approach was the positive role of philosophy, considered a general instrument for the elaboration of the integral theory of education specific to all subjects of secondary education. Neither the training of secondary education teachers nor the organisation of the philosophy faculty was omitted; his suggestions are still relevant today.

The conclusion young Vasile Băncilă arrives at, with all its ramifications, is by no means anachronistic or utopian. On the contrary. Its semantic core is represented by the exceptional educational value of adolescence, the simmering and luminous emergence of a higher humanity thus constituting the basis of man's moral, social, metaphysical, intellectual and, in part, even physical personality.

Just as in politics or in war the timing of an action is essential, so the way in which adolescence is organised and lived is important for the full formation of a person. Băncilă compares it to "a furnace heated to a high temperature, in which the hardest materials are melted into a unique creation". "*In the evolution of the individual*", he says axiomatically, "*there is only one moment when the maximum can be realised from the force of the soul*" (Băncilă, 2004, p. 138), so that such a moment must be known in advance, must be awaited, seized and exploited to the full.

3.3 Adolescence – personality cheetah

After childhood, this moment is none other than adolescence. Philosophy (as an active and unifying atmosphere) and adolescence form a vital binomial whose endosmosis contributes decisively to the formation of a personality. Here can be found another kind of cheetah, only this time not of pedagogy, but of the psychology of ages.

Băncilă was somewhat circumspect with his, so to speak, reformist assumptions and conclusions. The ideas put forward (illustrating an ideal that might actually prove to be impossible, unattainable), beyond their unquestionable value, were not complete, as they constituted exaggerations of modest truths, circumstantial intuitions that equated the professor of philosophy with a kind of superman with a superhuman soul.

*

All of the above are lines and ideas from Vasile Băncilă's youth, rough sketches or attempts on various themes, partially written, with a heavy style sometimes bordering on the edge of anxiety yet with an undeniable and intense intellectual combustion. Later, starting in 1938 and continuing in the post-war period, when Băncilă's soul was fecundly obsessed with the elaboration of a *system of philosophy* (which would spring from the Romanian ethos and, equally, from religion: September 1938), his meditation will contain an enormous number of unsystematised worksheets as such; the ones that should be mentioned first, given the present context, are those that have as their theme "The definition of philosophy" (see, Băncilă, 2008); then I will turn to the parts that make up a whole system of philosophy.

The conclusion I suggest is as simple as possible: judged, as Noica would say, by the grid of *Hermes' logic,* of the *holomere,* the fragmentary, provisional, occasional and summarizing notes of the student Vasile Băncilă can somehow be raised, through a forced and risky extension, to the power of a possible whole or of a part made up of other parts-subsections. In other words, guided both by a metaphysical instinct (which, according to Băncilă, is part of our biology) and by cognitive interests, the notes of this rich archipelago can be coagulated in the form of meaningful islands for the later intellectual exercise of the thinker.

Notes

[1] Creangă, I. (1837–1889). Romanian writer, one of the most valuable Romanian storytellers.

He wrote many stories, short stories, novellas, and an autobiographical novel.

[2] Băncilă quotes this eloquent passage: "*Mi-ți ni-vi-li, me-te-îl-o, ne-ve-i-le; me-te-o, ne-ve-i-le, mi-ți-i ni-vi-li. What's that, go to the wilderness! Some were rocking like madmen, till they were dizzy; others were only roaring, till their sight was failing; some smacked their lips as if having a fit. Most of the others were walking about in a state of stunned silence, and were thinking how they were wasting their time, and only sighed heavily, knowing how many needs awaited them at home. And I have never seen such headache and tongue-lashing as in these unfortunates; a terrible trick of tinkering, God forbid!*"

[3] Caragiale, I. L. (1852–1912). Playwright, novelist, pamphleteer, publicist, one of the most important Romanian writers. Among his writings: *Novellas, stories* (1908), *Theatre. Complete works* (1908), *Moments, sketches, reminiscences* (1908), *New sketches* (1910).

Chapter 4

Irony and its paideutic role

4.1 Towards a pedagogy of irony

A 167-page typed study on "The Pedagogy of Irony" (Băncilă, 2004, pp. 9–88), also dating from 1922–1923, is preserved (there is also a 42-page manuscript with many corrections and additions). On a note attached to the typed text (dated December 2, 1940) Ion Rădulescu-Pogoneanu, a lecturer in the Department of Pedagogy at the Faculty of Letters and Philosophy of the University of Bucharest stated that it was a "definitive work for pedagogical practice", presented by the student Vasile Băncilă at the University Pedagogical Seminaries in Bucharest, a text revised after a couple of years by the author.

Nearly a century has passed since Vasile Băncilă's notes on irony were written. The concept was not new at that time either. From Socrates to S. Kierkegaard (*On the concept of irony, with constant reference to Socrates*, 1841), without, however, avoiding German Romanticism, literature and philosophy have said essential things about the surface and the deep layers of irony. And from then until the postmodernists, the discourse on irony has been protean, with the subject being approached from various angles, particularly by the humanities. Among other things, there are still worthy studies such as Vladimir Jankélévitch's *Irony* (1950), or Jean Starobinski's constant studies; and in more recent times, one could even speak profitably of a poetics of irony (see *Poétique de l'ironie*, 2001, by Pierre Schoentjes).

I will not judge Vasile Băncilă, the young man of 1922–1923, inside the horizon of a century of philosophical and literary accumulations on the subject of irony. Moreover, in his introductory remarks, he barely connects with the various metaphysical and artistic meanings recorded, before him, by the discourse devoted to irony. He mentions, it is true, the names of some philosophers (except the Dane S. Kierkegaard), but only for their syllogisms on the psychology or science of education, on laughter or on a certain morality of irony.

Subtitled "Psychological outline applied to school life", the original and insightful approach, as I. R.-Pogoneanu appreciated in the Note, was a plea for a pedagogy of irony filtered through three veils: the nature of laughter, the practical philosophy of irony and the peaceful value of irony (the subtitles belong to the editor Dora Mezdrea).

Like the pages on the role of philosophy in high school, these bring an innovative, reforming conception about the status of school pedagogy (extension to university pedagogy may be illicit), a discipline imminently threatened by routine repetition. "Revolutionary progress, nowadays excluded from all fields by scientists, is especially inappropriate to pedagogy", the introductory words of the study say.

Moreover, the development of pedagogical ideas would have, through their history, the image of a madreporic diagram (the madrepore is a coral with a calcareous skeleton), and the revolutionaries who imagined that they were elaborating educational truths were deluded when they subsumed them to theoretical revolutions.

If pedagogy was monotonous, a kind of "universal and frenetic quasi-plagiarism", the young Băncilă set out to formulate a relatively new problem. To do this, he thought, we would have to ignore the past, which he did – but only partially – in his approach.

In the introductory phrases, he raises the problem of authority in the education process, which is not solved by various punishments but by a teaching strategy that is both fair and effective. He was not targeting the teacher who obtains such authority without minimal effort or, on the contrary, with difficulty, but was thinking of the educator with experience in several school environments, who adds to his educational action an imponderable means: irony.

4.2 Irony and laughter

Organically linked to the latter, we immediately discover laughter, the common meaning of irony being that of "making fun of someone, delicately and wittily, with the aim of touching him, like the invisible needle of an immaterial bee" (Băncilă, 2004, p. 13; I have already observed, the author's aptitude for comparisons and memorable lexical formulations – "to encircle", "to variegate", "to tenderize", etc.).

The problem of laughter was not new either, as it had been meditated upon from the ancients to the contemporary period. Vasile Băncilă highlights this aspect by invoking the pivotal ideas of the most appropriate essays. The following are mentioned in passing: Aristotle, Th. Hobbes, I. Kant, A. Schopenhauer, L. Dumond, Mélinard, H. Spencer and H. Bergson, authors who also interested him, some of them active in the field of educational psychology.

The nature of laughter has been variously described, including by science, and examples are given; but most philosophers' theories have focused on "*classical laughter, laughter containing intellectual conflict*" (Băncilă, 2004, p. 18). It is, in fact, laughter that is based on various forms of contrast and includes something almost insurmountable.

He adheres, as expected, to H. Bergson's construction (*Le Rire* had appeared in 1899), even if it is a "sociological and philosophical explanation of life" and less a "proper and definitive psychology" (Băncilă, 2004, p. 19) of laughter. He does not, however, remove from his choices the Schopenhauer-Dumont-Mélinard triad, authors from whom he draws the main elements for his own analysis, but from whom he stands out with insightful observations; and he also notes some of Bergson's exaggerations.

The young Băncilă bases his predominantly psychological approach on the dual nature of laughter: *intellectual conflict* and, equally, *contrast.* He identifies in laughter dimensions such as gradual absurdity and a nuanced logic (see Băncilă, 2004, pp. 20-21), for which he offers and explains vividly coloured examples (for example, the untimely and absurd appearance of a dog during a church service; it is an episode that is not laughed at by strongly religious people). Neither of these two features produces laughter, but taken together, organically, they generate contrast, a mechanism carefully deconstructed by Băncilă.

One of the author's conclusions is that laughter represents "the resolution in irrational, psychological and biological terms of a logical process that cannot be resolved in logical terms" (Băncilă, 2004, p. 25). Absurdity as an impossibility becomes possible through the logical filter, thus producing the necessary energy of laughter, which cumulatively has a "*biological, intellectual, metaphysical value*" (Băncilă, 2004, p. 26; here he offers the example of students who are prone to spontaneous laughter; elsewhere, he also speaks of an ideal laughter, one in which its synthetic character and "degrees of synthesism" shine through – Băncilă, 2004, p. 34).

The nature of laughter, as I have already suggested, is deciphered by the young Băncilă by appealing to the psychology of the person and of age, with examples that are mostly known and edifying. The nuances of laughter are based on the differences between individuals and, at the limit, even on the differences between peoples (laughter would be more specific to Latins than to Germans – Băncilă, 2004, p. 30).

The connection with Bergson's statements is activated from time to time, either to reinforce what has been said or to make some corrections. Moreover,

Băncilă believes with some emphasis that his explanations can encompass many other theories which somehow offer general characterizations, elements that can be "placed in layers from the outside in", or "reveal particular themes or linings of the laughable conflict" (Băncilă, 2004, p. 33).

4.3 Pragmatism of irony

From the nature of laughter as a constitutive element of irony Vasile Băncilă moves on to a *pragmatic* analysis of the latter. He asks which of the various forms of laughter is really part of irony, ruling out, from the outset, purely physical laughter (that would be obtained through tickling), nervous laughter or laughter through suggestion (even if one can speak of irony through suggestion). The following remain essential: laughter generated by logical conflict (he notes that irony is also a serious weapon in social life – see Băncilă, 2004, p. 35), laughter caused by a discharge of energy, or intentional laughter (also analysed psychologically).

The relationship between irony and laughter is not just theoretically important. Can irony be regarded as a more complex psychological value than laughter, or is it just a form of laughter, as it appears in Schopenhauer and Bergson? Băncilă chooses the first option, indicating a distinction made between laughter and those soul complexes that express it, which may or may not make laughter ironic or, on the contrary, favour an attitude full of humour. However, a precise delimitation of irony as a form of ironic laughter is needed, on the one hand, and of what distinguishes it from laughter itself, on the other.

Băncilă sees the characteristic of irony in "the tendency that laughter sometimes has to bring valid self-love damage to the subject of the irony, or to damage in some way the object of the irony" (Băncilă, 2004, p. 36). If laughter as such, pure and simple laughter, is something theoretical, touching someone tangentially, irony, on the other hand, is an obviously practical attitude, like laughter (not the general one, but the intentional one). The outward effects of laughter, those not aimed at one's self-love, are generated by the meanings conferred upon it by the social environment: "Society is vindictive and seeks the slightest pretext to air its resentments" (Băncilă, 2004, p. 37).

In other words, when it acquires a practical meaning, this is given afterwards to laughter; while if its primary intention is pragmatic, then we are dealing with irony. Here Băncilă departs from Bergson's assertion in *Le Rire* (essay on the meaning of the comic) that laughter always contains the unspoken intention to humiliate. Irony, says the lover of comparisons, is "a small mechanism set up for the offensive, a kind of spiritual projectile, in which the mechanism is given by laughter, and its force is given precisely by this added tendency to strike at something"; the finality as an *ironic reaction* "is not only a result, but is thought of as an end, it is therefore also a cause at the same time" (Băncilă, 2004, p. 37).

It insists on the intentionality and the practical tendency specific to irony, which is, in fact, a demonstrative phenomenon, as it reveals a background of practical instincts on the part of the producer of irony, instincts that are not implied by laughter alone.

From such an angle, the portrait of the ironist, not at all fanatical with his *projectiles* (and drifting into imprecation and sarcasm), is elementary: "a man with certain practical instincts, with certain likes and dislikes in life, but who retains his spiritual elasticity and freedom to laugh"; on top of that, somewhat similar to laughter, irony retains the certain character of an art, "something emancipated and disinterested" (Băncilă, 2004, pp. 38-39).

*

The hermeneutics of the pragmatism of irony did not stop there. Beyond practical instinct, irony presupposes the existence of intuitions, a kind of *ideation*, or a simple and unorganized practical philosophy of the representation and hierarchy of life's values, i.e., an ideal to which things are related, even if such a goal is present in an incipient, embryonic form, with a by no means unified and interested character.

At the risk of sounding somewhat paradoxical, Băncilă directs our attention to the abstract character of irony (whose aim is nevertheless practical, *id est*: concrete) understood as philosophy, but also to the personality of the one who uses ironies. Among others, he targets the one who transforms irony into a principle of conduct, an insider with a nimbus of superiority, who always displays an ironic smile; there are also those who "criticize everything, without becoming epic and dramatic, insinuate, consider matters with a sovereign and amiable certainty, believe themselves to be precious, to be august little beings..." (Băncilă, 2004, p. 43).

Băncilă assembles the determinations of irony into a synthetic definition: it is "*a spirit, or its equivalent, whose content is associated with pragmatic virtualities intended to condemn*". Through a fruitful symbiosis, the pragmatic brings with it laughter, giving irony "incisive presence, vigour, offensiveness, personality", while laughter gives the practical tendency "elasticity, generosity, means of expression, youth, variety and colour" (Băncilă, 2004, pp. 40–41).

A taxonomy of irony according to its cause or purpose is also developed here, emphasizing the pedagogical-moral factor as a mobile unit put to work by the various tendencies of moral life, tendencies which are opposite in nature and which may be either instinctive or deeply conscious.

Depending on the factors that determine it, along with the irony of those who have made it a principle of conduct, Băncilă invokes that form given by "the desire to accommodate either to society, to life as such, or to oneself" (Băncilă, 2004, p. 43). It is an opportunity to dismantle the social malaise in which man is caught up, the harshness or absurdity of life as such, besides the fact that the individual has his own oddities, contradictions and inabilities with which he feeds his discontent. Man instinctively seeks, says Băncilă, a kind of hygiene that supports him in his accommodation with society, with life, with his soul; a hygiene embodied, alongside creation or religion, by irony.

Băncilă deciphers a special and rare case through the irony generated by the *metaphysical* accommodation with the sphere of reality, especially with life as such, when the irony reaches "heights of philosophical vision in which the whole problem of existence is mirrored" (Băncilă, 2004, p. 50). For a concrete image of this form of irony, he suggests, through a subtle analysis, a comparison with the very expressive painting made by Leonardo da Vinci for a version of the head of Saint Anne.

*

Vasile Băncilă also finds types of irony important, depending on their *purpose*. The most common is irony aimed at others, at one or more individuals. Self-irony is not excluded, but is seen as a form that can be, in some situations, insincere, affected, as many use it not because they believe in their own faults, but to give themselves importance, as they say, in the eyes of the world.

For self-irony, he sends the reader to Fr. Paulhan, who had published a book on *La morale de l'ironie* in 1911; an author who had somewhat influenced him in his pedagogical observations, but also an exegete from whom he distanced himself. Irony in the face of life as such, a superlative form of irony, does not signify any formal philosophical system, nor any "awareness in scientific terms of its purpose, its objective" (Băncilă, 2004, p. 53). Just as it is necessary to distinguish such superior irony in its forms of manifestation from *humour*, which is also a way of accommodating existence that involves laughter, engagement of the spirit, other attitudes that all make up a kind of *philosophical vision of* life. While humour relies on a prior background of optimism and immunity, it is more depersonalised, more outward in form; irony, when evil penetrates the soul, means pain that is gradually reduced to a certain melancholy. In critical cultures, Băncilă observes, humour is increasingly rare, replaced by irony which represents "something more personal, more human, although, in its higher form, it is very difficult to achieve" (Băncilă, 2004, p. 56).

Not infrequently, Vasile Băncilă's analyses of the pragmatic philosophy of irony are pertinent comments on our collective mentality, with judgments stimulated by Constantin Rădulescu-Motru's lectures on the psychology of the Romanian people, on Romanianism.

4.4 Laughter, irony and education

After this preliminary propedeutic detour through which the predominantly pragmatic determinations of irony are traced and encircled, Vasile Băncilă arrives at the actual moment of its practical application, in other words, at the relationship between irony and the fact of education. The biography of irony up to this point and the already established prerequisites make it much easier for him to continue his demonstrative approach.

Through laughter, irony seems to be eminently educational, laughter being called by H. Bergson *a social gesture*. But it is not laughter in general, but ironic laughter or sometimes sarcastic laughter. It is true that it is laughter which, through comic theatre, for example, corrects social mores or customs, even the way people behave. But we are dealing here with a specific kind of laughter with moralising effect, which does not justify, observes Băncilă, the generical affirmation that theatre has such a virtue, because there are situations when the comic art being promoted leads to rather immoral effects. In this sense, he asks rhetorically: "Did Caragiale's social comedies ever straighten out Romanian society, be it with a tinge of nuance? Who would dare to say?" (Băncilă, 2004, p. 57).

Vasile Băncilă questions the moralizing enthusiasm of dramatic art, as spectators experience more often the *entertainment* function of those portrayed and ridiculed on stage. One does not correct oneself if one laughs at another's defect, assuming that he has one himself; one can even gloat with pleasure at seeing what happens to another person. Even Pristanda, if he were to watch *A Lost Letter*, would laugh heartily and somewhat naively. Băncilă does not admit any delayed effect, a belated correction, "in the course of life", because that would mean relying on rather precarious probabilities.

This is not an exclusively negative attitude of the author, but a desire to delineate as precisely as possible the pragmatic function of laughter. To this end, he returns to Bergson's characterization – laughter is a social gesture – and makes some annotations. First, the social character is given by the fact that it is only man who laughs. Then, the pleasure it brings is important for education, in that laughter is a "hedonic element, which is a recreation, a tonic" for man; such a feature expresses great social importance, laughter thus becoming a mechanism for bringing people together, a very powerful element of socialisation. Finally, one could speak of the practical, socially transformative power of laughter, but only in an indirect way, that is, through the *irony* to which it, laughter, is constitutive.

Băncilă insists, afterwards, on one of the objectives of irony, *the self-love* (real or supposed) of the one being ironized. The irony of an idea, the irony of life as such and the irony involved in the act of education all presuppose the substratum of self-love, through which we are at the heart of a profound, irreducible reality, in possession of a force that does not slide over things at all (self-love also exists in children).

He invokes John Locke, because he claims *honour, dishonour* or *reputation* stem precisely from self-love, for these "give wings to the soul". An opportunity to temper the slightly exaggerated claims of the English philosopher, but also to make fair observations about English morality, conceived particularly as "of good reputation, as a mechanism, a morality of good manners" (Băncilă, 2004, p. 61).

The structure and functions of self-love are examined from various angles in order to capture as accurately as possible the productive two-way relationship between it and society, at the level of which occur the benchmarks of *public morality* (the equivalent, let us say, of public opinion).

*

In connection with other elements with a paideic function, neither the school nor its teachers are excluded from the equation of self-love. School education is much better than the best education acquired in isolation from school, even if the teachers are mediocre.

In school, however, the inner social environment in which the pupil's personality develops is of enormous importance. It is essential for pupils to have not only good teachers as genuine *colleagues*. This is also why the educator must be interested in the school atmosphere. Irony will work to the full in the school environment, and its special pedagogical role will be truly central, alongside self-love.

Vasile Băncilă, who believes without reservation in the effective work of *indirect education,* continues his approach to this specific educational role of irony. He distinguishes irony from honour in general, but also from its educational function, noting that honour sometimes facilitates the progressive emergence of vanity, which in some cases can serve as a means in the educational process.

Irony is not to be confused with social contempt or violence, without totally excluding the existence of cases when students reach a state of deep depression precisely because of an educator who unconsciously shows a form of cruelty. Or cases, also rare, when the teacher's attitude borders on cynicism, when there is a total failure of education, "for the human soul, too much despised, awakens its thwarted canine instincts" (Băncilă, 2004, p. 63). However, contempt in school is not a moral method of education; it is, in Băncilă's opinion, an invasion of the way education is carried out in a society.

Distinct from irony is also the self-control of students, a *device*, according to Bergson, of modern pedagogy, although such self-driven collectives have existed in previous periods and, according to Băncilă, will become even more important in the future.

But it is not the student's self-consciousness that irony appeals to; it works with a more intimate and finer element, from which it draws its freshness and power: *a sense of modesty*. Modesty is not synonymous with the raw feeling of shame, it is a "delicate and persevering vibration" in which a kind of "principle ennobling the soul" is hidden. Modesty is thus not alien to the genesis of social life, as Băncilă associates modesty with religious feelings, "two forces of the soul, perhaps the most significant, which have brought man out of his primitive state" (Băncilă, 2004, p. 65).

The endosmosis between modesty and self-love is fundamental. Hence the pedagogical effectiveness of modesty as such (in fact: of irony), which is emphasised in the adolescent phase, an excellent opportunity for effective education. Moreover, this stage greatly develops pupils' solidarity and can put the teacher in difficulty, especially if he does not know how to use the method of irony, saturated with wit and inspiration, and thus transformed into a sovereign means.

*

From the pedagogical significance of irony, the student Vasile Băncilă moves on to its value in the intellectual field. The teacher-student binomial vibrates at the emission of irony, a superior one, and at its reception. Irony is gymnastics of the mind through its points of view and its relativities, through the nuances it suggests and through its abstract representations of reality, a strategy that demands from pupils *spiritual hardening* and a change of attitude.

Speaking about this role of irony, somewhat monopolizing and intensely sovereign for the specific intellectual foundations of the student, Băncilă engages in his discourse much of the complexity of the pedagogical process. Of course, the various strategies of irony are not a *factotum*; in addition to them, there are other equally pedagogical methods at work that can ensure educational performance in a school. And an educator with the knowledge and art of irony is, for a class of pupils, a great gain, both for the knowledge he imparts and for the meanings that transpire "from his gestures, from his imponderable reactions to life, from the way his intelligence breathes, from his wit, his words, his ironies" (Băncilă, 2004, p. 67). In other words: from everything that emanates from the multiple folds or faces of the professor's personality.

Inevitably, irony provokes laughter, a passing effect, a kind of *volatilized comedy* as Bergson would say, to which Vasile Băncilă refers again. And just as laughter in itself has no educational force (unlike ironic laughter), so there are certain forms of irony that lack pedagogical energy. This is also the reason why I propose to analyse the specific pedagogical conditions of irony.

4.5 The limits of irony and pedagogical comfort

Not all ironies are to be followed. As Fr. Paulhan states, there are many undesirable variants: "There is a rude, heavy-handed and despicable irony, there is a winged and subtle irony. There is a malicious irony and a contemptuous irony. There is a naive irony and a disappointed irony, there is the irony of the misanthropist and that of the philanthropist, the irony of the assassin who mocks his victim and that which, perhaps, inspired Jan Huss at the stake" (the French translation is by Băncilă). The list of ironies is, of course, not complete.

The string of formulations by Fr. Paulhan gives Băncilă some of the negative conditions for the existence of an irony, from which he also starts in his comments. First of all, he points out the dangers that irony in education generates; for example, irony out of malice which can degenerate into sarcasm or zealotry, as well as other harmful types of irony such as that which "ironizes everything in principle", a "negativism through irony, and not through pessimism proper"; or the superior irony, which persiflates life and invokes *fatality*, an idea that is both "useful and fatal", ultimately leading to "moral passivity" (see Băncilă, 2004, pp. 72–75).

If we agree with the pedagogical significance of raillery, we will, however, take with great reservations assertions such as "a culture degrades itself by cultivating raillery", a "reprehensible product, part of the morbid concretisations of intellectual environments, sometimes found even in the peasant world", "one of the most depressing attitudes for its spectator (...), because it gives a glimpse of the impotence of the soul from which it springs" (Băncilă, 2004, pp.71–72).

I do not believe that, later on, Vasile Băncilă himself would believe such allegations, not to mention the reaction that Caragiale, who knew all too well what the specific difference between *mockery* and authentic raillery is, would have when reading them.

Other negative pedagogical conditions of irony emerge indirectly from the section on the *didactics of irony*, where its positive conditions are formally listed and synthetically commented upon. Among them: "a strong and broad background of natural goodness"; "to involve an intellectual background as appreciable as possible in depth, horizon, finesse and spirit"; "the authority of the educator" (Băncilă, 2004, pp. 76–78).

To which are added other conditions not as serious as the first three, but indispensable to pedagogical irony. It is a question of dosing the irony in order to reach the threshold of objectivity as complete as possible in terms of what is being ironised, because there is a risk of exaggeration. At the same time, it is necessary to individualise the irony so that it is equivalent to the pupil's mistake or defect, without eluding the features of the pupil's distinct personality. Then, any irony should be timely, demonstrating an adequate knowledge of the pupil whom the teacher has approached with effective *human intimacy*.

Through this, the road to a supreme goal is advanced: the moment when teachers and students will constitute a unique community, a "living factory in which the ideal man is frantically being created" (Băncilă, 2004, p. 81). This is the stage when irony has expressed its pedagogical function most effectively.

*

To be truly useful, irony has to accept certain *educational limits* that it must not exceed. Even if it has as its soul motive the self-love of the one being ironized and never reaches the sphere of moral law, pupils must be stimulated to engage in purely moral exercises in order to develop their specific moral function, "as one would give a stomach pebble to digest in order to fortify its power of assimilation" (Băncilă, 2004, p. 82; the comparison is too harsh, I doubt it achieves its purpose). It is, more precisely, a method of converting extra-moral strategy into something of moral value, a procedure that pedagogy exercises in many cases other than irony (which thus becomes a "principle of heteronomous morality").

Secondly, irony is not effective for any student, regardless of age, just as it cannot be applied in situations where another pedagogical procedure might be needed. Adolescence, not primary school, is the right moment for using irony.

At the same time, not every teacher is apt to indulge in ironies, even if he is a good educator due to pedagogical skills. Irony requires a certain mastery (let us not associate it with the degree attained by ironists in literature), a talent that a person does not get by the very fact of being a teacher. But this character joins others with the gift of irony, so that all pedagogical vocations provide: "the aristocratic character of the occupation of educator" (Băncilă, 2004, p. 85), in an attempt to apply science and art of education.

Such an ideal is established not by the common man, but by the social elites. The emphasis, therefore, is on *man*, not method (the time for a magic of method is over), however metaphysical or mechanical it may be. This explains the demands made on those selected to provide education, in order to avoid transforming the school, as Băncilă interrogatively observes, into "a place of refuge for powerless creative accommodation, an asylum for bureaucratic pensioners who imagine they hold the world at their little finger" (Băncilă, 2004, p. 85).

With the help of his readings and his observations as a school practitioner, the student Vasile Băncilă criticizes, without mincing his words, some of the shortcomings of high school education, but also praises the educator and education, which are decisive functions in the life of a society. The field of education was not lacking in scientific pedagogy (sometimes in the guise of "vanity or doctoral naivety", which reformingly provided "pedagogical pills"); the misery of the school consisted in the fact that it was often entrusted with "a superior function to inferior people" (Băncilă, 2004, p. 86).

*

Vasile Băncilă reached his final conclusions about a pedagogy of irony by rehashing, for the most part, teachings he had previously drawn. Whether positive or negative, no one can oppose the manifestation of irony in the school environment, particularly in the case of adolescents. Whether there is too much or too little irony, this mechanism cannot be controlled, although the student practitioner believed that, without being left to chance, irony should somehow be *legislated* in order to avoid negative tendencies (drawing attention to and studying the latter).

It emphasizes the positive value of irony, its aristocratic-supremacist pedagogical function in the process of moral and intellectual education. It is "a more formal means, if we consider it in its direct results, to produce atmosphere and stimulus in the classroom, reminding us that in this form, once created, the educator puts his knowledge and his soul impulses" (Băncilă, 2004, p. 87).

Finally, he does not overlook the paideic complexity of education, comparing education to "a fine and precise wheel, whose fragile circle is linked to the centre by countless thin spokes, like spokes of light" (Băncilă, 2004, p. 88). To which he adds again the determining role of the vocational educator's personality.

Chapter 5

Eminescu: romantic and pragmatic optimistic

5.1 Starting frames

Two or three years after graduating from university, in 1924–1925, Vasile Băncilă conceived the projects of a few conferences on Mihai Eminescu. It is important to note how, at that historical moment, he was reading one of the greatest Romanian poets and gazetteers, an author in whom Lucian Blaga saw the embodiment of the "Platonic idea of the Romanian", while the private thinker Petre Țuțea[1] called him an *absolute Romanian* or a *lyrical sum of Voivodes*.

First, let us take a look at how the two aspects of Eminescu' personality were perceived at the time. Titu Maiorescu said essential things about the poet and his pessimism, and after the critic deposited at the Academy Library the box of Eminescu's manuscripts (preserved and untouched from 1884 until January 25, 1902), Nicolae Iorga exclaimed: "A new Eminescu has appeared!"

Shortly afterwards, in 1905, the exegete Ion Scurtu published a critical edition of Eminescu's texts written between 1870 and 1877 (see *Political and Literary Writings*, vol. I), after analysing the periodicals and manuscripts brought by Maiorescu (a bunker in which many critics of Eminescu's work would toil). In the academic years 1912–1913 and 1913–1914, Garabet Ibrăileanu[2] held at the Faculty of Letters in Iași the course "The Eminescu Era", the last in the *History of Modern Romanian Literature*, where he mentioned episodically, in one of his lectures (15 March 1913), the conjunction between optimism and pessimism.

This is the period of Eminescu, the end of the nineteenth century and the beginning of the next, in which and after which Eminescu's image will be synchronous with the *Zeitgeist*. Eminescu's gazetteering will be taken over by the traditionalist orientation initiated by Iorga, rebuilding his moral portrait, pushing the journalist and prophetic pamphleteer to the foreground, as Pompiliu Constantinescu remarked (see *Works*, 1967, p. 537).

Simultaneously, Eminescu is vindicated by the radical nationalism promoted by A. C. Cuza[3] (who would also publish a corpus of Eminescian *Works*, 1914), thus opening the way to the ideological marks applied to the poet and publicist by the subsequent history of Romanian politics.

With such a context of the reception of Eminescu, we are now practically at the beginning of the Romanian interwar period. About five years after the Great Union (1918), the liberal Constitution adopted in 1923 was already in force. In the spring of 1924, Vasile Băncilă proposed a conference on Eminescu, in the not merely circumstantial conviction that one could talk endlessly about this author. Especially since, in discussing Eminescu, "we speak, in fact, of ourselves; for he has entered into the fabric of our being, as he has entered into the soul of this earth" (Băncilă, 2004, see pp. 304–318).

But the self-referential discourse, believes the lecturer, is one of the most difficult types of research works which is why Eminescu, unanimously appreciated, should be lived, rather than just analysed.

Băncilă's exposition (a text which, by its parentheses, is not in a definitive form) has a dual character: it is interested both in Eminescu and in the study of a phenomenon of *Romanian collective psychology* (a dimension only tangentially and sporadically mentioned).

It begins with expounding a thesis, not at all new at the time, that the author of *Luceafărul* is a romantic. The criterion with which he wants to operationalise the last term will be one of substance, and not a formal one, as Nae Ionescu used when he distinguished between Romanticism, Classicism and Baroque (with the addition that the second criterion is naturally included in the first).

Items of Romantic culture: "irrealism and aformalism", "refuge in dreams", "collective and creative Freudianism", "dissatisfaction with the present" (detailed by geographical-biological and social causes, with examples of the collective mind).

The conclusion, only sketched, was that Romanticism "is not something purely literary, but is an integral phenomenon: social, literary, philosophical, economic" (Băncilă, 2004, p. 306). He advances the thesis that such a cultural tendency can be likened in its features to *adolescence*, a reason (familiar to the pedagogue Băncilă) why such a stage of life is called romantic.

5.2 I am a romantic, therefore I exist!

Before ascertaining why Eminescu is a romantic, Professor Vasile Băncilă dwells on the idea that romanticism pleases people in general. Without being romantic, the ordinary man is mostly positivist, has a common-sense logic and is mystical, but "when he makes poetry, when he dreams, then he wants to make it romantic. In art, the common man loves either *the jolly* or *the romantic*; the one because it entertains him easily, the other because it gives him refuge in the happiness of dreaming" (Băncilă, 2004, p. 307). There is at its heart a "7-8 o'clock evening romanticism", as H. Ibsen would say.

With a good psychological culture (he had just attended Motru's courses), Băncilă explains (with examples) this double nature of man: through the law of psychological compensations. The justification comes immediately: "we are condemned to live one-sidedly and precariously, in slices; the law of compensation gives us the opportunity to taste, at least sporadically, something of the complete prototype personality nostalgically dreamed of by man" (Băncilă, 2004, p. 308).

The lecturer's syllogisms decipher in romanticism not an accident of existence, something ephemeral, but a profound human *longing* which fulfils an imperious and fundamental hygienic function, thus ensuring that man obtains a wholesome life – at least in theory. He extends this hypothesis to the level of humanity, which as a whole would be romantic – "romanticism is what animates humanity", it is "the philosophy of history", it is "the essential Platonism of existence" (Băncilă, 2004, p. 309).

With this detour, he comes to the question – and the answer – of why Eminescu is a romantic. The question, I repeat, was by no means new, nor was the justification novel. One would expect an approach that was not social-biographical, centred on the man Eminescu, but maybe a bit deeper, with a metaphysical stake. A way to mirror Eminescu's knowledge and the poet's romanticism.

Băncilă wants to compare the romantic Eminescu with the Russian writers, who also rebelled against society through political or moral, sometimes even literary romanticism. Moreover, he believes that the romantic orientation of a personality is determined by his social status: if you come from *below*, from *the people*, you are a romantic, an attitude that is not found in those *at the top* – Vasile Alecsandri,[4] Duiliu Zamfirescu, I. L. Caragiale – despite the appearance of romanticism or a partial romanticism found in some of them.

At the same time, in order to introduce the listener/reader directly into Eminescu's world, the lecturer Băncilă appeals to the background of his poems. To which he adds, this time a little more profoundly, other characteristics of Eminescu's romanticism: "the extraordinary power of feeling and imagination, to the point of enchantment and hallucination" (Băncilă, 2004, p. 310; hence "aesthetic sincerity"). Pessimistic Romanticism (contrary to Nae Ionescu, he also finds an optimistic, practical or philosophical Romanticism - in Hugo, Fichte or Hegel), but also a cosmic-philosophical one ("The evening star", "Poor Dionis"; another departure from

Nae Ionescu concerns the trait of megalomania, a dimension he attributes to Romanticism; Băncilă discovers it only in philosophical Romanticism).

To justify all this, he invokes the subjects of Eminescu's poetic meditation: philosophical, erotic, social, poetization of the past, finally asking himself if Eminescu is somehow a popular poet. Not at all, concludes Băncilă; Eminescu is difficult to understand, because he has profound thoughts and a great power of information even if he is clear, classic, defined.

Băncilă's reception is different, perhaps diametrically opposed to that of G. Călinescu:[5] the divine critic noted in Eminescu (the model was Maiorescian) a decompression of the abstract, a sensorialisation of it so that it could be deciphered by as many receivers as possible. Referring in particular to poetry, G. Călinescu spoke of two faces of poetry: one of linen and the other of silk. But even in his theoretical texts, Eminescu "translated" the abstract into terms that are easier to understand (as I said, he had learned this lesson from Maiorescu).

Distorted by his readers in certain poems ("I have just one last wish", "Near the unpaired poplar trees") whose meanings demand a particular power of abstraction, Eminescu is actually very aristocratic. And if the same Romanian people love him, this is possible because the genius of Eminescu gives the receiver the pleasure of admiring the hardly accessible grandeur of genius.

The seduction of Eminescu's greatness has another side, however, deciphered by Băncilă through the grid of ethnic psychology, more precisely by tacitly appealing to the law of psychological compensation. Eminescu impresses us with what Romanians as a people do not have: "epic character, virile pessimism, racial melancholy – the Romanian has melancholy, but a more serene, lighter melancholy – hallucinatory imagination and above all deep, cosmic, elementary faith" (Băncilă, 2004, p. 314).

5.3 A pragmatic journalist

Eminescu's role in Romanian culture is also evident, according to Băncilă, in the pragmatism of the gazetteer, who was not a kind of tool of the conservative party, even if the publicity engendered for the *Time* newspaper was not without benefits for this political party. Without expressly referring to Eminescu's publicity, Băncilă sanctions both Eugen Lovinescu ("a frivolous and *Westernist* sociologist") who underestimated the political articles, and those who saw in the performance of the conservative newspaper a "party passion (Eminescu and the party!)" (Băncilă, 2004, p. 315).

According to Vasile Băncilă, the pragmatism of Eminescu's personality is expressed by practical instincts, by strong energy, traits that make the gazetteer a kind of hallucinating pragmatist. He also has a contradictory nature: pessimistic and sceptical in his theoretical work, dogmatic in his practical one. And "Romanticism made him see in what he criticized a *cosmic entity*" (Băncilă, 2004, p. 316; in another entry, in October 1963, Băncilă finds in Eminescu "pessimism on the metaphysical level and optimism on the historical level").

Without using, in his linguistic euphoria, the term xenophobia, Băncilă touches on it asymptotically: Eminescu "did not hate certain people, even if he named them – but certain symbols". And then, a few lines later, he states that "*his thesis that the foreigners have ruined us is correct*, whatever one may believe today, whatever Motru, who has no sense of reality, may believe" (Băncilă, 2004, p. 317, my emphasis).

Eminescu's social-political thought would have gradually evolved from the publicity of the Iași period to that of the capital city and *Time*. From such activity was born his nationalist doctrine, Eminescu remaining the political thinker "with the greatest *Lendemain*, the most influential of us, and the most authentic Romanian sociologist" (Băncilă, 2004, p. 316).

Vasile Băncilă's conference plan, not yet finalized, raises in its last part ("not yet studied") the question of Eminescu's value for Romanians, but also for those outside Romania. From these few lines can be seen the extraordinary level reached by Romanian poetry in Eminescu who, for those from abroad, gave us the right to exist, made us, in other words, a historical people.

5.4 Differently, about pessimism

The following year, 1925, Vasile Băncilă was also concerned with Eminescu's personality. On August 3 and 4, he held two lectures at the "N. Iorga" Popular University in Vălenii de Munte, on the pessimism and pragmatism of the poet and publicist (Băncilă, 2004, see pp. 354–363).

He had started to prepare since March of the same year, writing the notes entitled "Eminescu's pessimism" (Băncilă, 2004, see pp. 319–325), from which he used some ideas in the summer. It is a composition that seems more methodical, polysemically identifying the theme as such and indicating some possible answers to certain problems. In the summer lecture, he will only add some nuances, the substance of the ideas remaining the same.

He takes a questioning look at Eminescian pessimism from several angles, trying to find its specific code. He wants to break away from the prejudice that there is pessimism in Eminescu. Of the poems, he thinks that only three are truly pessimistic, "the rest are elegiac, or even humorous" (Băncilă, 2004, p. 320). And he asks, rhetorically: How pessimistic can something read by teenagers be! To the general public, pessimism appears in the form of melancholy. Cautiously, he takes into consideration feelings and ideas, the man, the poet and his philosophy. Alongside a strong pessimistic mood, these reveal both optimistic facts and objective judgment.

Under the impulse of the law of psychic compensation, Băncilă's thesis is simple: pessimism implies optimism, which is why this attitude has arisen in "pragmatic races or races with glowing vitalist instincts: Germans, Anglo-Saxons, Slavs, Italians (French; they too have a national inability to grasp pessimism)" (Băncilă, 2004, p. 322).

Compared to Western pessimism, Eminescian pessimism, even if it has, for us, the meaning of the white raven, is a minor phenomenon. Băncilă wonders whether Eminescu's pessimism can really be compared with that of Leopardi or Byron (a critical exercise carried out by some exegetes, with undeniable benefits for Romanian literature).

Indecisively balancing Eminescu's pessimism between being or not being, trying to explain how Eminescu is pessimistic, indicating arguments for or against, Vasile Băncilă remains on the edge of a choice: "perhaps pessimism is one of the *main affections*" (Băncilă, 2004, p. 323; my emphasis). Hence a radical conclusion: it is not possible to establish, from his poetic work, whether Eminescu was a pessimist or not, nor does his work provide us with sufficient arguments in this regard; therefore, the problem of Eminescu's pessimism is insoluble, officious.

It is no less true that, after so many approximations, after establishing four conditions of a genuine pessimism, after rejecting biographism or scientific criticism, Băncilă almost certainly indicates the core of the concept: pessimism is a tragic philosophical conception, theoretically formulated, not to be mistaken for anger, banal sadness or bitterness. Therefore, it is not literary criticism (Maiorescu, C. D. Gherea, D. Caracostea, M. Dragomirescu) that can pronounce a conclusion on pessimism, but practical philosophy.

If Eminescu had only been a poet, things would have been much simpler. But he was a full intellectual, with parallel vocations (poet and journalist, but also writer of philosophical reflections), so he must be judged in the totality of his personality, which does not exclude some internal contradictions. Eminescu "is not a morbid figure with a gentle and encouraging face, crowned with cherry blossoms", just as he is not "the spring of living water, to which some went too early in the morning and found it shrouded in misty pall" (Băncilă, 2004, p. 358; the allusion was to the poet's contemporaries).

*

The lecture on Eminescu's pragmatism did not bring many new aspects compared to what Băncilă had already said a year or so before. Invoking William James's conception that *truth is useful in life*, pragmatism is defined as being created by "the poet's soul elements, which form a doctrine of struggle in practical life" (Băncilă, 2004, p. 359).

Somehow recalling Iorga's characterization of the complete man of our culture, Băncilă sees in Eminescu a complete man, with practical inclinations manifested early on, but also later in his activity; as a man of action, school reviser or gazetteer. All this proves the existence of active instincts in two areas: moral and national.

At the same time, Vasile Băncilă wanted to outline some sociological ideas in Eminescu. From the age of 16, he says, Eminescu had a social doctrine (!) that he would later develop in *Time*, namely: *"solidarism"*, the understanding of society as a unitary whole, a structure in which its members serve each other. This is the justification for Eminescu's criticism of the so-called *overlapping layers*, of forms that are without substance, alienated, that interrupt organic growth; and it is also the source of his opposition to the Rousseau-ist idea of the social contract.

Eminescu's reaction to foreigners cannot be explained, according to Băncilă, by the gross confusion that C. Rădulescu-Motru makes: having lived as a young man among non-Romanians, on his return home he identified in foreigners his enemies. Eminescu, says Băncilă, had a critical spirit and some Slavic blood, which implies "intellectual nihilism and metaphysical contemplation on the one hand, and an inclination towards activity on the other (Tolstoy, etc.)" (Băncilă, 2004, p. 360).

The lecturer suggests the value of Eminescu's social doctrine needs to be carefully researched, because the publicist has often been misunderstood. Here I will reproduce a few critical tendencies that later became spearheads against Eminescian social-political and economic texts. He has been characterised as a chauvinist, when in fact, he loved his nation and did not hate others, understanding by the concept of humanity a set of specific national aspects. It was said that Eminescu's journalism openly expressed party passion, by inventing a theory to combat the Liberals ("reds"); or that he was reactionary and overly praised the past, to which he wanted to return.

Nothing true, notes Băncilă, in all these anathemas and accusations that, since then, have become commonplace in the criticism directed against Eminescu. The publicist was an advocate of organic development based on the healthy part of our tradition, and his texts, particularly in *Time*, confirm that he was not "a man who fights out of party passion"; still, it is true that "the practical political struggle is not fought with scientific definitions alone, but with strong and increased breath; a practical exaggeration is required in the struggle of political life" (Băncilă, 2004, p. 361).

*

The young professor Vasile Băncilă read the publicist, but also the poet Eminescu with great empathy. He was vibrating in front of Eminescu's social-political and economic doctrine, in which he discovered something salutary for the Romanian nation, for the professional journalist based his syllogisms on the principle of nationality, in sync with the trend present at that time in the Western world. Eminescu's writing offers a model for expressing ideological truth in literary form, namely, society seen as an organism and as a form arising from our national space.

In the latter sense, in his 1934 monograph G. Călinescu described Eminescu as a "conservative progressive"; Vasile Băncilă spoke, a decade earlier, of a "conservative evolutionist - the wisest social doctrine" (*evolutionist* does not refer to Darwin's theory, but to organic development). To which he adds further correctives: "He respected in the minority active elements of the nation; the foreigner who wanted to remain a foreigner but do his work honestly was welcomed; he hated only those who left their nationality, so that he could speculate all the better" (Băncilă, 2004, p. 362).

Hence another principle of Eminescu's gazetteering, dear to Vasile Băncilă: the ethnic principle, also in keeping with the spirit of the time, with European social and moral trends.

Notes

[1] Țuțea, P. (1902–1991). Romanian philosopher of Mircea Eliade's generation, publicist, economist, adherent of different political orientations, victim of the communist regime in Romania. Among his writings: *Between God and My Nation* (1992), *Religious Reflections on Knowledge* (1992), *Metaphysical Anxieties* (1994), *Philosophical Writings* (2 vols., 2005–2006).

[2] Ibrăileanu, G. (1871–1936). Romanian literary critic and historian, novelist. Among his writings: *Critical Spirit in Romanian Culture* (1908), *Writers and Currents* (1909), *The Literary Work of Mr. Vlahuță* (1912), *Romanian and Foreign Writers* (1926).

[3] Cuza, A. C. (1857–1947). Romanian professor, far-Right politician, anti-Semite. Among his writings: *Verses* (1887), *The Fight Against Alcoholism in Romania* (1897), *On the People. Statistics, theory, politics. Economic-political study* (1899), *The teaching of Jesus, Judaism and Christian theology* (1925).

[4] Alecsandri, V. (1821–1890). Romanian poet, playwright, folklorist, politician. Among his writings: *Popular poems. Ballads (old songs). Collected and directed by d. V. Alecsandri* (1852), *Boyars and nouveaux-riches* (1874), *Complete works* (1875), *Prose* (1876).

[5] Călinescu, G. (1899–1965). Romanian encyclopaedic spirit, literary critic and historian, one of the most important writers and publicists, along with Titu Maiorescu and Eugen Lovinescu. Among his writings: *The Works of Mihai Eminescu* (1934), *Principles of Aesthetics* (1939), *History of Romanian Literature from its Origins to the Present* (1941), *Impressions on Spanish Literature* (1946), *Poor Ioanide* (1953), *The Praise of Things* (1963), *The Black Chest* (1965).

Chapter 6

Religious reflections

6.1 Loneliness and faith

Among Vasile Băncilă's early writings, there are many pages that refer to religious phenomena. These are meditations that were certainly stimulated by the influence that the spirit of his professor, philosopher and theologian Nae Ionescu – to whom he refers both directly and indirectly – had on him. For the Christian thinker Vasile Băncilă, these religious reflections also constitute the prerequisites of his spiritual being.

Like other attempts, these texts do not seem to have a final form, the author noting, from time to time, suggestions for further development. Băncilă's interest is directed towards the state of religiosity of the Romanians, towards social life organised by religion, towards Orthodoxy and the specific difference between it and Catholicism.

A note by the student Vasile Băncilă surrounded an essential conjunction: "Loneliness and religion" (Băncilă, 2003, pp. 31–32); trying, from a few lines, to trace a portrait of the former. Of course, when religion is under consideration, then it cannot be carefully examined in the absence of solitude, prayer or asceticism, or without implying a relationship with the Saviour, just as the idea of communion cannot be excluded, seen as communion in the same faith as one's neighbour.

The student Băncilă specified what he considered to be the types of solitude, starting with the biological one ("the falling asleep of all conscious thought: *an absolute maturity*") and continuing with others: cultural, metaphysical, the creation of great personalities, morality and happiness; he arrived at "positive, harmonious, sweet, creative solitarism", which is possible through religion.

It is not the precarious features of these kinds of loneliness that are important, as they are insufficient for detecting specific differences. It is hard to see where the connections laconically invoked by the student lead. One must simply try to grasp, if possible, the value he places on religion, which guarantees solitariness and thus facilitates, for example, musical creation; and even if in the modern period "there is no more religion" (?), "one can also create without religion" (Băncilă, 2003, p. 31).

The major purpose of this sketch seems to be to signal a subject worthy of research: the way both society and solitude need to be examined. In order to create, the philosopher, says Băncilă, isolates himself, "voluntarily breaks off from society", his mind being "more contemptuous of the social than the artist's" (Băncilă, 2003, p. 32). At the end of this virtual approach, he points us towards Vasile Pârvan's Hymn to solitude.

*

Also dating from the same year are the pages in which Băncilă tries to meditate on the question of faith (December 1921). It is a longer text, about 17 pages written in pencil, designed on the borderline between logic and faith.

Applying logic everywhere seems to him not to be ... logical: "you think *in* logic, not *of* logic" (Băncilă, 2003, p. 128). This is why, says Băncilă, religion does not need logic; the problems of religion are, it is true, significant for logic, only it is incomplete, just partially known. It is true that the grid of logic seems to be universal, because it is by its fluidity or cosmopolitanism that most human needs are judged.

It is not so much God or the content of faith that is logical, but sophisticatedly said, faith itself. But in being logical, faith has reserved the right to realise its own content. There is a procedural flaw here, in that faith is already being judged with a logical instrument, and the fault lies precisely in the instrumental universality of logic as such; a universality that is not as extensive as that of religion.

Reading this text by the student Vasile Băncilă (of course stimulated by Nae Ionescu's courses on the philosophy of religion), a key consideration is the phrase; "believe and do not investigate". He does both, in a positive sense: he both believes and investigates the logical fibres of faith, even proposing further steps, as I will examine in due course.

His appeal to logic in the sphere of religion stems from the fact that religion has ideas and provides man with truths. In such a hypostasis, from the perspective of the "unity" of the self as a whole and without the threat of contradiction, two options are equally admissible: religion as a good belonging to the nature of the soul, and religion as expressing truth. However, if we agree with the truth of religion, then it is necessary to eliminate from its sphere those assertions relating to the domain in which science is expressed, on the one hand; and to refute logic's claim of expressing truth in the sphere of metaphysics, on the other. The incompatibility between the truth of religion and the truth of logic is thus removed.

Băncilă's remarks did not stop there. Logic is not just a formal instrument, but needs a certain content with which to operate its judgments and syllogisms. As a psychological product it needs, like religion, sensation (experience) and a logical instinct. This is why Băncilă also wonders whether faith is biological in nature, or whether it is not, along with logic, a gnoseological faculty.

God is also a product of logic, and religion has given man faith in Him. To this end, Băncilă expressly and somewhat syllogistically constructs a syllogism, in which the premises are *"Faith is logical"*, *"God is the content of faith"*, the conclusion given by the middle term being *"God is ... logical."* (Băncilă, 2003, p. 131).

But he does not agree with this anthropomorphic and phenomenal mechanism of deduction, and this is because God is conceived within the framework of faith, the latter admitted by logic and therefore capable of constructing and providing truths. Thus the gnoseological significance of faith is indirectly admitted.

*

Let us nuance that last sentence. There are three variants, says Băncilă, three possibilities for faith to be a gnoseological faculty: either an independent one (in continuation of the logical one), or an indirect one (by the right to give itself a content), or by constituting a faculty of knowledge, like logic, but without having anything in common with it.

The desired option of the student Băncilă would be the first one, but this is not true. Even if it were true, it is superfluous because of the one-sided knowledge it achieves, given the isolation of faith from logic. So he admits the second case, faith as an indirect gnoseological faculty; but here too there is a split between faith and its problems.

Logic allows the existence of faith itself, but not the nature of its problems: "If it were to say that the problems of religion are logical, of the same nature as those of scientific logic, then it would be condemning faith, and therefore contradicting itself."

And again he resorts to a syllogism, where the premises have an unusual form: *"Either you don't admit faith – and then you don't admit logic (logical necessity) either"*, *"Or you admit faith – and then it has a right to give itself content"*, followed by the conclusion, *"So God is legitimate, like logic"* (Băncilă, 2003, p. 132).

But a primary condition of the logic of faith and God is that they are not logical, which gives authority to scientific truth. The intermediary between these two sides, however, is man: "Choosing between logic and faith is not a

matter of logic, but of biology, because ultimately both are biological values"
(Băncilă, 2003, p. 133). The logical conflict thus no longer arises between faith
and science, but between two constituent parts of our soul.

Băncilă's notes have the physiognomy of a game with various sophisms and
signs of logical fractures in judging the religious phenomenon, the essence of
which is given by the belief in God, just as the student's notes are also the
logical confrontation of religion and science. The attempt is to prove that
they, religion and science, are equally logical, that is: you can believe in each
of them, their conflict being only of a psychological nature.

But here we come across a kind of tragedy, because if we fail to adapt
biologically, then we have no choice but to struggle until we die. However,
with these two devices, as Băncilă calls them, the human soul is more
completely satisfied than if it had only one of them. And the optimal situation
is for each to retain its autonomy.

For there to be a congruence between religion and logic, it would be necessary
for us to be able to know *the absolute* - which man does not attain, *the thing in
itself* being unattainable. What we are left with is the accommodation of needs.
Religion and science thus tolerate each other, and modern man needs a lot of
metaphysics or epistemology. This is where man's malady, called *metaphysical
illness*, comes in.

The dilemma of religion or science is thus resolved: the complete man
needs both, even if he is always in one of them; he must not limit himself to
religion ("but there will always remain a coefficient of it"), but study science,
stopping where he must, and then believing. And if he cannot be in any of
them, let him forget. Therefore, instead of "believe and do not investigate",
the student Vasile Băncilă creates another injunction: "investigate, believe,
stop, forget"! (Băncilă, 2003, p. 134).

It is surprising, however, that the student Vasile Băncilă does not take
advantage, in his syllogisms concerning religion and logic, of *speculative logic*,
which he must have come across in the courses of his mentor Nae Ionescu.
He would thus have avoided those logical dead ends and would have
accredited a different logic, where the *coincidence of opposites* (coincidentia
oppositorum) in particular is accepted.

*

Investigate, believe, stop, forget! This attitude seems to express both lucidity
and a kind of Christian tolerance, traits that we also see in the way Băncilă
perceived the logic of a Young Men's Christian Association – "Psychology and

the Rationale of Imceism" (Băncilă, 2003, pp. 135-136), founded in 1921 as a branch of the Young Men's Christian Association (YMCA, London, 1844).

Editor Dora Mezdrea, in a note, says of this American-funded organization that, "although it wants to serve ecumenism, it soon becomes the spearhead of the neo-Protestant movements" (Băncilă, 2003, pp. 435–436).

Opinions seem to have differed at that moment in history. Mircea Vulcănescu, a member of the Association of Romanian Christian Students ("Asecere"), confessed the influence that Nae Ionescu's courses on the philosophy of religion had on him (see Vulcănescu, 1990, pp. 41–45). He remembers the transformation of his soul he was going through at the time, having recently come out of the cruel atheism that placed the *Bible* and Geology in an unresolved conflict. He was trying to "rebuild on his own the conversion to a Christian vision", even though, says Vulcănescu, "our philosophical material was weak and heteroclite". He remembers a religious experience that sprang from "from the exaltation of a 22-year-old Welsh girl who one day left her father, mother, fogs and cliffs to come and preach the word of God at the foot of the Carmel".

In these moments of Christian warmth, over that confused and generous religious élan, Nae Ionescu's lectures came like "a shower of cold water". His attitude to evangelism was hostile, making a distinction between the heavenly and earthly aspects of Christianity and the intellectual promiscuity that was presented as Christianity in some youth circles (including the *Ascetics*). The Christianity that Nae Ionescu accepted was a metaphysical one, "harsh, asocial, entirely oriented towards the afterlife, in which the kingdom of God is realized only at the end of the world, through a kind of eschatological catastrophe of the whole cosmos".

The religious enthusiasm shown by Mircea Vulcănescu can also be found, perhaps a little paler, in the student Vasile Băncilă when he talks about the psychology and the purpose of *imceism*. From a moral point of view, even if "religion is a self-serving form of advertising for American finance" (Băncilă, 2003, p. 135), it does not seem so serious because it is not a premeditated thing (a volatile assumption, I think). Alongside interest (emphasised by an Albert Schinz), leaving aside "the mentality of the vibrating bourgeoisie", Vasile Băncilă proposes that a fragment of faith should also be taken into account, that Wundt's law should be applied: "out of something bad can come something good; out of interest a good religion can be born" (Băncilă, 2003, p. 136).

It was therefore a question of faith, of religious spirit, and not of the relationship between Catholicism and Orthodoxy, the latter being philosophically superior but unfortunately not better from a practical, social point of view. It was not the superiority of Orthodoxy that should be invoked, as Nae Ionescu did,[1] but the core given by the doctrine of Jesus, even if *Imceism* was much closer to Protestantism than to modernism.

There was no knowing whether America would provide the civilization of the future, and the YMCA brought just what Romanians lacked: "faith in all matters; with it, we would perhaps be superior even to the Apollonians, whereas today we are very cursory, but very sterile bipeds" (Băncilă, 2003, p. 136).

Only rarely does one see the criticism that Băncilă makes of our infatuation, platitude and stubbornness, ignoring that intellectual promiscuity attributed by Nae Ionescu to such religious manifestations.

6.2 Oriental religiosity

From March 25, 1925, another manuscript of Vasile Băncilă is preserved;[2] 24 pages, entitled by the editor Dora Mezdrea "Romanian Religiosity" (Băncilă, 2004, pp. 326–342), a text with later additions. It is an outline developed in about eight sections, methodically thought out and progressively conceptualised, with the precise aim not to summarise but to mediate – or reconcile – a controversy that arose in the press of the time (the publications are called *The Free Word* and *The World*, on the one hand; and *Word* and *Thought*, on the other). It was about the controversy: whether or not there was a *Romanian Orthodoxy*, to which was added the perplexity of Professor Băncilă in the face of "presumptuous and fractious young people" who radically affirmed, in the Capacity exam (4th grade high school), that "the Romanian people are not religious" (Băncilă, 2004, p. 326).

After the First World War, our religious area was taken by surprise by the problem of confessionalism and nationalities, which were also to be the main themes of the interwar period. In fact, after the war which, as Thomas Mann said, had put Germany on edge, two great questions were raised about human beings: whether they were still capable of believing in God and, secondly, whether poetic creation was still possible after the tragedy that had occurred (questions that were also valid after the Second World War – see a book by Hans Jonas on the concept of God after Auschwitz).

*

Like many of his generation, Vasile Băncilă experienced spiritual turmoil and inner changes when he came into contact with the religious spirit that was emerging in the historical moment of Greater Romania. His approximations may seem banal if they are separated from the context of their elaboration. He wanted, first of all, to trace a conceptual clarification of religion, distinguishing it from science and philosophy. He does so by naming the relationship between the *fragmentary* (science describes the phenomenon, the appearance) and the *whole*, which is specific to philosophy, a discipline that has not reached a scientific threshold (or did so only partially, in psychology and logic), remaining at the stage of brilliant hypotheses.

But what is religion? asks the philosophy teacher. It brings us what philosophy cannot, because it builds for man an "absurd or unintimate (cold, alien, inhuman) universe" (Băncilă, 2004, p. 327). Religion comes from the heart (a possible path to the ultimate truth), and is rooted in scepticism, in distrust of the results of science. In theory it builds a rational universe, with a beginning and an end, with motivation and harmony; in practice, it addresses human instincts, giving them meaning and offering something familiar, intimate, humane (this explains why "a monk can be alone in the wilderness; here there is just him and God, without him being bothered by the priests and the world"; Băncilă, 2004, p. 327).

Loneliness, whose anatomy the student Băncilă traced, still occurs. Man needs a supreme being who listens to him and consoles him. This is why religion cannot exist in the absence of the concept of an *anthropomorphic divinity*, on the one hand, and of a more direct relationship between man and God, on the other.

He is interested in the Christian religion of the West, through the process of alteration to which it has been subjected. Intimacy has been damaged by the interposition of the Pope and the priests between man and God, a sin from which Protestantism is not exempted. All the religions of the West have "*basically the same attitude to life, whatever their dogmas*" (Băncilă, 2004, p. 328), because each of them has become a social morality or a social technique (C. Rădulescu-Motru is quoted for his idea of social determinism specific to the evolution of religious psychology, a determinism from which Băncilă dissociates himself).

I will not dwell on the causes that would have led to such an alteration, I only mention those that are also related to the Romanian religious space. Without commenting on it, he draws the conclusion that our Orthodoxy shows that Romania is equally Oriental and Latin.

Next to the Papacy, the most important cause of the degradation of the Western religion is its orientation towards social-political activity (with emphasis on the political factor), an inner logic that also worked in our country, with the calendar reform (about which Băncilă wrote dense articles in 1924–1925; one of them was praised by Nae Ionescu).

Should Romania imitate what was happening in the West? There is no question of such an influence, apart from one similarity: the Latin substratum, but not as pure here as there – "indeed, itself *oriental*". The influence of the *Orient*, not the Western influence (which will be felt in a few hundred years' time), was dominant here, in religion, politics and folklore. The Romanian soul bears the imprint of the Far East, of the Indian spirit. But there is no denying that the most important element was Latin.

What else is specific to Romanian religiosity, this *original religious phenomenon*, as Blaga would say (invoked by Băncilă)? First of all, an original feature, namely, a direct and personal relationship between the believer and God. Then, other features: the form of our religiosity is more intellectual than sentimental and pragmatic, a dimension imprinted by Latinity and the fact that "we are Levantines, a mixture, and mixing annihilates the affections, the instincts, and sharpens the intelligence" (Băncilă, 2004, p. 331).

The intellectual nature of our religion is not an impediment in representing "something *essential* and universal" for the Romanian peasant who, like the primitive, "lives permanently with the concept of divinity"; and the Romanian people, Băncilă theistically states, "does not have deep feelings, formidable instincts, epic, dramatic affections" (Băncilă, 2004, p. 332).

From this, he draws two conclusions that are not at all conformist: Romanians do not need priests in their role as divine authority (Romanian Orthodoxy does not have priests who are directors of conscience, as in the West), but only as a kind of intermediary mechanism; Băncilă thus finds the explanation for the fact that the church is rarely attended, which paradoxically favours pure religiosity. Moreover, our religion has no social character and, partly, no moral character.

Consistent with himself, Băncilă adds: the moral charge is, in part, rejected because the religion of the Romanians is pure, since it is possible for a religion to be without morals; he invokes the religious philosophers in whom the religious dimension dominates the moral one (he refers us to the Westerners, to the French Protestant reformer Jean Calvin); in order not to seem inconsistent this time, i.e., to be accused that he would eliminate morals from religion, he specifies that the purely religious phenomenon inevitably implies an intimacy with morals ("morals and religion can rhyme admirably").

It is apparent, in the avalanche of these notes, that there is a paradoxical deviation from the canon of common sense (the attitude of the theologian Nae Ionescu was contaminating). Professor Vasile Băncilă's judgments and syllogisms are lively, they incite us with their reformist accents, they ask us to agree or disagree by engaging in a virtual dialogue. It is true that this is not a study, but only the outline of an approach whose completion was somewhat overdue. However, a feature that seems to be vital to the author's discursive strategy can already be seen: the intuitive grasp of the essence of a theme (of *holomers*) and the suspension or postponement of the full, comprehensive development of the discourse as such. It is a consistency that takes the unusual form of inconsistency, to give another name to discontinuity or discursive delay. I am not saying, by this, that various ideational contradictions occur in one text or another; just that nuances or enrichments of meaning, changes of perspective, sometimes even unnecessary repetitions, take place over time.

*

Vasile Băncilă's perspective on religion is not one of common sense, but a philosophical one. Based on faith and the concrete, religion represents an accommodation of man with the universal in order to achieve an intimacy with it. And as this relationship grows in intensity (I would even say in purity), religion takes on an increasingly asocial character. Of course, religion is also implicitly moral only if it does not separate itself from "purely religious living" (the influence of Nae Ionescu is certain), that is to say, if it remains similar to primitive Christianity, without becoming a social technique (and it becomes one, as it does in the West, when morality is too exaggeratedly practical-social). This is where Vasile Băncilă discovers the superiority of the religion of the Romanian people which, in order to provide us with religious thought or thinking, cannot be conceived as "an organ of civilization for the barbarians, as something political, therefore, as a tool of socialization in the bourgeois civilization of man" (Băncilă, 2004, p. 333).

From the sphere of our religion Vasile Băncilă does not exclude (how rightly!) a hatred for the Papists manifested not only by the priesthood but also by the common people; an attitude, he says, generated by the Schism, a hatred which, in certain areas, was also due to the situation of the people of Transylvania, who perceived the churches of the West as a national danger, but also a reflex facilitated by the instinct of the Romanian people ("between all religions there is hatred, and especially between related religions"). An instinct that led the Romanians "to ally themselves closely, on religious grounds, with the Orthodox peoples of the East, in a kind of brotherhood" (Băncilă, 2004, p. 334).

And yet, it has been said about the Romanian people that they are not religious (without reference to any source). Seven causes are mentioned, some of them rephrased: not much respect for the priest, sporadic church-going, the non-social character of Orthodoxy, the absence of epic psychology, the middle and upper classes are not very religious, neither are the intellectuals, the mixture of races and religions (which produces a mutual annihilation of moral-ethnic-religious instincts – as recounted in *the Gospel*), finally, publications and the press, through the indifference and contempt they cultivate towards religious faith.

Băncilă proposed a further development: to stop at the religion of the Jews, a fully socialized one, from which the purely religious thought is completely absent; the Jew, he says, is not a religious being, and "the Jewish intellectual is the least religious of all – he does not even believe in his religion" (Băncilă, 2004, p. 335).

*

Vasile Băncilă noticed some tensions in the Romanian religious phenomenon, a series of symptomatic attacks made by printing books of a social nature, by the announced visit of some Scandinavians, by some rebellions (the examples of the calendar and of the priest in the primary school are given), a tendentious pan-Orthodox or pan-Christian congress held in Sinaia, as well as an inappropriate approach to monastic life (he proposed to address, in the future, the role of monasteries in pure religiosity).

All this led him to note a tendentious-Western orientation of the Romanian church, a threat described by some 15 causes (see Băncilă, 2004, pp. 336–339; the influence of Nae Ionescu is also evident here): The spread of the morals of the Western civilization to the villages, the tendencies of a modern life with all that such a mentality implies for the diminution of pure religiosity; the lack of firm faith among the intellectuals and the word of order that the unbelieving middle and upper classes had for the church; politicianism, drawing the church into various traps by putting it in the pocket of the politicians; the opportunism of the clergy, through which political licentiousness was cultivated (the campaign in the Saxon town of Reghin for the election of Octavian Goga,[3] a way in which Miron Cristea[4] proved his activity as a patriot, without having any religious faith), the church and the university becoming a monopoly of the liberals; secularisation, the worldly mentality of the prelates and popes; three other causes: the Uniates and the Greek-Orientalists, the Shagunists in Transylvania (he met some refined and very sceptical Transylvanian students: for example, Ion Chinezu); finally, the existence of several confessions, which transformed the church into a political and social issue.

Despite these dangers for the spirit of the church, Vasile Băncilă wondered if there was not something anachronistic in Romanian religiosity. In any case, amidst some social slippages, the church was subject to transformation, in order to come out of its passivity and to act.

But he draws attention in particular to the tendency towards socialization with its many harmful consequences, among which: an *"ethnic disunity"*, an "ethnic strife"; "the destruction of the religious function", because by *"straightening out the state, religion risks losing itself"* (Băncilă, 2004, p. 340); the loss of the originality of the Romanian soul, as our Europeans have raised the cult (from Gherea to Motru); the removal of the spirit of folklore and religious books, in which the old Romanian language is preserved.

However, if something is to change, then it is necessary, says Christian professor Vasile Băncilă, to respect certain conditions: "a religiogization of society, not a socialization of religion" (Băncilă, 2004, p. 341); an organic change, not a sudden, radical one; these tendencies presuppose a series of reforms (discussed, more than once, by the theologian Nae Ionescu): the renovation of seminaries and theological faculties (priests should be religiously and philosophically cultivated, with a religious spirit), the reorganisation of the church and monastic life, the separation of the church from politics.

Vasile Băncilă's conclusions were firm: Romanians are a religious people, but not of Western origin, because there is in their religiosity a certain specificity and something oriental; yet a concord can be found between the spirit of the church with the trend of the age, in accordance with the interest of religion and of the Romanians, without damaging their originality.

6.3 Socialisation of religion

The notes on the relationship between church and society were not an isolated episode in Vasile Băncilă's reflections. In the same month (March 1925), he developed the theme of the socialisation of religion (see Băncilă, 2004, pp. 343–351),[5] and the following year (April 1926), he outlined a plan for the organisation of social life through religion.

The evolution and harmonization of religion with the spirit of the times seemed to him to be inevitable. The idea always arose that the church could not stand aside; it had to mix with society, but also to develop it spiritually. This is the original propagandistic nature of religion, which it does by *preaching:* "To know how to conjugate this verb in practice, that is the whole social side of religion; but it is conjugated with the heart and spirit of God, not with the prosaism of bourgeois accounting." (Băncilă, 2004, p. 347)

But what about that certain resistance to religious modernization! The main thrust of the outline study was, *roughly speaking*, the difference between Eastern and Western religiosity. To this end, as he does on other occasions, he successively sets themes to be researched and points out master ideas.

First, it would be necessary to look at the psychology of secularization, as the phenomenon began in 1864. He does not ignore the fact that there are also good signs in the process of church organization, and especially in the approach to church issues (C. Rădulescu-Motru, N. Iorga, Nae Ionescu, Ivanov, L. Blaga are mentioned). And because of the way religion was conceived, politically and socially (as a technique), he had to resort to antiquity, to the religion of the Jews, which is not only profoundly anti-Christian, but even anti-religious; Jews "have become transcendental in the diaspora, as a necessity to take refuge in the world of the dream, of the ideal", they "breathe desire and contentment for life here" (Băncilă, 2004, p. 343).

The approach that Vasile Băncilă projected through these notes was one of metaphysics and religious logic, but also of religious psychology. He wanted, for example, to analyse the psychology of the religious instinct (by appealing to A. Comte, Fechner, Renan, Plato, Plotinus, etc.), but its identity was not very clear: was it instinct, or a combination of instincts, or was it feeling!

Băncilă did not advocate a return to the Middle Ages, nor to any other type of social and political organisation. But he believed that religious synchronisation was needed, and that the social should no longer be exaggerated at the expense of religion.

About the way the socialization of religion was carried out in our country, he refers to the relationship between the priest and the teacher in the villages: they fight between themselves over who has power in the community. And with the calendar reform, many peasants, turned against unworthy priests, opted en masse for Adventism. The peasants were tempted to make no distinction between the man-priest and his office, the justification being in the propaganda that the Western sects engaged in.

*

Orthodoxy is, after Băncilă, at a historical turning point, precisely because of the degradation of the role played by the priest; his sins represent a kind of cataclysm for Orthodoxy: "priests have always been the ravens of religion (historically)" (Băncilă, 2004, p. 346).

The portrait of the priest is painted in grim colours: he is opportunistic and biological, hypocritical and petty, has a lot of self-love, is prone to being a cheap politician. Hence a host of arguments against the socialization of religion.

Thus, Romanian Orthodoxy was in danger, being attacked by the ethnic enemies of the nation: minorities, Bolsheviks, etc., but also by Americans and sects. It is important, however, that religion be in contact with the transcendent. No one can be religious unless they have a metaphysical vibration, and for that "one must therefore be primitive, or a man of metaphysical sensibility – that is, a sensibility which feels the intense need of a rational universe" (Băncilă, 2004, p. 347). This is the case of creators such as the *faithful* Caragiale or Eminescu.

Here, in fact, lies the ingratitude of religion - there are now people who lack strong metaphysical needs (the example of the philosopher P. P. Negulescu is given), which is a reflection of the tendency of the transcendent to disappear. This is why people are becoming selfish and characterised by narrow materialism at a time when there is an increased need for the transcendent, a symbiosis between the transcendent, i.e., life beyond and the phenomenon of life here, in order to make life as harmonious as possible.

It is true that Băncilă also felt the need to introduce the transcendent into social life (the Hellenes also made use of this element), because an ideal society is congruent with authentic religiosity (see the social transcendent in Emile Durkheim's sociology); such a society would profit even by an "unsocialized authentic religion, seen as an exercise of the transcendent"; or, at most, a fruitful synthesis, combining the transcendent with social instincts, which "no bourgeois religion can offer" (Băncilă, 2004, p. 352). Let this mechanism not be confused, therefore, with any politicization of religion, as happened in Catholicism.

*

But what is religiosity: instinct or feeling? It is a synthesis of innate instincts, plus a soulful mixture of ideas and feelings. That is why, says Băncilă, mankind has been dominated by two great creative forces: religious instinct and ethnicity. This also includes the stages through which peoples have passed in their evolution: the religious and the ethnic phases (see the Orthodoxy-Romanian conjunction in Nae Ionescu).

In order to make religion compatible with society, an ethical transcendent was also sought, as is found in W. Wundt. But it is not possible to work with categorical imperatives, because people need concrete things, i.e., sentimental impulses, God. Man feels the lack of the religious transcendent, and when religion no longer offers it, he ends up making an idol out of the categorical imperative. This is the idea with which Băncilă ends his notes: "God must be concrete. Even if you don't believe, the idea of God plays its part, it brings you a benefit, so it works *by itself*, it's not as if you didn't have this idea at all: then it would be madness" (Băncilă, 2004, p. 353).

*

Professor Vasile Băncilă's religious troubles did not end with these notes. A year later, in April 1926, he would draw up a plan and write about the way in which social life could be organised through religion. Moreover, because he was also a teacher, he was concerned about the organisation of religious education in schools. It would be the last part, the fourth, of a more extensive study, which also included ideas on: the genesis of social life and religion; religion in uncivilised as well as civilised societies.

The old notes were continued with new proposals on the role of religious instinct and religion (in the evolution of society and of the psychic stages as the matrix for the formation of man, spirit and humanity). Once more, the influence of Nae Ionescu's or C. Rădulescu-Motru's courses, with their own developments and, implicitly, with accents of detachment, can be seen.

He invokes, for example, the phenomenon of the decline of religion in the modern period because of the positivist spirit, in which he does not see anything modern; on the contrary, it is "the primitive spirit of man, in fact the uncultured, barbarous spirit"; and "primitive religions are not, in fact, religions, for they have nothing transcendent, the afterlife is still earthly life, only it is placed on a mountain, or underground": "The Creation and Organization of Social Life through Religion" (Băncilă, 2004, pp. 383–390); this advanced an unusual idea: the link between primitive religion and scientists working in the laboratory: "Today's physicists and chemists are the elder brothers of the priests of primitive religions" (Băncilă, 2004, pp. 384–385).

The proof, of uncertain validity, was found in the way contemporary primitives adhered to positivism and the benefits of material civilization. And the Russian peasants who made this change also moved very quickly from faith to Bolshevism and religion.

On the other hand, primitive man believes Băncilă, cannot approach the transcendent and the vision of integral reality, hence the drama of his turning to Christianity. But Băncilă makes, as he himself says, a more serious claim: "true religion is not for primitives, nor even for common people" (Băncilă, 2004, p. 387).

The reason? Through religion, there is an intensification of the religious soul (which some religious people do not have), the experience of a higher spiritual state (the discrimination is partly debatable, even if it takes into account the biological endowment of the individual).

It is, in fact, authentic religion, whose conditions are specified: "man must have a strong metaphysical life" (if he is a captive of everyday life, of the phenomenal, "he is unfit for religion"); hence the aptitude for the transcendent; "to see that, metaphysically, reality is absurd, that life is impossible, and to suffer from this almost to the point of hysteria"; "to find comfort in religion, to see the rational completion of the representation of the world through God" (Băncilă, 2004, pp. 388–389).

These are demanding imperatives that lead Băncilă to consider religion as a dimension of the future, with the hope that human society will truly progress: the *future will be religious* (the creation of most philosophers, who somehow include a religious system in their work, shows this), or we will witness the *barbarization of humanity.*

In the crisis of the modern age, there is, in fact, a distancing from traditional religions and a tendency to impose new religions, such as Marxism, which are in fact false or negative religions, based on hatred and lacking transcendence.

The mixture of religions betrayed, for Băncilă, a symptom: could it be time for a new religion? If so, there are three possible solutions: either a new religion, or a universal religion that will be imposed everywhere (the phenomenon of missionaryism is a good example), or this phenomenon of synchronism will continue. He gives a few options and then presents his proposal: "to experience religion itself, in the form of our historical religions, and through them to escape to the same sublime reality" (Băncilă, 2004, p. 386). And let us renounce false religions, in which Protestantism or scientific religions are included, interrogatively.

With many parentheses, Vasile Băncilă's excursus ends with other opinions about religious instinct (determined by metaphysical torment and including biological reasons, see p. 390), about ethnographic ethos (idyllic elements, folklore etc.) contained in religion, about the religious perspective of a higher humanity (not possible without religion, metaphysical culture and ethics), or about the non-religiousness of some peasants or intellectuals when they suddenly turn to culture.

6.4 Orthodoxy and Catholicism

Almost on the same date, April 15, 1926, Vasile Băncilă writes some notes on "Orthodoxy" (Băncilă, 2004, pp. 364–382) provoked by a dialogue with his friend whom he calls Kiko, alias historian P. P. Panaitescu.[6] The latter raised some objections, specifying the characteristics of Orthodoxy: "imperialism, in the sense of Alexander of Macedon; the idea of monarchy by divine right; the lord of the country is half-holy, is one of the gods, is a tyrant, and seeks to maintain his power indefinitely" (Băncilă, 2004, p. 364). There is here an oriental character reflected in Orthodoxy. The second feature, inversely oriented: decentralisation, decomposition into local units; religion thus becomes a political-social weapon of defence (defensive regionalism, says Băncilă).

In other words, the historian specified the Roman or pagan features of Romanian religion: utilitarianism, symmetry of spirit, sense of measure, remnants of pre-Christian religions. Kiko, says the friendly Băncilă, is right as a historian, but he approaches religion from the outside, that is: he does it phenomenally; and not from the inside, that is metaphysically. He points out the historical vicissitudes through which Orthodoxy has passed, and the two characteristics cannot reflect the essence of Orthodoxy, because they are contradictory. It is more a matter of Eastern political atmosphere or political mentality. Vasile Lupu, invoked by the historian, and any Oriental ruler, Christian or not, wanted to be, if possible, an imperialist.

What is needed, however, is the syllogisms of a philosopher doubled by a historian and a psychologist. Only in this way can the soul of the Romanian peasant be intuited. This is what Băncilă does through a series of approximations on Orthodoxy, judged against the Western religious phenomenon, Catholicism in particular, deconstructed in a partly theistic and tendentious way.

He notes, first of all, that the religion of the Romanians is situated in an anonymous transcendentalized atmosphere, with the supreme duty of *salvation of the soul*, but not as those so-called heroes of Catholicism do; in Orthodoxy, "salvation is pure, it is the very living spirit" of it, "that is, of detachment from the world, of serene vision, of spiritual tranquillity" (Băncilă, 2004, p. 366). In this way, it is superior to any form of Christianity, and it departs from biological placidity or platitude.

Professor Vasile Băncilă then breaks down such a general characterization of Orthodoxy into its underlying features. First of all, he takes up the idea of detachment from things, an attitude of broad contemplation, an almost anonymous or almost personal one. In principle, contemplation has a decisive bearing on the nature of Orthodoxy. The phenomenology of the world has to be perceived philosophically, as a transient reality of little importance to man. He compares, in parenthesis, the German people with the Orientals through the grid of the transcendent, which for the latter is lived for its own sake, whereas for the Germans it is completely different: "Heaven is for earth, not the other way round" (Băncilă, 2004, p. 367).

A second feature is identified in the almost Platonic idea of divinity, one without practical effectiveness, not being at all an incentive for action; it was an explanation for how rarely the Romanian peasant goes to church, but also an unusual justification for a thief, for example, who can be a good Christian, provided he believes in and worships God (it would also be a bit funny: with his right hand he worships, and with his left he steals...).

Another characteristic of Orthodoxy: even if it is not antisocial, it is asocial. Hence, unlike Catholicism, the lack of organisation ("like an army") and a low emphasis on church hierarchy. The Orthodox priest is an ordinary man, as are church leaders, and the church does not canonise saints. It would seem that the idea of freedom in Orthodoxy also derives from such a trait.

*

Orthodoxy, however, also has its antinomies. This would explain, for example, the contrast between such subtle, refined authenticity and the practical, mundane character it often has. Existing in all Orthodoxy, the antinomy would be due precisely to the esoteric nature of Orthodoxy, which is why "it risks being something not perceived and therefore remaining external or mundane" (Băncilă, 2004, p. 368). It is the practical, worldly dimension that has generated some adhesions between Orthodoxy and Protestantism, the latter being "the consecration of the lay spirit in religion", which brings with it "personal freedom and liberation from the iron discipline of Catholicism" (Băncilă, 2004, p. 375). Băncilă brings up again the *case of* the Transylvanians and of the Patriarch Miron Cristea, the Transylvanians being the means by which the Protestant spirit penetrated, as far as it did, into the Old Kingdom; he recalls, however, in his end notes, the popular character of the religion of the Romanians of Transylvania: "and in so doing they, after the war, helped us to reform" (Băncilă, 2004, p. 382).

Such a portrait of Orthodoxy is, for the most part, an ideal one. Vasile Băncilă himself senses this, because he wonders, at a certain point, how up-to-date those characteristics were and whether some adjustments were needed.

The comparison with the Western attitude to life is definitely in favour of Eastern superiority. For example, the asceticism of our people, also attributed to the "frugality of the Romanian peasant", compared to his Western counterparts – who "eat like the bourgeois" – is a mixture of economic criteria and the use of time. But asceticism really takes place in the monastic space.

An old antinomy is thus creeping in: the Romanian people are either too religious or not religious at all, the first notion in particular requiring a philosophical attitude. The asceticism of Orthodoxy is "something popular and serene", it has in it "something classical", it is "not passionately exaggerated"; and, together with religiosity, these traits make up something natural, they "grow out of their natural soil", without resembling the "mysticism of the cultural factory of the medieval West" (Băncilă, 2004, p. 370).

Thus, Băncilă believes the *stamp of* the psychology of the Romanian people can be explored, a psychology that is not morbid at all, without technique, without being a cultural product, as things happened in the West. And this crucible is the sum of Romanian spirituality, spiritual harmony, generosity towards things, a spirituality keeping as close as possible to the landscape (a reasoning that excludes the people of Transylvania, however, where the influence of *Western biology* is felt).

Why this detachment from life, from things, why the attitude of renunciation or resignation, of spiritualization of a people who have gone through so many historical vicissitudes? It is curious how Vasile Băncilă leaves aside the meaningful reservoir of Romanian folklore (he will come back to it later), at a time when Blaga, Mircea Vulcănescu, Mircea Eliade (see Cosmic Christianity) etc., treasure popular creation. It is true that many ideas are only laconically stated by Vasile Băncilă, left to be specified in such words as "I have to show...", "have to study this fact...". or "I will have to study it thoroughly...".

As has already been noted, Băncilă's writings concern the East-West binomial, more precisely: Orthodoxy-Catholicism, the latter being exposed through its attitude towards life, particularly through its social and political characteristics: "Between Orthodoxy and Catholicism" (Băncilă, 2004, pp. 291–298).[7] Băncilă finds the essence of Catholicism in its imperialism and organisational activity, with obvious Roman similarities in its intrinsic logic. And with the observation that Plato can be claimed by Orthodoxy ("vaguely, unconsciously, for such is Orthodox logic itself"); and Aristotle, "consciously" this time, by Catholics, "both as a means of expression and legitimation" (Băncilă, 2004, p. 374). The Schism was thus something fatal, an exclusivist relationship between two types of religious logic, fundamentally different as states of mind, despite the fact that their dogmas are similar.

Situated at the antipode of Catholicism, Orthodoxy is not at all imperialistic, on the contrary, "it is something *static*, it is an *eternal attitude*" (Băncilă, 2004, p. 377), something similar to the image of a Buddhist in contemplation (which Băncilă would have seen in a museum). This is why Orthodoxy does not engage in practical, political competition (see the subjection of the church by the state).

This is how the danger of the politicization of religion among Romanians can be understood, which Băncilă mentioned in a different context from the one dealt with here, since any involvement in politics amplifies the worldly dimension and greatly weakens, if not outright destroys "the intimate aspect of religious vibration", just as "exaggerated asceticism destroys life". And also dangerous for Orthodoxy is "the modern invasion of sects and irreligiousness" (Băncilă, 2004, pp. 378–379), a feature also mentioned by Băncilă.

*

After all this, what should one do? By morally ennobling the believer, Orthodoxy implicitly becomes active and social, a kind of school of human virtue. Such a tendency, however, must be well measured, together with the power of Orthodoxy to defend its rights against those who touch them and to organize its Church in the spirit of tradition, by protecting its intimate being.

And there is something else that, according to Băncilă, should be changed with maximal enthusiasm in the Orthodox garden: the external or worldly spirit. One could write many pages of irony, of pain, of *religious medicine* about the sins of our Church: what goes on at the Romanian Chapel in Paris, country priests who dance in cassocks at the ball or at the altar (where they also read newspapers), priests who wear canes and gloves. These are shortcomings that are, whether we like it or not, linked to the essence of the contemplative force of Orthodoxy.

And yet, Orthodoxy is superior to Catholicism, whose correction is even more difficult, if not essentially impossible. This is why it needs to be more attentive to its own virtues, by which it "guarantees a pure religious life" and practically dissociates "between the theoretical and the worldly life", saving itself through synchronism with modern society, through "inner elasticity and complexity". It is, however, an ideal hypostasis, because "Orthodoxy is full of rubble, debris, weeds", "it is weak, sometimes dusty, like that mischievous horse in the story, full of blisters, wretched, who sat forgotten in the stable" (Băncilă, 2004, p. 381).

Notes

[1] Dora Mezdrea believes that Băncilă was referring to a lecture given by the philosopher at the students' hostel in Brăila, because until that time Nae Ionescu had published only one text in which he spoke of the superiority of Orthodoxy ("Pascalia", *European idea*, April 1920). But what if Băncilă implicitly refers to this very source, but also to Professor Nae Ionescu's lectures!

[2] At that time, Vasile Băncilă was a professor of philosophy and pedagogy at the Normal School in Brăila (he worked there until 1941), where Badiu Vizireanu, who had prematurely passed into the world of the righteous, was director – see Nae Ionescu's obituary in *Word*, 9 May 1927.

[3] Goga, O. (1881–1938). Romanian poet, publicist, politician with fascist and anti-Semitic tendencies. Among his writings: *Poems* (1905), *Mr. Notary. Drama in three acts from the life of Transylvania* (1914), *Cries in the Wilderness* (1915), *The Boiling Wine* (1927), *Precursors* (1930).

[4] Cristea, M. (1868–1939). Publicist, philologist, politician with anti-Semitic tendencies, theologian, first Patriarch of the Romanian Orthodox Church (1925–1939).

[5] Dora Mezdrea, who researched the philosopher's archive, mentions Băncilă's intention to defend a doctorate on such a topic – another doctorate variant was the subject of Schopenhauer.

[6] Panaitescu, P. P. (1900–1967). Romanian philologist and historian. Among his writings: *Michael the Brave* (1936), *A history of Romanians* (1942), *Dimitrie Cantemir* (1958), *Common peasantry in Wallachia and Moldova: the feudal order* (1964).

[7] Most of the ideas of that time will be taken up again in the present notes.

Chapter 7

Back to René Descartes!

7.1 A philosopher at the crossroads

Immediately after graduating from university, in September 1922, the young Vasile Băncilă writes about Descartes, the thinker who fundamentally marked the modernity of European philosophy. It is a 25-page manuscript, with six sections, in which he outlines Cartesian philosophy and the method of the French author. If I dwell on these pages, I do so as in other cases, not so much for the waning novelty that the approach might have today, but for its contextual importance.

Initially, Băncilă dwells on antecedents offered by the classical philosophy of Greece, by the dependence between philosophy and science, by the mutual impulse they had in their evolution. After Aristotle, however, Băncilă believes, the Greek people "had lost their philosophical nerve, just as they had lost their political nerve, and even earlier their artistic nerve" (Băncilă, 2003, see pp. 180–203).

This is why science could no longer receive any influence, and ancient philosophy, especially Aristotle, would have to wait a while before being put back into the circuit of ideas of other centuries (Băncilă partially avoids the Middle Ages, when philosophy would have been interrupted, and mentions only the Arabs and the Renaissance; he was probably unaware of Étienne Gilson's work on *Philosophy in the Middle Ages*, printed in 1922). Under the Renaissance enthusiasm, a new, scientific spirit arose, with an extraordinary power of synthesizing the latest scientific data, a spirit capable of developing a method of searching for truth independent of any external authority. This *patronage* was given to R. Descartes (1596–1650), or Cartesius, a French philosopher and mathematician.

The only true philosophy, according to Nae Ionescu, is the one the author lives. A process that takes place, after all, even when you want to receive, to understand the philosophy of a creator, as happened with Professor Vasile Băncilă who, in his notes, wants to provide authentic grounds for a real interpretation of Cartesian philosophy. Even if he does not say it directly, he discreetly utters an exhortation: *Back to Descartes!*

*

The thinker Descartes took an unusual initiative compared to other authors: before developing his own philosophy, he developed a lucid and efficient *method*, free from confusion, in his search to find the truth. Alongside his acknowledged contributions to mathematics and physics, *Discours de la Methode* (1637; the title is longer) remains to this day a cardinal philosophical landmark for modern European thought. Three hundred years after the appearance of this unique metaphysical approach, the *Journal of Philosophy* published a special issue devoted to Descartes (see No. 4, Oct. –Dec. 1937), and in the same year, the International Congress of Philosophy was held in Paris under the patronage of the spiritual figure of Descartes, with the presented papers printed in no less than twelve volumes.

In his lecture at the Romanian Academy (November 5, 1937), the philosopher Ion Petrovici praised the legacy of a philosophical genius like Descartes, its fruitfulness not only for the history of philosophy, but for many other spheres of the human spirit. He had "direct followers" (Petrovici, 1937, see pp. 365–376) like Malebranche or Spinoza, but "even heterogeneous philosophers, like the empiricist John Locke or the materialist Lamettrie, have put Cartesian vines on their hearth – feeding their fire". He recalled the substantial lecture on Descartes in W. Wundt's History of Philosophy course in the 1905–1906 semester. The same Wundt who, some ten years later, during the war, writing a negativist pamphlet on everything that was not German philosophy, accepted an exception: the famous Descartes.

Uncontroversial, the French philosopher was valued everywhere, even by people who could not stand the French. He was the seedbed of modern philosophy, the one who gave the signal for its beginning. It is said that when Victor Cousin visited Hegel on a trip to Germany, he told him: "France has more than done its duty to world thought by giving it Descartes". Also, at that time, the not at all modest Schopenhauer placed Cartesius alongside Plato and Kant, two philosophers in whom he believed enormously.

In his festive exposition, Ion Petrovici risked to *state* that there are some similarities with the spirit of Cartesian philosophy, among them common sense, "that natural balance which instinctively flees from extremes and exaggerations, that attitude of finding the right note, guarding against the glare of paradoxes and the temptation of adventurous plotting". He was quick to overlook some of the concessions made by the French philosopher in his own work, but he could not escape the spirit of synthesis of the scientist, the one who sees the image of knowledge as a tree whose roots are metaphysics, the trunk being physics, and the branches – mechanics, medicine and morality.

*

In the same anniversary issue of the *Journal of Philosophy* can be found writings by Mircea Florian (on Cartesian dualism), Grigore C. Moisil (on the stages of mathematical knowledge), Dr. Al. Tillmann (on Descartes' ethics), Lenormanda Benari (on the commentators of Cartesian works).

The exegetes of Cartesian philosophy are, quantitatively speaking, extremely numerous, in relation to a not so extensive corpus of works. They were very interested in the man Descartes, but also in the philosopher's primary thought, intentions, feelings and beliefs that inspired the work. It has also been said, as Gouthier states, that *Cartesianism* is one thing and *Descartes' thought* another. The latter belongs to history, whereas the former is to be re-acknowledged by the various followers or epigones of the philosopher. The important thing is that the spirit of the philosopher should be properly understood by the spirit of the person who comes into contact with his work.

In a letter, Descartes thought disappointedly: "*I am so disgusted with the trade of making books that it pains me just to think about it*" (to P. Mersenne, 20 April 1646). He was anathematised in the Netherlands, where he had found the peace and quiet that was conducive to creation. He was accused of scepticism, Papism, atheism, of attacking church and state. Even his favourite disciple, and an intimate commentator on his work, Regius, broke away from Descartes' metaphysics to retain only his physics.

Nor was France any the worse off, various exegetes, some occasional, of his work accusing him of dwelling too much in the spirit of scholasticism, of being too complicated, heretical, Protestant, of being too syllogistic with his "*cogito ergo sum*", of being somewhat confused in arguing for the existence of God. Even Blaise Pascal had some objections to the connection between the philosopher and the divine creator of this world, these being added to those coming from the Jesuits, his former teachers, the same Jesuits who once approved of him as a good Catholic and a directing spirit. Paul Valéry may have been right when he considered the effort of commentators to decipher the secret of Cartesian thought to be futile.

However, to his contemporaries, Descartes appeared antinomic: atheist or follower of the Church, on the one hand, traditionalist and revolutionary on the other, that is: two diametrically opposed angles of view, "of religion and of science, each with its followers and deniers" (see Lenormanda Benari's synthesis of Descartes' reception, in the cited issue of the *Philosophical Review*, pp. 456–463).

One thing is certain: criticism from Descartes' contemporaries will be reflected, in a small way, in the history of the subsequent reception of the man and his work. For three centuries he was considered a metaphysician, physicist and theologian alike, with the emphasis on his *Metaphysical Meditations*, and the anathemas were often repeated.

Thus, in the first half of the nineteenth century a positivist Descartes is in fashion; later accused of anti-intellectualism as the mystical and religious tendencies of the post-1900 period bring him back to the same Jesuit objections of the seventeenth century.

In the Romanian space, in a virtual dialogue with Motru and under the umbrella of a mystical revolution, Nae Ionescu was very categorical: "In other words, for the time being we are merely liquidating rationalism; not the true rationalism with which mysticism has always lived in the most fruitful peace; but Cartesian rationalism, which is an overthrow and, further, a one-sided falsification of the true one." (Ionescu, 1990, pp. 21–25) Then he explains, in detail, how it is liquidated: in philosophy and politics, in art and religious life.

In order to criticize Descartes and his creation, you need the object of criticism, i.e., the *complete work*, which was only achieved between 1896 and 1912, with the famous Adam et Tannery edition. In 1886, L. Liard gave the first scientific and philosophical synthesis of the Cartesian system of thought. And the twentieth century would be one of disorder and unusual hypotheses, when Cartesian studies abounded (between 1900 and 1937, there would be around three hundred Cartesian exegeses; in France, about eighty of them). The reason is simple: it was a work and a thinker who offered some answers to the concerns of the time, when exegetes were preoccupied with the metaphysics of ephemerism or the pragmatics of deciphering illusion.

7.2 Living in Descartes' philosophy

How much and how deeply did the young Vasile Băncilă understand the man and thinker Descartes, the character – or, in his own words, the "patronal personality" – that Professor Nae Ionescu did not like? Băncilă's empathy with Descartes is explicitly formulated as soon as he aims to identify himself, through experience as both "actor and historian", with the latter's philosophy, its character and its influences. This is why he proposes an outline showing the features of this philosophy, its causes and precedents, and the effects and importance it has had. And this without giving us much, if any, indication of its sources.

He lucidly notes the sea of confusion in which the new philosophy was immersed at the end of the Renaissance, when the vectors of the Middle Ages and ancient philosophy were mixed in equal measure. Descartes was confronted not only with this atmosphere, but also with the various philosophical systems that preceded him, elements that were enough to feed his intrinsic scepticism (as distinct from true scepticism): "To doubt all that he had learned is to doubt the very power of men hitherto to find the truth" (Băncilă, 2003, p. 183).

But he did not depart from the spirit of the Renaissance, which his method proposed as a continuous way of thinking about life and the world in equal measure. This marvellous way of finding the truth was, says Băncilă, a kind of *Ars Magna* that Descartes made available to the science of his time.

Vasile Băncilă also intuits the believer in the person of Cartesius, his need to establish an absolute faith. As he keenly observes another feature of Cartesian thought, namely that of being in sync with the individualistic imperialism of the Renaissance, of being an intellectually conquering spirit, animated by a proud self-consciousness; we should be attentive to nuance even when, under velvet opportunism, Descartes writes *humble phrases* (political tactfulness played tricks on the French philosopher).

Descartes believed himself to be an absolute initiator through his personal method, which he miraculously discovered through a crisis (following the Greek meaning of *krisis*), occurring while he was on a military expedition. There, he would have had the revelation of that single criterion which guarantees truthfulness, as Băncilă observes; but, according to him, the formulation "*truth is that which is clear and distinct*" must otherwise be deciphered through the threads of Cartesian psychology: "*the adherence of the will when something seems clear and distinct*" (Băncilă, 2003, p. 185).

*

The phrase *clear and distinct* seems to Băncilă to be a tautology, the conscious criterion being reduced to that of absolute clarity. The only guarantee of truth remains rational clarity expressed by immediate evidence, a condition of truth rather than a criterion.

Trying to explain the sufficient reason of Cartesian truth, Băncilă submits the latter to a minimal logical analysis, deciphering a passage, mediated by will, from logical possibility to logical necessity. Only in this way will we have a positive mechanism for finding the truth. It is not difficult to see in Băncilă's remarks his familiarity with the human device of will which he assimilated from Schopenhauer.

Descartes' belief that his proofs of the existence of the self, the world and God would "exceed in certainty and evidence the proofs of geometry" seems precarious to him. This leads Băncilă to say that Descartes' simple propositions would make his criterion "insufficient" and "open to distortion" (Băncilă, 2003,

p. 187). The Cartesian criterion thus seems vulnerable to him; the philosopher should have found an *extra-volitional means* of avoiding the illusion of clarity given by will.

Băncilă then briefly comments on the four secondary rules specific to the Cartesian method, to which he adds two more. He notes deductive speculation and its role in the affirmation of human subjectivity, as opposed to induction, which makes the man "a marvellous telluric excrescence, with some pragmatic capacities, but limited and confused" (Băncilă, 2003, p. 188). With an observation: Descartes *doubted everything by his method, but he did not doubt itself* (the proof that his ego thinks if it doubts was, I believe, sufficient reason).

It details the steps by which the French philosopher declared the idea of God, one of our ideas, to be something clear and distinct. Descartes thus gave "two great blows, catching its metaphysical anchor on two rocks: the existence of the self and the existence of God" (Băncilă, 2003, p. 190). Most of the truths of man and of the world are determined by the idea of God, including high morality which is theological; alongside it, Descartes also places a practical morality regulating the relations between the individual, the laws and customs of society, its decisions and the will of its power.

Praising Descartes' personality, Băncilă sees in him a realist spirit, a "metaphysical or ontological rationalist realist" (Băncilă, 2003, p. 193), placing him next to two other representatives of ontological realism: Plato and Spinoza. In his use of abstractions, he was a dogmatist (dogmatism that becomes ontological realism), just as, in his conception of matter as being distinct from the soul, he is a dualist, doubled by a deist.

Vasile Băncilă is also concerned with the prerequisites of Cartesian philosophy, with its historical precedents to which the thinker explicitly referred. The criterion of experience and the deductive method did not belong to him. Only Descartes enriches the principle of evidence by that of "*the honesty of knowledge*: do not let the will affirm an idea until it appears perfectly clear in the intellect", thus claiming to obtain the truth from "the *domain of moral facts*" (Băncilă, 2003, p. 194).

But Descartes' scepticism is not unusual. These thinkers cannot be ignored: Augustine, Hugues de Saint-Victor, François Sanchez, even Campanella. The questions concerning the existence of divinity were also not very new, its hypostases in the Cartesian grid of ideas being found in Aristotle, Thomas Aquinas, St Bonaventure, the psychologist Vives, St Anselm, Duns Scotus. And the question of the immortality of the soul is in the lineage of the dualistic Christian vision and also of Plato's ideas.

For his mechanistic conception of nature, Băncilă refers to the spirit of the Renaissance, but also finds a predecessor in Robert de Grosseteste, who looks at physics through the study of figures and movement. And for ethics, Descartes is indebted to Duns Scotus and Occam, while in analytical geometry, his precursor is Nicholas Oresme.

7.3 Cogito ergo sum – a sophism

After these filiations that yet do not diminish the Cartesian spirit, Vasile Băncilă continues to apply the critical filter through which he receives Descartes' method and philosophy. He could not fail to hermeneuticise the cardinal proposition: *cogito ergo sum*. He asks himself: is it an intuition of some state of mind or of the depth of the ego, similar to the intuition of freedom, or, as in Schopenhauer, of the will? Or are we dealing with reasoning? If it is truly an intuition saturated with evidence, then what of that *ergo*? (Băncilă's Renaissance linguistic spirit says nothing more to him here). If it were a reasoning, however, Băncilă says that the second part of it would thus be included in the first: *I think, therefore I exist* (Băncilă, 2003, p. 196). That is equivalent to an analytical judgement, one that makes Cartesian demonstration superfluous, as it falls into a vicious circle (the error called *petitio principii* or *circulus in probando*, identified by Aristotle), the conclusive proposition being implicitly contained in the premise. Or the second part is not contained in the first, but then the validity of the reasoning is questionable.

This would be, according to Băncilă, "the most intimate point of Descartes' error and, at the same time, the original and fruitful error of his system" (Băncilă, 2003, p. 197). But let's follow its deconstruction. Let us not admit that the first term implies the conclusion. The *cognition* has the sense of *self-conception* and tells us nothing, logically speaking, about the *self*, which is something transcendent to the cognition. This is where the philosopher's naive realism comes in: thought would imply a kind of substratum called the I, but, adds Băncilă, "*Thought can only be in the self,* and if thought exists, the self exists" (Băncilă, 2003, p. 197).

We cannot deduce that substratum from thought in general, because it would be necessary to do it also through thought, therefore, "we would remain in the same place" (is it tautological or redundant that thought thinks about itself!).

However, a hypothesis that the French philosopher would not have considered is put forward, namely: can *cogito ergo sum* not be an *aprioric intuition* in Kant's sense? And Băncilă is also one who doubts, psychologically speaking, even if such a point of support can be ignored in a logical or metaphysical approach. However, he believes that such an intuition would only have a phenomenal objectivity, as in Kantian philosophy, and not a metaphysical one, as Descartes would have wished.

Băncilă concludes, finally, that the Cartesian sentence "it is nothing but a sophism, with a great power of persuasion, in that it is a mixture of intuition and judgment, being neither one nor the other, but imposing a subjective certainty of both" (Băncilă, 2003, p. 197).

It seems strange, to say the least, that the young Vasile Băncilă is exclusively focused on *cogito ergo sum*, without ever mentioning *dubito ergo cogito*, the epistemological doubt that Descartes' intuition expresses. This was not a completely new cognitive attitude, for the history of European philosophy had known similar episodes. What is unusual is the specific radical character of Cartesian doubt, the fact that it is under the control of a precise method in its constitutive steps (the four rules for "guiding the mind"). Doubt thus demands the renunciation of any presupposition or prejudice considered true, demanding imperatively that one must start from thought, and only by means of it can one arrive at something true.

Descartes doubted the truths in books, doubted education or what others said, he even doubted his own sensations or representations (things that we see in our dreams seem real). He doubted everything and anything, but he realised that he who doubts must exist: *I doubt, therefore I think; I think, therefore I exist.* This is the final point of *methodical doubt.*

*

But if there is any sophism, it creeps into Vasile Băncilă's demonstration. He ignores, in order to save his discursive mastery, the character of true intuition of each of the sentences: "I doubt", "I think" and "I exist". In his *Meditations on First Philosophy*, Descartes states that "This sentence I am, I exist, whenever it is uttered or conceived in thought, is necessarily true".

Just as Băncilă ignores or evades the fact that *ergo* does not have, in the statements in question, the meaning of a deduction, since this would invalidate the principles of methodical doubt. Deduction is a way of knowing for Descartes, alongside intuition. In Descartes, we are not dealing with a syllogism, as Băncilă thinks, but with a cascade of *intellectual intuitions*, as my professor of symbolic logic, the delightful Radu Stoichiță, observed.

Closer to us in time, there has been more discussion of the *incognito ergo sum* statement (in Derrida, Lacan, Barthes, or photographers and writers such as Camus or Kundera), which studies the role of memory in the foundation of identity. If the subject is grounded in language, then the topos of identity is in the imaginary, through an *imago of the self.* But language establishes the veracity of a continuous present, while memory refers us to its relation to the past. Thus, in the end, there is a precariousness of identity recovered through memory. This is not a philosophical approach, but rather a behavioural-psychological or philosophy of language approach.

7.4 The function of Descartes – a kind of Luther

Returning to Vasile Băncilă's criticism, I will consider the objections he raises to Descartes' theology from the perspective of principles of pure logic. Firstly, the proofs of the existence of divinity: the path through the first cause refers to Kant, while two other arguments "confuse the subjective and objective realms"; from the comparison that Băncilă invokes, I understand something else, namely that it is the specific difference between the *ideal* and the *material.* Here are the sentences: "It is the same as if I wrote to someone that I was giving him a large sum of money and he believed himself to be rich, as if the letter were also the money" (Băncilă, 2003, p. 198).

Descartes would get entangled in some logical improprieties, often encountered in the history of philosophy, especially in the absurdity of the principle of analogy. The error consists, on the one hand, in the confusion between "what an idea indicates and the nature of the idea itself", and, on the other hand, in straining "the idea of causality to the point of making it incomprehensible or destroying it" (Băncilă, 2003, p. 198).

As far as the ontological argument is concerned, he considers the essential criticism made by Kant and Schopenhauer to be complete. With one *caveat* concerning the flaw in this type of argument: "*logical* existence is confused with *objective* existence: in truth, once we have the idea of perfection, we cannot *deny* its *existence* (and here is the sophism of the partisans of the ontological argument), but it is an *existence of the same nature as the idea,* i.e. logical, therefore subjective" (Băncilă, 2003, p. 199).

Still being a critic of Cartesian philosophy, he formulates another reservation concerning the ethics of the philosopher: as a *strictly logical theologian,* he conceives of morality as something relative, when in reality it is, for humans, something absolute.

*

Why would Descartes remain in European philosophy? As the founder of modern philosophy, he used a spirit of synthesis of the latest data in science and logic, doing away with the principle of authority in thought. His reform in philosophy is likened to what Luther did in the sphere of religion. Of course, the greatest merit is that of instrumentalizing a method of "thinking verisimilitude", expected by the spirit of the time, which wanted "a kind of simple and effective *gnoseological panacea*" (Băncilă, 2003, p. 200).

Closely linked to the method is the gravity of a sceptical vision understood in its own tragic way in relation to the enthusiasm brought by the Renaissance. With the methodical doubt formulated by Descartes, the world stops believing as simply and as easily as it did before. Although the dogmatic temptations of the Middle Ages sustained by Renaissance euphoria did not end, for the need to believe was still there, now the people wanted to do it in a more intelligent and subtle way. Here was the almost insoluble question facing Descartes: the congruence of dogmatism with scepticism. He didn't solve the problem, but he did manage to infuse the mentality of the time with a host of beliefs.

It is impossible to get past Cartesian dualism: both mechanism and spiritualism at a time when the world was tempted by science and mysticism, a mysticism that was not superficial but, on the contrary, intellectual and monotheistic. And Descartes' merit was to try to *accommodate the* scientific spirit with the mystical tendency.

*

Having gone through so many trials and successes, the philosophy of Descartes, notes Băncilă, through its ideas, had a long and *active* posterity, generating a school and philosophical systems with superior, creative spirits. Cartesianism, as a complement to Descartes, marked the great direction of the development of philosophy up to Kant; Kant himself was later to take over that supremacy, but only after Descartes "poured himself into it". The two, Descartes and Kant, disputed the same founding role, the same philosophical *function*: one for modern philosophy, the other for contemporary philosophy.

Descartes gave the canon to his contemporary epoch, he is a historical philosopher: "To have corresponded to his time, both to its tendencies and to its virtualities, and to have remained, through this time, active in its subsequent evolution, is the happy fate of Descartes' genius" (Băncilă, 2003, p. 203).

One would have expected Vasile Băncilă to mention, at least in a parenthesis, the influence of Descartes on the spirit of Romanian philosophy, at least on the

Transylvanian Cartesianism of the seventeenth century, introduced there by young Hungarians who had studied in universities in Holland.

Many of the French philosopher's ideas, Băncilă noted in 1922, still retained their aura of actuality, such as the idea of evidence or immediate intuition in the sphere of knowledge, as well as the role of the will in formulating a judgment. Or the discovery of analytic geometry, the undulatory form of motion, the prescience of the Kant-Laplace system and other ideas which, says the traditionalist metaphysician Băncilă, are in keeping with the French ethnic genius.

*

In a later note, in 1941, Băncilă again expressed his reservations about the Cartesian *cogito*, somehow reprising his older observations. The existence of the ego or non-ego cannot be deduced either by direct intuition or by reasoning, the latter being touched by the error of *petitio principii*: "*I* think. But the thing to prove was the *self*. How do you know *the ego* exists? When you postulate the ego, you also postulate the non-ego." (Băncilă, 2009, p. 16)

And if he deduces the non-ego from thinking, then he can also deduce it from feelings or from the mind: I feel, therefore I am, I hate, therefore I am, or I suffer, therefore I am.

Starting from the premise: "he who thinks exists", Descartes could not know what exists and what does not. Moreover, you cannot prove that something exists by appealing to time but to space, whose existence becomes the "*central point*" (Băncilă, 2009, p. 16) in philosophy. Băncilă's conclusion was that the French philosopher had spent most of his life trying to discover something and had stumbled upon a chimaera. This reconfirmed his opinion that *cogito ergo sum* was nothing but a sophism.

Chapter 8

Ethics, sociology and politics in Schopenhauer

8.1 A terrific *up date*

About the German philosopher Arthur Schopenhauer (1788–1860), Vasile Băncilă left us two texts: one of about 12 pages, which constitutes the second thesis (evaluated by G. Antonescu and Mircea Florian, examining professors, with the highest mark); and another one in three versions, one of which, about 140 typed pages with corrections by the author, is a final form, an excursion that materializes his intention to get a doctorate in philosophy.

The dissertation proposed a three-part analysis of Schopenhauer's well-known work *The World as Will and Representation*, written when he was 31 (1818; the second edition, with additions, appeared in 1844, then in 1859 and 1873). But it will not be an examination detached from the rest of the work, as in other cases; even if the essence of all the author's writings is condensed in this main work, the book will be received through a "whole Schopenhauer" (Băncilă, 2003, pp. 209–215).

Until 1922, little was written about Schopenhauer's work. There were some examples, such as Mihai Eminescu, with his doctoral thesis *On the Fourfold Root of the Principle of Sufficient Reason* (*Über die vierfache Wurzel des Satzes vom zureichenden Grunde*); Titu Maiorescu, who also translated a series of aphorisms from *Parerga und Paralipomena* (published in 1851); C. Dobrogeanu-Gherea, the critic using him in his course on Eminescian pessimism.

Known for his criticism of Hegel, with whom he would teach philosophy at the University of Berlin, influenced by mystics such as Meister Eckhart and Jakob Böhme, initiated into Buddhism and Hinduism as well as the mystics of early Christianity, Schopenhauer was a thinker who left a serious mark on the spirit of his time.

Vasile Băncilă did not ignore Schopenhauer's biography (a thinker who, as Cioran would say, *rubbed himself against life*), a dimension more important in a philosopher than in an artist, according to the German thinker himself. The life of a philosopher, says Băncilă, is converted, through intellectual syllogisms, into tendencies of character, according to which he constructs a new ideal universe.

Without resorting to an analysis of Schopenhauer's life, Băncilă confines himself to drawing conclusions about the character of the philosopher[1] (a sort of demiurge), who had, above all, "a strong intuition and necessity of life", therefore also "intuitive thinking", and a "direct, concrete, persuasive vision" (Băncilă, 2003, p. 210). Alongside this, he discovers, in the personality of the philosopher who confronted the whole of reality, something contrary: a tendency to silence, withdrawal and denial, metamorphosed into a rare power to understand not only his own pain, but pain itself. A contradiction that marked his affectivity and his way of knowing the world.

Thus temperament, character impose a certain way of knowing, the intensity of which will be resumed by the intellectual capacity of a thinker (a little later, Băncilă will say that Schopenhauer's philosophy is a kind of enthusiastic codification of the expression of his character). Here, however, we have a hypothesis that is not generally valid, but specific to Schopenhauer's nature – a thinker in whom "suggestion, the presence of life" are decisive – as in his system of thought we find "good mental hygiene against intellectualism" (Băncilă, 2003, p. 215).

Some of Schopenhauer's influences should be mentioned, cultural influences to which Vasile Băncilă adds a few others: the theory of Platonic Ideas, the positive sciences of the time, but also a social imprint from the landed romanticism of his epoch. In fact, the German Romantic movement and, alongside it, Kantian philosophy left a decisive mark on Schopenhauer.

The student Băncilă advanced the thesis that "*philosophy is the struggle against scepticism*" (Băncilă, 2003, p. 211), a hypothesis verified, more than once, in the history of philosophy. When a system of philosophical thought is called into question, the consequences can only be sceptical. The closest case was that of Kant, studied by Schopenhauer in relation to Plato, even if the author of criticism, says Băncilă risibly, gave us no metaphysics, not to mention the human split between pure reason and practical reason.

*

Today, almost a century after this summary written by the young student, infinitely more is known about Schopenhauer. We thus smile in the face of the intellectual terribilism typical of his allegations, but we cannot deny him the courage of his value judgments, even in the presence of not many, and not very profound, arguments. His remarks on Kant's metaphysics and the fracture of the Kantian system are juvenile and must be taken as such, coming as they do from a small rebellion haunting the young man who was venturing, with ease, into the realms of universal philosophy.

As the determinism of temperament in relation to the work must still be taken with some reservations, for there is a risk of too categorical an influence on the ideas of a thinker, it may seem to us that the nature of the author's syllogisms exhibits a sensitivity coming from his character.

Thinking of a possible metaphysical unease, Băncilă says at one point: "A passionate man, in whom life flows intensely and proteanly, *will not be able to think systematically,* nor will a quiet man, with few feelings, be able to have the power of intuition of the former, but, on the other hand, he will be able to have strong, discursive thinking." (Băncilă, 2003, p. 210)

It is true that he validates his own opinions, finding in Kant's philosophy either an encouragement, by the implicit fructification of the social instinct, or an accreditation of the positive sciences producing necessary and universal truths. Kant began the process of scepticism, but the real battle with this school of thought, Băncilă believes, was to be waged by the German Romantics, Fichte, Hegel and Schelling, as well as Schopenhauer.

Not marked by any complex, Vasile Băncilă attempts to deconstruct the Schopenhauerian philosophical system. Without having a gnoseology similar to that of Kant and without being his disciple, the author of *The World as Will and Representation* differs markedly from Kantian thought. But this does not erase any influence coming from the latter, because it is present, subtextually, in the criticism he will offer on Hegel. Schopenhauer develops an original physiology of perception: the external world exists only insofar as it is perceived and present in the human mind as a *representation*, the foundation of the world being in the power of *the will*, which has no reason or purpose.

For Schopenhauer, the world as such, like the history extolled by Hegel, does not have a terminus, a final ground. And the will is the meaning-giving factor for the organic and inorganic world alike. The primacy of the will is to be found in the animal sphere, through the vital force and the instinct of perpetuation of the species. This idea has not been abandoned; on the contrary, it has fertilised the history of philosophy from the second half of the nineteenth century to the present day.

Băncilă identifies four characteristics of Schopenhauerian philosophy: understanding and reason constitute a single faculty; the 12 Kantian categories are reduced to three aprioric structures: time, space, causality; the last one, causality, has the status of an intuition, which is why it is also found in animals; finally, the fact that the thinker from Danzig is among those who "give a *physiological* interpretation to apriorism", the body being "a deeper reality and prior to intelligence" (Băncilă, 2003, p. 212).

The central category of Schopenhauer's metaphysics is therefore *Will*, the first and last reality, lying outside the three categories and being transcendent, unique, indivisible, uncreated and eternal. From Plato he inherits the Ideas, also situated in the transcendent and expressing the code of every individual: "*to every man corresponds an Idea*" (Băncilă, 2003, p. 213), and the universe, in phenomenal terms, is *my representation*.

Schopenhauer has some radical statements from which he draws a conclusion about the nature of life: human will *is* effort, effort implies desire, desire means lack, lack is pain. It follows, finally, that life is pain. And if we consider that we have here a positive reality and that pleasure is the negative reality, then happiness is not possible, because life is effectively pain and preparation for death. And how can we avoid pain, which has its source in the will? Through creation, art and morality, after which, says Băncilă, "we enter the bliss of death" (Băncilă, 2003, pp. 213–214).

The last part of the synthesis of the dissertation is reserved for critical observations, more precisely put in other words: how Băncilă understood Schopenhauer. First of all, this is the kind of philosopher in whom contrasts are to be found: his thinking is both pessimistic and voluntarist.

Then follows an avalanche of unanswered questions. How does Schopenhauer argue that man ultimately has the intuition of his existence as will? Should the limit of this intuition be reality itself? Can we equate the "intuition of *my* ultimate reality" with the reality of the world? And how can will, as metaphysical reality, be something outside of time if will is activity? And if the will creates phenomena through Ideas, it is no longer something simple, unique. Then, lack is not, invariably, just pain; it can also be pleasure if we take the case of the realisation of an ideal, not to mention the fact that, psychologically, pleasure and pain cannot be quantified. Finally, the formidable contradiction of Schopenhauer's thought: if the will is the *will to be*, how can we destroy it?

In accordance with the formulated hypotheses, Băncilă emphasizes that Schopenhauer's philosophy is congruent with his character, personal idiosyncrasies and various influences, being essentially a contradictory type of thinking. And the philosopher's posterity is atypical: he did not create a school, but had only a few *minor* disciples, who either corrected his system or overemphasized certain elements of it. And he lists a number of names that the history of philosophy has not really remembered: Frauenstaedt, Bilharz, Bahnsen (best known), Hellenbach, Mainländer, Petres, Lange, Dühring, Noiré, Du Preel, Taubert, Schneitewin, Venetianer, Bovies, Koeher, etc. (he refers to Hartmann: "L'école de Schopenhauer", *Revue philosophique*, August 1883).

But perhaps the most significant author influenced by Schopenhauer was Nicolai Hartmann, the founder of critical ontology in the twentieth century and an important historian of philosophy. Schopenhauer's influence on H. Bergson and Nietzsche cannot be ignored, the former also being suspected of plagiarism: both see the mechanism of knowledge (intuition) and metaphysical reality (will or vital impulse) as identical. Despite the accusations, there are essential differences: for Bergson, intuition is a conscious factor, not something implicit, and the vital impulse is not something timeless, but *duration* itself.

8.2 A German philosopher read in French

The summary of Vasile Băncilă's undergraduate thesis is merged into the other manuscript, the possible doctoral thesis, *Schopenhauer's Ethics, Sociology and Politics* (Băncilă, 2007, see pp. 216–429), written in 1922 and revised the following year.

As I noted above, Schopenhauer's philosophy was not researched in Romania until then. Titu Maiorescu, a Herbartian, had considered it when he was influenced by the philosophy of I. Kant (between 1872–1890, as Simion Ghiță observes). Among Titu Maiorescu's lectures on the history of universal philosophy, there is one called "Transition to Schopenhauer" (Maiorescu, 1980, see pp. 84–102), reproduced from the lecture notes taken by I. S. Floru.

First, a note is important: "We are expounding Schopenhauer's philosophy at greater length, because in today's philosophical movement (which is very small compared to the first third of our century) this philosophy is still in the public eye as a continuation of Kantianism, while Fichte, Schelling and Hegel are disappearing from public consciousness" (Maiorescu, 1980, p. 267).

Through his pessimism Schopenhauer is, for Maiorescu, a symptom of the times and has "a splendour of style such as has never been seen in the philosophical literature of any people, a depth of ideas characteristic only for him"; he biographizes him, appreciates his ethics and logic, his grounding in morality, and his aesthetics as Schopenhauer is reviving, in the context of sensualist materialism, "the pessimistic but idealistic tradition of Indian Buddhism" (Maiorescu, 1980, pp. 88–89).

Maiorescu emphasizes Schopenhauer's desperate nature, citing, for example, a letter from his mother sent from Weimar (1807), a city in which she does not wish to live with her son: "For my happiness, I need to know that you are happy, but not to witness that happiness... Your unpleasant despairs, your lamentations on the world's stupidity and on human misery make my days too dark." (Maiorescu, 1980, p. 90)

Maiorescu gives many biographical details of his intellectual biography (the critic holds two lectures on this), as well as his reactions to his teachers; for example, to Schleiermacher, who seems to have said that every philosopher is inevitably religious. Schopenhauer noted: "No religious man comes to philosophy, he has no need of it; no true philosopher is religious, he needs no restraint, but walks freely." (Maiorescu, 1980, p. 91)

Maiorescu insists on the philosopher's life with autobiographical expositions from "About philosophy in the university" (negative opinions about official philosophy) and from "Aphorisms", the first appearing in the journal *Literary dialogues*, the others – in a printed collection ("Aphorisms for wisdom in life", Socec Publishing House, 1890), after some of them were published in the same journal.

The World as Will and Representation (November 1818, Brokhaus) comprises, the critic observes, the exposition of the logical-metaphysical structure (in the first two parts), then Aesthetics (Part III) and Pessimistic Morals (Part IV). Before the book appeared, Schopenhauer left for Italy, where he was to be in the company of the three (with him four) great pessimists of the nineteenth century: Lord Byron, Leopardi, Châteaubriand (the fifth pessimist is mentioned in parentheses: Eminescu, 1849–1889).

After its printing, Schopenhauer's capital work was "almost unknown", apart from a few remarks from Herbart and "some dithyrambic words of praise from Jean Paul" (Maiorescu, 1980, p. 92).[2] Years later, in 1835, the publisher Brockhaus wrote to him saying that the book was not in demand, for which reason he was obliged to sell the remaining copies as *scrap* (!).

The following year, Schopenhauer published *On the Will in Nature*, in which he developed critical syllogisms against philosophy teachers and the reading public. Neither this nor the second edition (with "supplements") of *The World as Will and Representation* was a publishing success until 1853, when an English magazine, the *Westminster and Foreign Quarterly Review*, published an extremely laudatory article on Schopenhauer, which was later translated in the Berlin-based *Vossische Zeitung*.

The Germans were now beginning to take an interest in the work of the hitherto ignored philosopher. In 1857, at the University of Breslau, the first lectures on his philosophy were given, and the Berlin Academy offered him membership, which he refused. The last six years of Schopenhauer's life were marked by "the light of celebrity, too late for warming the heart of the great pessimist" (Maiorescu, 1980, p. 94), who will die just as he lived: in solitude (in his will, he will leave a small capital for the care of his faithful dog).

Maiorescu presented the sequence of Schopenhauer's writings and translations of the philosopher's works made in Romania and France, indicating, at the same time, as an important source Th. Ribot, *La philosophie de Schopenhauer* (Paris, 2nd edition, 1884; he is an author judged negatively by Băncilă).

He then tackled the philosophy of the German thinker, read, of course, in the original (lesson 23 of manuscript 1521, 31 May/12 June 1891 is reproduced), dwelling more on his aesthetic theory, of which he also published fragments, "without the music part", in *Free Romania*. He does, however, summarise the aprioric forms (space, time, causality), insisting on how comparative anatomy confirms Schopenhauer's philosophy, the manuscript stopping somewhere on page 160, the rest of it being lost.

*

Let us return to Vasile Băncilă's text on Schopenhauer, designed to be spread over three sections, with a methodical introduction and presentation of the genesis of the German philosopher's work. The ideas in the thesis now gain breadth and depth. First of all, I would like to point out that, unlike Maiorescu, Schopenhauer's work and his exegesis are read by Professor Băncilă in French. The following are quoted: many specialist journals with studies on various aspects of the work; A. Schopenhauer, *Le Monde comme volonté et comme représentation* (trans. by Jean Cantacuzène, 2 vols, Leipzig, F.A. Brockhaus, 1886–1889); A. Schopenhauer, *On Religion* (1906); A. Schopenhauer, *Le Fondement de la Morale – Mémoire non couronné par la Société Royale des Sciences de Danemark*, à Conpehague, le 30 janvier 1840 (1897); Émile Charles, *Dictionnaire des sciences philosophiques* (1563); Théodore Ruyssen, *Schopenhauer* (1911); Th. Ribot, *La philosophie de Schopenhauer* (13th edition, 1914); S. Reinah, *Essai sur le Libre Arbitre* (1907); Alfred Fouillée, *Critique des systèmes de morale contemporaine* (1883); Paul Janet, *Histoire de la science politique dans ses rapports avec la morale*; W. James, *Philosophie de l'expérience* (1910); Harald Höffding, *Histoire de la philosophie moderne* (1906); Spencer, *La bases de la morale évolutionniste* (1880) and others.

Schopenhauer's writings are considered by Băncilă as a reference point for an introduction to general philosophy, to the history of philosophy and especially to practical philosophy. Just as the German thinker remains a fundamental reference for philosophical creation, for the philosophy of life, of the will, of intuition, for the general resolution of the question of the moral fact. We are dealing with a kind of contradictory mosaic, since "the concept of the will links him to Schelling and Böhme, the primacy of the will over intelligence to Fichte, subjective idealism to Kant, objective idealism to Palton" (Băncilă, 2003, p. 216).

Therefore, according to Théodore Ruyssen, Schopenhauer is characterized not "only by his opposition to a system, but also by the highly original amalgam he made of Eastern and Western philosophies, of Platonism and Kantianism, of Christianity and freethought, of classicism and romanticism" (Băncilă, 2003, p. 439).

Vasile Băncilă abruptly asks himself (and will do so at the end of the work) what remains as a definitive legacy of Schopenhauer's ethics, sociology and politics. By constantly referring to the context of the twentieth century, his perception concerns the writings as a whole and is a critical perception, one that involves clarifying and justifying the negative criticism made of the work, but also advancing new solutions to the vicious and unsatisfactory problems presented by the philosopher.

He was, as Maiorescu pointed out, more or less understood during his lifetime; and when he was, readers were sentimental dilettantes, in keeping with the fashion of the time. A fashion which, says Băncilă, turned the philosopher either into a bizarre pessimist, or saw in him an absolutely clear thinker who was placed in "the type of German philosophical obscurantism" (Băncilă, 2003, p. 218), as C. Dobrogeanu-Gherea did.

It is no less true that Schopenhauer has also been read by official philosophers, but with little or no empathy, and sometimes by introducing foreign ideas into the argument and thus favouring error. This is how Ribot, for example, proceeds when he sets out to talk about the philosopher's morality and does so by discussing something else, the problem of love. This kind of confusion is often encountered among French thinkers, for whom ethics appears to be assimilated to the philosophy of life (see Ruyssen; Băncilă also suggests such an approximation somewhere), as a kind of pragmatic metaphysics that is generous with what it encompasses. But even the ancient Greeks would have confused the moral with the truth and the beauty (without Băncilă explaining how; *truth, good and beauty* is an irreducible triad, not at all contradictory, if sophisms are eliminated), just as the same factor of the moral was substituted by the English with the useful, or by the Germans with the theological transcendent or with what the state religion represents.

8.3 Five ethics

Băncilă notes, however, that Schopenhauer's sociological thought has not been discussed at all, even though it is one of the originalities of his approach. Just as he has not dealt with the question of politics in the German thinker, even though his strong points are metaphysics and ethics.

If ethics and sociology are intimately related, the relationship between sociology and politics is not, the latter studying "the *social organization best suited to the realization of ethical ideals and biological goals*" (Băncilă, 2003, p. 221). The idea of an ideal, for politics, is borrowed passively from ethics and biology, thus becoming a normative discipline (most sciences are passive, even ethics, as it merely ascertains "the commands of concrete moral reality"). However, politics is transformed from passive into active by a complex of means (taken from sociology) with which it pursues a goal as understood by ethics and biology, to which is added the intuition of the politician, something irrational which, together with other elements, makes politics both a science and an art. This is how politics comes to be logically linked to sociology, which is why the two will be approached without any radical distinction between them.

After Băncilă, until 1813–1818 sociology had not been rigorously discussed. Moreover, Schopenhauer himself "gave us at most a politics, and not a sociology" (Băncilă, 2003, p. 223). Even the ancients, says S. Reinach, are not a reliable source in this respect, because they too had no clear idea of free will or of the reality of the external world. The nineteenth century is the century of sociology,[3] when the foundations of a science of the social were laid, even if judgments made since antiquity were fructified with a kind of retrospective generosity.

Schopenhauer the man is above the philosopher, because the cypher of his work is, as already seen, character: a theoretical individualism, "perfect, comfortable and prudent" (Băncilă, 2003, see pp. 225–226). He was bereft of friends, family, even homeland: "He almost died because he was German", as one exegete puts it, or, according to another, Germany would have been for him: "a wasteland of ink and a wasteland of words" (Băncilă, 2003, p. 440). But he was a split character, "varied and disparate to the point of drama and anarchy"; hence an "impressive conglomeration of adverse virtualities, and his philosophy, to the keen observer, a veritable explosion in the potentiality of disparate tendencies". To which was added a volcanic temperament, through the absolute living of every idea.

Traits which, as I said earlier, determined the Schopenhauerian way of thinking: intuitive, analytical and synthetic, contradictory. This is why his work is, ideologically and ethically speaking, a seemingly endless string of antinomic tendencies. Băncilă sets out to identify, in the philosopher's five or so ethics, the authentic, legitimate one; but all of them are unconnected and contradictory.

The first would be the ethics of glory, Schopenhauer being exasperated, as he wrote to a friend (2 July 1858), that he knew only half of what was written about him. It is an ethic underlying his letters in particular. He was flattered when disciples gathered to debate his work, or he advised them to popularise it, each of them having distinct, well-established roles, as is also evident from his correspondence.

Then comes the ethics of a moralist, one who was inclined towards "the concrete, intelligent, colourful grasp of moral facts, the painting of characters, of habits", a dimension that gives him a *French writer* status (Băncilă, 2003, see pp. 228–229).

But much more important are the other three ethics, which are also dealt with by Băncilă: general ethics (where pessimism appears), personal ethics (one of an informed, theorized and wise Epicureanism) and Schopenhauer's ethics proper, the one that deals with "the psychology and principles of moral facts".

*

In 33 paragraphs, Vasile Băncilă presents Schopenhauer's ethical ideas in the first part, then his sociological and political ideas in the second part. It sums up, first of all, the author's metaphysical determinations for what is necessary in order to understand his ethical, social and political thought. It insists on will, a fundamental Schopenhauerian concept. Metaphysics appears to him to be congruent with both a pessimistic and an optimistic view of life, and the philosopher's arguments "are mostly concrete, literary, persuasive, because of his intuitive intelligence, without lacking the rational armour" (Băncilă, 2003, p. 232).

These are arguments that revolve, as I have already said, around the relationship between six essential terms: life, will, effort, desire, lack, pain; those that make up the sequence of statements that leads to the conclusion that everything is pain, with a couple of exceptions to the rule. Băncilă details them and gives conclusive examples, expressing the discord between human nature and the nature of life (he illustrates with long quotations in French from *The World as Will and Representation* and *The Foundation of Morality*).

Pain, however, is something positive, while pleasure, which consists in forgetting the will and which is also perceived as pain after it ceases, is negative. The positivity of pain is achieved as long as man comes closer and closer to the will, and pain itself is not only pain, but something positive. The suffering in the world, determined by the will, and its consequences are framed by Schopenhauer in what he calls *eternal justice*. And one more thing: "If desire is pain, the greatest pain is the very absence of pain," wrote the German philosopher.

Through a succession of quotations, Băncilă portrays the world as a colourful and contradictory spectacle offered by the will, a world in which happiness is illusory and people are born to be simply devoured by sadness and other positive misfortunes... With sentences from the philosopher: "In the hours of melancholy, of hypochondria, the world appears, from an aesthetic point of view, as a museum of wrecks; from an intellectual point of view, as a madhouse; and from a moral point of view, as an inn of rogues." (Băncilă, 2003, p. 443)

Also eloquent are the pages describing that doctrine of salvation, which Schopenhauer envisages through six hierarchical steps: egoism, art (Băncilă is not interested, as Maiorescu was, in the aesthetics of the philosopher), pain, morality and asceticism (the essence of which is the mortification of the body, with its fulcrum in the morality of the Vedas), with which man takes the road to salvation, to the denial of the will (without this resembling suicide).

Stylistically speaking, Vasile Băncilă finds himself in Schopenhauer's writing, as the philosopher's texts, dripping with images and memorable comparisons, are a happy combination of literary and philosophical genres. And the thinker's plethora of arguments confirms the endosmosis between his biography and his work.

*

In *Aphorisms on the Wisdom of Life*, Schopenhauer formulates in serene, impersonal and archaic terms a personal ethics, unrelated to other ethics or to his metaphysics. It is more a discourse for all those who have not had access to his philosophy, a kind of practical guideline that he followed through his conduct, with the aim of achieving some personal satisfaction using such means as "health, youth, tranquillity, freedom and intellectual activity" (Băncilă, 2003, p. 251), all active on the warp of a willing temperament. And in *The Moral Foundation,* Schopenhauerian ethics is condensed in a representative way.

Băncilă refers to them in distinct and dense paragraphs, noting exaggerations or confusions in Schopenhauerian metaphysical discourse (see the confusion of happiness with morality). He considers Schopenhauer's metaphysics to have its phase of innocence and suspects it of not being a genuine morality, as the thinker said of Giordano Bruno's philosophy. Moreover, no exegete has spoken of Schopenhauer's ethics proper, which is made up of the psychology of moral facts and the principles of moral facts.

Interesting is the commentary on the theory of freedom, with its fulcrum in the statement: "I can do what I want." People, Băncilă observes, believe themselves to be free for three reasons: they confuse the intuition of *I can do what I want* with *I want what I can do*; they are then mistaken about deliberating between possible alternatives, they decide for one of the paths, forgetting the others, thus believing themselves to be completely free. Only, says Băncilă, from the union of these three errors is "born the practical error of freedom" (Băncilă, 2003, p. 256).

Apart from this outward, physical freedom given by conscience, there is another way, one indicated by reason. Man encounters, in this way, an extremely rigorous determinism (to which character is added), which, Schopenhauer says, only those "brainless philosophers" ignore, or the so-called "undecided and floating discursives" (Băncilă, 2003, p. 448) who take a middle way.

However, in the economy of freedom, the feeling of responsibility for our actions comes into play: a phenomenon for which Schopenhauer refers us to Kantian freedom theory (perhaps the only one that is protected from Schopenhauerian criticism), "the greatest idea that man has come up with. This and transcendental aesthetics, these are the two beautiful diamonds in Kant's glorious crown; they will never lose their brilliance". Just as freedom is no stranger to free will, which turns it, as Malebranche says, into a mystery.

8.4 Between politics and sociology

Băncilă writes extensively about Schopenhauer's moral foundation, but also about the ethics of principles. I am interested, however, in aspects less commented on up to that point, namely Schopenhauer's sociological and political ideas. The effort of the exegete is great, since the German philosopher rarely and indirectly discusses social problems in *World as Will and Representation* and in *Aphorisms*. Băncilă does not interpret Schopenhauer's various approximations of the social, but rather wants to recirculate the philosopher's ideas about social reality and the possibility of science describing it; he does this above all through the criticism he undertakes.

Human society is made up of individuals, who are its phenomenal part, and in each of whom the whole will is manifested: "The essence of the world, the will to live, exists whole and undivided in each individual being. The microcosm is equivalent to the macrocosm. *The masses comprise nothing more than the individual.*" (Băncilă, 2003, p. 452)

Therefore, the human individual represents a profound reality, each human being has an intelligible character in his depths. In other words, as Băncilă stated, "man is an autonomous reality" which "cannot merge into society to form a larger, organic reality" (Băncilă, 2003, p. 274). Society is more an arithmetical sum of individuals, and not a dialectical one. The German philosopher emphasizes individual life, its unity, and the people appear to him as an abstraction, a pure fiction.

In a superfluous bout of criticism, Schopenhauer considers that individuals, as Băncilă observes, "cannot melt into a superordinate object"; the formation of a society is, for the time being, subject to failure: "Everything in the individual and the individual in the Whole, that is the permanent inclination of Schopenhauer's spirit" (Băncilă, 2003, p. 275), concludes Băncilă. Just as Schopenhauer himself contests the existence of an individual psychology which cannot be, if one disregards the will, the essence of the world.

Băncilă was grasping Schopenhauerian ideas about history and, indirectly, about the nation. The object of the former is the individual, but an individual of little importance, something of the nature of appearance, obliterated, superfluous, meaningless and even petty. The historian practises the "science" of the configurations that clouds take in the sky, structures in which he identifies "groups of people and animals", history narrating "what existed only once and will never be again" (Băncilă, 2003, p. 452). Schopenhauer's contempt for history resembles that of Descartes, one exegete observes.

Hence the conclusion: history cannot be a science of the individual, such a thing is a pure contradiction, but it can be a *chronicle* of the succession of facts. Since the historical fact is not in itself scientific, history, says Băncilă, is in Schopenhauer's view a "logical monstrosity". It is possible, at most, to have a Platonic philosophy of history, one that "will deal with that which always *becomes* and never exists (...); it must bind itself to that which always exists and never becomes nor ever passes away" (Băncilă, 2003, p. 453).

In Herodotus, Schopenhauer finds enough history for the needs of philosophy. Then, asks Vasile Băncilă, what role can history play? Having been overcome by art, it has, in the end, an honourable role, giving people the opportunity to know its past and to make predictions for the future. Not to mention the fact that it is the same history that distinguishes man from animal.

Schopenhauer did not, however, have total contempt for history, as his more aesthetic appreciation of historical monuments shows. And in adopting a middle way, he does not ignore the practical function of history.

*

Schopenhauer also has shocking ideas about the nation or ethnic feelings. No concessions to chauvinism, he says, and patriotism seems to him "the most foolish of passions and the passion of fools". Today it is apparent only too well what patriotism – or nationalism – meant in the context of the nineteenth century, that of the affirmation of the national spirit, just as the specific difference between chauvinism and patriotism cannot be overlooked.

Ethnic instinct seems to have been indifferent or foreign to him, since he found it appropriate that national pride is the easiest form of pride. Just as he no longer gave any meaning to the crowd, and this in an age in which, towards its end, the *masses* would become the main actor in the logic of history. Cynically and humorously, Schopenhauer says in an aphorism: "Each nation mocks the others, and all are right" (Băncilă, 2003, p. 278).

Schopenhauer, notes Vasile Băncilă, speaks about society indirectly, through his syllogisms on man's social instinct. But he does so from the perspective of social psychology, just as he did in the case of ethics. Băncilă constructs an intelligent hermeneutic of the social instinct, based on the ideas that emerge, particularly, from the *Aphorisms*. He again brings in Schopenhauer's biography, his sincere loneliness with which he vainly uttered a kind of prayer: "Give me a man!" but he also brings back the somewhat communitarian attitude for, says Schopenhauer, "I rejected no one, I ran away from no one who was truly human in spirit and heart"; he thought he would find one man out of hundreds or thousands, so that, in the end, he was convinced that "nature is endlessly greedy and that I must bear with dignity and patience the 'loneliness of kings'; a desperate loneliness" (Băncilă, 2003, p. 453). Which is, in fact, *the tragedy of the lonely man*, loneliness restoring to man the Adamic condition of his natural, primitive happiness.

All this has not prevented him from identifying in the social instinct the generative factor for human society. He establishes the essential determination of the social instinct: *selfishness*, to which are subsumed four types of individual interests: economic, vanity, sexuality, boredom or hatred, with vanity or ambition accompanying man to the last moment of his life. As his exegete Th. Ruyssen says, perhaps no one equalled him in the depth of his observations on boredom, in which Schopenhauer paradoxically saw a source of sociability, even though many identified in it "a public calamity, for official institutions are created out of political prudence to prevent it, because this evil, like its extreme opposite, hunger, can drive the people to the most harmful excesses: bread and circuses, that is what the people need" (Băncilă, 2003, p. 454).

It is not so much ideas as sympathy of wills that bind people together. And friendship has its source in people's character, because, says Băncilă, choosing extremes, a genius will never befriend an imbecile (Cioran would be of a different opinion; he was looking for *the secondary*, he was almost seduced by the *little* man).

*

Many excerpts from Vasile Băncilă's possible doctoral thesis expose questions of *applied sociology*, especially those that seem bizarre in relation to the general theories specific to Schopenhauer's thought. Among them: property rights; religion; the state (he rejects anarchy and despotism, even if republics are close to the former and absolute monarchies to the latter); politeness as a social phenomenon (with the unusual example of the hedgehogs who, in order to protect themselves from the cold and to live together, find a way of distancing themselves from each other); social conformity; the problem of the sexes (a metaphysics of love); war; the enslavement of factory workers.

Just as passionately does Băncilă dwell on the theory of law and social reform, embodied in Schopenhauer's applied politics. The idea of the state is confused, in the German thinker, with that of law, having, despite all these errors, a particular importance for the political vision of the philosopher. The right Schopenhauer opts for is a right in itself, paradoxically situated outside the law but which is not something artificial since, according to the philosopher, there is "no moral right, no natural right and no pure doctrine of right" (Băncilă, 2003, see pp. 455–456). It is a positive right, which Băncilă captures in a series of details.

Schopenhauer's judgement of *penalty* in a state is interesting. The purpose of a law is the prevention of crime, but what is punished is not the perpetrator but the act. And this is to prevent future crimes. Schopenhauer departs radically from the law of retaliation and from Kant's understanding of punishment as an end in itself; for him, the penal code is "a repertory, the most complete possible, of the reasons which can be opposed to all criminal actions supposedly possible".

In Schopenhauer, Băncilă also deciphers the spirit of a philosophy of social reform. The thinker is an advocate of organic evolution of a people, in accordance with its character and past, even if, in the final analysis, social reform seems to him somehow impossible, the causes being in his own fundamental pessimism, in the fatality specific to the will and the unchangeable character of the people. We cannot oppose the prevailing evil and, through it, unhappiness.

Schopenhauer also has total reservations about the possibility of educating people, or about the force of real progress. In all of these cases, what changes is only the *form* (see also the option of a convinced Schopenhauerian Eminescu). Hence the philosopher's detestation of philosophy teachers, of women, of optimists of all colours, the story of history being nothing but "a long dream, the heavy and confused nightmare of mankind".

A diatribe is addressed also to material progress, and this in the last years of the thinker's life, when he defined it as a chimera, a dream of the nineteenth century and when his criticism was devastating, *ad personam:*

> Miserable parvenus, enriched with what you have not earned, proud of what does not belong to you, arrogant beggars, who glean the stock of the first inventors and plunder their ruins, compare, if you dare, you, who celebrate your discoveries with such pomp, your algebra with language, your printing with writing, your science with the simple calculations of those who first gazed at the sky, your *steamers* with the first boat to which a daring man put a halyard and a rudder? What are your engineers and chemists beside those who gave you the fire, the plough and the metals? You have made all these divine gifts, you were right. Why then are you so arrogant? (Băncilă, 2003, p. 456).

This is a longer fragment in which Schopenhauer pours out his critical verve on "bourgeois optimism" in a dialogue, a few months before his death (cf. P. Challemel-Lacour, "A contemporary Buddhist in Germany. Arthur Schopenhauer", *Revue des deux-mondes*, 15 March 1870). He was anathema, I repeat, to material progress, not intellectual progress, as, like a pure-blooded conservative, he hurled scornful arguments at the crowd.

8.5 Splitting with some division

This is how Băncilă concluded the mainly expository part of his approach to Schopenhauer's ethical, sociological and political ideas. An extensive section whose declared critical aim is to deconstruct Schopenhauer's hypotheses and theses follows, with interpretations that have been partially made up to this point.

It again reveals an obvious feature of ethical thought: its contradictory nature, its lack of unity, dimensions of which Schopenhauer would not have been aware. It is clear that the German philosopher was not possessed of scientific objectivity, but rather of a speculative mechanism, of fertile and ingenious sophisms.

In the general ethics hides an oriental philosopher, more precisely: a Buddhist; in the ethics itself, we are dealing with a Christian thinker; in the personal ethics, a Greek speaks (perhaps under the influence of Goethe and ancient culture); a Jesuit expresses himself by absolute contempt for his fellow men, and by converting the means into ends of self-satisfaction. Hence his oscillation or slippage between apparent neutrality and various tones: moral, amoral or immoral.

Schopenhauer offers us a therapeutics of pain, obviously of an intellectual-philosophical nature, coming as an influence of Stoic thought or Epicurean doctrine, with the author uttering syllogisms, especially in aphorisms, like an ancient sage; perhaps the last, says Băncilă, that mankind gave us. "It is strange that the most unbalanced philosopher should have written the most balanced book"; just as Nietzsche, "*because* he was sickly" (Băncilă, 2003, see pp. 300–301), apologised for force through writing. A sort of liar's manual, Schopenhauer's aphorisms are in "good company with Machiavelli's doctrine and we recognize in him the translator of that *Art of Prudence* of the Jesuit Gongorist Gracian", an author often quoted and who influenced his thought.

Băncilă's criticism is aimed above all at general ethics, in which metaphysics and ethics proper are also structured. Even if he takes up the cascade of questions raised in the introduction against Schopenhauer's metaphysics, without going into detail, Băncilă believes that metaphysics should not be criticised; a metaphysics such as Schopenhauer's should be judged according to its value in terms of *allogical elements*: congruence with the author's character, the scope of the character's generality ("i.e. the extent to which it satisfies many people"), its persuasiveness, the conclusions or practical applications drawn from it, "the degree to which it serves as the transcendent foundation of his ethics" (Băncilă, 2003, p. 302).

8.6 What is pessimism?

Vasile Băncilă focuses his analysis on Schopenhauerian pessimism (not once placed face to face with pessimism in general), characterizing it as sincere (even if it had several morals), absolute and metaphysical. The philosopher's sincerity has been questioned by those who have highlighted the opposition between *work* and *author*, between creator and man (see Kuno Fischer). Professor Băncilă, however, has always relied on a synchronism of the substance of the German thinker's writings with his character – a grid, it could be said, of the psychology of creation. And if there is a contradiction, and there is, it manifests itself during, so to speak, the emission of ideas as such.

*

But one thing is certain: Schopenhauer experienced his pessimism and the glory of his work in equal measure. There may be reservations about Schopenhauer's sincerity expressed through his role as an *artist*, even if Băncilă believes that the pain of artists is as genuine as that of children. But there are grounds for scepticism about such a type of sincerity, especially since it came, as Schopenhauer's exegete points out, from an excessive, susceptible, contradictory character, although arising from an anxious soul, which perceived pain acutely and with a certain generosity, having, moreover, an "unusually adequate intuition" (Băncilă, 2003, p. 303).

Guarding against some distortions, Băncilă defines pessimism: it is a conception according to which, by universal judgment, the essence of life is represented by pain. It excludes, out of hand, individual judgments – made, for example, by a man whom a great misfortune has befallen. He is not a pessimist, but something else, for what happened to him in no way affects the life of people in general.

There are two forms of pessimism: a relative one, which unconsciously implies the existence of optimism in the world, and an absolute pessimism, which has either metaphysical or psychological grounds.

Schopenhauerian pessimism is hampered by the absence of an explicit clarification of the concept of Nirvana, which is not to be identified with Buddhist Nirvana, Buddhist pessimism being relative. Schopenhauer's Nirvana "must be conceived in the sense of pure non-existence" (Băncilă, 2003, p. 308); the will to live, which is the Will, i.e., the essence of the world, is destroyed. Man, as a result of this loss, is left with nothing but pure representations, his consciousness of the relationship between *self* and *non-self* disappears; he has, as H. Bergson would say, a transient "annulled consciousness", "until the organism is destroyed by the withdrawal of the will" (Băncilă, 2003, p. 309). By renouncing life, *essence* and *phenomenon* are destroyed in equal measure, and happiness is no longer possible. Having a metaphysical basis, Schopenhauer's pessimism is absolute.

Băncilă admits that it is difficult to logically define pessimism, or to admit a certain scientific validity to it. The most important criticism of pessimism has been its opposition to optimism, a pragmatic, not a scientific strategy. It is true that pessimism needs to be empirically proven; after which it can be founded in a metaphysics of its own, thus providing it with a transcendent horizon.

*

It has been shown how Schopenhauerian pessimism is logically and metaphysically dismantled (but also criticized), in a slightly speculative way by using arguments from everyday life. The theory of the ideal is invoked in order to use a judgement such as "lack is pleasure" and also to point out a flaw in the philosopher's famous reasoning, which concludes that everything is pain, a conclusion that could become: everything is pleasure.

Băncilă analyses metaphysically, biologically and psychologically, through pragmatic reasoning and generalizing, the relationship between *pain* and *pleasure* in life, as features that can be positive or negative only from a metaphysical angle. And all this in a finite life, man being frightened, says Băncilă, of an infinite existence, full of endless troubles. The example of Ivan Turbinca is recalled; punished to have an endless life, forgetful of death, an optimistic character willing to spend his days "with vodka, with snuff, with singing, pranks and what have you" (Băncilă, 2003, p. 321). Pessimism has an important place in popular and religious culture, evil and unhappiness coming from the gods or evil geniuses.

Methodologically speaking, it is not the appeal to pure speculation that proves that pain or pleasure constitute the substance of life, but the appeal to experience, even if it cannot validate the truth that one of them is predominant (as Băncilă shows through various critical combinatorial hypotheses). Truth, in this case, is sociologically conditioned: "truth is what is admitted as necessary by all normal people" (Băncilă, 2003, p. 329; Edmond Goblot's *Treatise on Logic*, 1920, is invoked here). It is a criterion of truth, but, I believe, by no means the only one and perhaps not even the most valid one, if we were to take into account the relativity of the phrase "all normal people", i.e., the impossibility of a complete induction.

Vasile Băncilă concludes that neither pessimism nor optimism can be justified (the causes are logical). There are other reasons besides the absence of the sociological basis mentioned above: there are no statistics of pleasures and pains; their internal logic suffers from a fundamental flaw. Which means that pessimism and optimism are only *non-philosophical ideas*, non-logical ideas, like the convoluted form of meliorism; still, they can be fertile from a spiritual and practical perspective.

Therefore, pessimism, says Băncilă, is not a matter of philosophy, but of art and religion, which do not tend to express universal ideas (with a Kantian meaning) *in an absolutely logical sense* (authentic art, achieved in the highest artistic degree, acquires, however, a degree of universality, though admittedly not in a logical sense).

However, Băncilă finds psychological grounds for these ideas: the origin of pessimism and optimism seems to be in one's *temperament*, just as one cannot ignore one's experience or experiences. Moreover, as personal tendencies, they are innate, these being aspects Schopenhauer did not take into consideration. Along with temperament, "thought and egoism or subjectivity" (Băncilă, 2003, p. 338) also contribute as secondary elements.

This is also true in Schopenhauer, whose pessimism, not at all based on logic, is as *reflexive and dispositional* as any genuine pessimism.

*

So let us admit, with Băncilă, that pessimism is true. Does this lead to Schopenhauer's *theory of renunciation*? Is it possible? And so arises the great contradiction of the Schopenhauerian philosophical system. On the one hand, the Will, an irrational factor; on the other, its possible and necessary destruction, a rational factor. Băncilă sees such a contradiction more as a motive for artistic creation. It is not scientific, which is why Schopenhauer takes an epic approach to the problem. Will cannot be destroyed for an elementary reason, namely, it is the ultimate reality: "Who can destroy it if there is nothing but it, and in it is the will to live?" (Băncilă, 2003, p. 341). And to this end, he puts forward arguments, both for and against; in the final analysis, these can in no way affect the specific *inexpugnability* of the will.

Moreover, Schopenhauer does not separate the fate of man from the fate of the universe, which no other philosopher has done. No one, says Băncilă, "has thought of making man's salvation conditional on the destruction of the universe" (Băncilă, 2003, p. 343), of its essence. Having seen in man the nothingness as such, Schopenhauer, with a sentimental-romantic logic, elevates him above the world, thus making renunciation impossible, just as the destruction of the Will is impossible. The Philosopher of Danzig "has invented this curious renunciation, which postpones death until the desire for life has first been killed, even if this requires an infinity"; for Schopenhauer, therefore, renunciation (a "kind of aesthetic revenge") "is nothing but an ingenious accommodation between his pessimism and his desire for life" (Băncilă, 2003, p. 344). A poet not identified by the editor Dora Mezdrea is quoted in this regard: "before my death, the death of the love of life...".

*

After an excursion with a multitude of hypotheses favourable – or not – to Schopenhauerian pessimism, Băncilă draws the line and summarises its undeniable merits. Schopenhauer expounded pessimism systematically and suggestively, and from a logical point of view, "it remains no less a non-philosophical idea"; he gave it a double opening: towards theoretical debate and towards practical application; he also showed that "pain grows with intelligence", which is not the case with the power of resignation, which seems much greater in an ordinary man than in a refined one; he expressed, implicitly, through the doctrine of renunciation, a great "confidence in man's initiative, the power of the idea over the conduct of life" (Băncilă, 2003, see pp. 345–349); and if man can do anything, the orientation of this extraordinary force must have a positive meaning, not towards the destruction of life, but towards its ennoblement; finally, Schopenhauer made us understand that man's contentment is given not only by the satisfaction of needs, but also by the *lack of* them. Băncilă reminds us here of the philosopher W. James, who, in a psychology textbook, established a fraction with *desires* (D) as numerator and the *degree of satisfaction* (S) as denominator, the result being *happiness* (F); F will be asymptotic to the ideal either if D is less or if S is greater.

At the same time, Băncilă also draws from pessimism about six practical rules more or less applicable in life, some formulations reaching the symbolic threshold of aphorism.

*

The following paragraphs of the possible doctoral thesis deal, one by one, with the relationship between pessimism and morality, with the problem of freedom in ethics proper, with the foundation of morality, and finally with the historical place of Schopenhauer's ethics.

However, the section in which Vasile Băncilă proposed his critique of the philosopher's political and sociological ideas is missing, only the outline of some ideas is left on a manuscript page.

At the basis of the German philosopher's ethics are sympathy and egoism (not understood as a degradation of altruism); his is a voluntarist and naturalistic ethics, which is close not to perceptual intuitionism but to English intuitionism; it is an original construction (with certain influences from Plato and Kant). Schopenhauer remains, at the same time, an ally of Rousseau, in whom he recognises the greatest of modern moralists, one who *knew the human heart* in depth.

Notes

[1] He will quote in this connection, in his second manuscript on Schopenhauer, from W. James's *Philosophy of Experience*: "A philosophy is the expression of a man's character in what is most intimate to him, and any definition of the universe is but the reaction, voluntarily adopted, as far as it is concerned, by a particular personality (...). If we examine the history of philosophy as a whole, the systems are reduced to a small number of great types, which are all ways of feeling the total movement that life brings with it." (Băncilă, 2007, p. 439)

[2] "A brilliant philosophical work, courageous, multilateral, full of penetration and depth, but often of a depth without borders and without taming, comparable to the melancholic lake in Norway in whose depths one never sees the sun, but only the starry sky and above which no bird or wave moves" (*apud* Maiorescu, 1980, p. 92).

[3] A discipline through which, in our country, Eminescu's journalism investigates, perhaps unpublished, the Romanian social-political space – see Bădescu, I. (1994). *Eminescu's sociology*. Constanța: Porto-Franco Publishing House.

Part II.
An essay in spiritualist metaphysics

Chapter 9

Pars pro toto

9.1 Part and whole

To describe or analyse a characteristic part for a whole is a figure of speech called synecdoche, one that, I believe, can be applied to the style of Vasile Băncilă's long notes. The thinker's worksheets, by their analytical and synthetic-summary character, look like a whole that comes into being by its own unfolding upon itself. A successive whole, approximated, resized, reconstructed, so that the partial-whole progresses, sheet after sheet, towards an ever more complete whole, towards a virtual whole that can be finally filled.

We will thus see how the system of philosophy that Vasile Băncilă dreamed of all his life has as its beginning a Socratic-Voltairian principle: let us define our terms before discussing them. In other words, we will know what a system of philosophy is as long as we understand the meaning of the two terms that make up the phrase: *system* and *philosophy*. For the latter term, we now have a whole volume of 175 worksheets and two finished texts (from 1938–1979) that deal mainly with the definition of philosophy.

But let us not forget that the student and then the new professor Vasile Băncilă left, among the notes of his youth, some on philosophy and ethnic philosophy. It is important and interesting to study the cognitive relationship established between these early writings and the ideas captured by the thinker in the records of the last four decades of his life. Băncilă himself does not forget this vein, as shown by the fact that, writing on the nature and method of philosophy (in February 1940), he refers to his work on *The Role of Philosophy in High School*, written in 1922.

Philosophically speaking about himself, the thinker Vasile Băncilă places himself, on the one hand, "in the middle of the *village*", in other words, "in the middle of the attitude towards the cosmos as expressed by the village, folklore and religion" (Băncilă, 2008, p. 9); and on the other hand, in the lineage of two philosophers he held in high but unequal esteem: C. Rădulescu-Motru and Lucian Blaga, distancing himself, in 1938, from the young Noica, then an essayist in full bloom (he would quote him several times and invoked, in this context, his work *De caelo*).

Noica had made his publishing debut with *Mathesis or Simple Joys* (1934) and was, writes Băncilă, from the family of false Pekingese; yet two years later (Nov. 1940), after Noica had also published other works, he was classified alongside Nae Ionescu in the *critical* orientation of Romanian philosophy (Băncilă, 2008, p. 13). Nor does he forgive his former teacher C. R.-Motru who had quoted the Ecclesiastes, but later criticised it and turned to personalism, thus reconciling himself with nature.

And there is another boundary of origin, or a nuance: Băncilă aspired to an organically situated philosophy "in continuation of the psychology and communitary attitude of the Romanian people from its patriarchal, folkloric but transfigured phase" (Băncilă, 2008, p. 10), as he says in a projected preface to his system of philosophy. He wanted, in other words, to define a type of wisdom founded on the *ethnical*, on the phenomenal level where a philosopher's creation takes place, but also reaching towards another goal above all, the essence, the transcendent, the totality where salvation takes place, a privilege granted only by God. In other words, an endosmosis between the ethnic and the spiritual. In short: "Creation in this world, salvation in the next" (1938).

He does not forget Blaga, to whom he will also reply, in correspondence, that he ignores salvation in his philosophy; he will treat this subject in a conference on "Blaga and religion", arousing, by the ideas being put forward, the philosopher's reservations and irritation.

*

Vasile Băncilă starts from the bottom, from metaphysical reality, in order to reach the top, the Absolute. It is the philosophy of one who has a spiritual sense for that which stretches beyond the immediate (Băncilă, 2008, p. 11; he often quotes Nae Ionescu, a favourite source). Or it has a *philosophical vocation* manifested by a *sense of the transcendent* in its general acceptation (30 Oct. 1950).

Thus, in philosophy, he starts from the "*critical* transfiguration of the attitude of the *village community*", from the Romanian ethos and from religion, being at the same time in community relations with the cosmos and wanting to know God. And he does so without feeling any fear when he is faced with (metaphysical) reality, nor any depression or crushing feeling if he thinks about the cosmos and time (like Motru or "so-called" Noica, an "egotist").

On the contrary, Băncilă is satisfied and stimulated, reassured and encouraged to work as soon as he is involved in a hierarchy. Moreover, in contrast to the moderns, he has a sense of major intimacy with the cosmos, like the primitives who are not yet denaturalized. The Cosmos, Vasile Băncilă believes, inspires humility (it makes you see your smallness), just as it gives you a "power that you draw from sharing with the infinity of the All", as in the case of religion; in this way, you are protected from two evils: pride and that personal nothingness in which modern man, however, is steeped, a "presumptuous puppy", "a cardboard Prometheus" (Băncilă, 2008, p. 10).

9.2 Philosophy – Second Genesis

Vasile Băncilă meditates on wisdom in two registers: either he speaks of philosophy, or he has the philosopher by his side. There are also instances in which he expresses himself impersonally. His notes detail, in an original way, the ideational and problematic load of the great chapters of the disciplinary understanding of philosophy: ontology, gnoseology, axiology, praxeology, or the 11 sections that comprise his own system of philosophy (early 1942).

Philosophy and the philosopher point towards the same chapters of ultimate philosophy. One thing must be said, however: in Băncilă's literary aptitude, his notes often have the gift of plasticising ideas through the wording and examples given, without, or only rarely, reducing the degree of conceptual combustion through ambiguity of meaning. He is much interested in *intensity* of expression, in concentrated (militant, as he says somewhere) and memorable forms and formulas.

The reasons or grounds, according to Băncilă, for which we truly philosophize are multiple: the being who has cultivated an extra spiritual sense, i.e., that of a reality other than the immediate one, needs an overall intuition of reality, at the level of which he distinguishes between appearance and essence (Kantian speaking: noumenon-phenomenon), between subject and object (as Nae Ionescu did in the *History of Logic*, a source mentioned by Băncilă); then the philosopher wants to know how to live (thus elaborating an ethics), or is interested in the problem of death (February 1940), of the problems of freedom, destiny and salvation (1941), of the idea of infinity and eternal time (1942).

Depending on how dominant one motive or another is, Vasile Băncilă also sketches a typology of philosophers (incomplete, if we take into account other impulses of philosophical meditation), for which he also invokes Jaspers and Masson-Oursel: cosmologists, metaphysicists, epistemologists and pathologists or *experientialists*.

*

After a while, in the 60s and 70s, Vasile Băncilă wondered why a lot of philosophy was being created at the time. The causes naturally stemmed from a kind of *up-datedness* of the collective mind, from the stage reached by the social, religious, educational, ethnic structures, by love, art and the mixture of peoples and cultures; the culprits for *ideo-logy* were, among others, "the Jews – the never-sleeping worms of intelligence, of ideas" (Băncilă, 2008, see pp. 114–115).

Philosophy, concluded Băncilă, invaded almost everything, so that every man, no matter how intelligent, had the opportunity to engage in a kind of poaching of ideas to justify a social or academic position. "No one discusses mathematics, chemistry, etc., unless he has studied them; but everyone discusses philosophy".

The philosopher is also obsessed with beginning and end, with origins and goals, he fraternizes with the absolute in order to understand and evaluate the relative in which he lives (July 1944, November-December 1945; pp. 28–29); or he is preoccupied with time, thinking about the essence of the world and our purpose in passing through it.

Concentrating on the nature and method of philosophy, Băncilă takes positivism (P. P. Negulescu and others) to task, as it suffers from a kind of selective blindness. In the philosopher's files, there are countless passages in which the vulnerability of positivism as a philosophy – but also that of superficial scepticism – are explained from various angles. Philosophy is not the philosophy of positive, clear-cut facts, but it begins with the *twilight*,[1] being "enlightenment in the dark" or "*the virtue of piloting in the dark or at least in the clear*" (Băncilă, 2008, p. 11).

Genuine philosophy is at the same time preparation for death (1941), the approach to the essence of our soul, but also a meditation on death,[2] the latter being a principle of knowledge (April 1973); just as philosophy is "the rationalization of the irrational and the irrationality of the rational" (idem, 2008, see pp. 27–28; ten years earlier, in 1934, the philosopher D. D. Roşca published *The Tragic Existence*, an essay related to the rational-irrational binomial) or preparation for life, in that: it gives man a certainty in the face of reality (different from the certainty of science), it frees him from loneliness, by communicating with an ontological world (metaphysical *semen*), and it gives him a mission, i.e., it projects a role (1945–1946).

In fact, according to Vasile Băncilă, philosophy was born when the human being became aware of his miserable condition and a specific form of loneliness (the impossibility of knowing the absolute of things), thus being the great indiscretion. Philosophy came to offer an antidote, to overcome the irrationality of life, its absurdity and metaphysical-moral tragedy, by fashioning – or: re-creating – a bearable cosmos (alongside art and science), as a kind of *second Genesis*, as the great fable, offering us "the system, the myths, thus "revealing" the positive "truth" to us". "*Philosophy is the pearl that covers the grain of the unknown*", but it is also a kind of science of those who "cannot resign themselves to not knowing what cannot be known" (Băncilă, 2008, see pp. 30–31).

As man's response to existence, philosophy represents a re-intervention or a critical entry into the harmony of total existence, after a revolution has first taken place, i.e., "man has stepped out of the game, has distanced himself from the vegetative living of the cosmos and of life". Scepticism and positivism remained at the latter stage, while Descartes and Comte developed a philosophical system which burned out the second stage as well.

*

It was neither the first nor the last time that Băncilă sanctioned scepticism, which is not a philosophy, but its abortion or degeneration beyond its initial value (see Descartes' methodical doubt); such a current of thought is a remedy against dogmatism and fanaticism; it offers the spirit the guarantee of freedom, subtlety and tolerance (through these privileges one could grant scepticism at least the role of therapist of metaphysical thought).

Vasile Băncilă thus makes a concession to scepticism, finally acknowledging its philosophical dimension: the truth accepted by sceptics is that which serves their own interest. He sees here a form of practical valorisation, one that would make these thinkers *the first pragmatists* (22 October 1948).

Since, in the case of scepticism, we are talking about its reception, can Băncilă's attitude be judged by the grid he himself set in a quotation: "in order to truly appreciate a work of philosophy one must have a spiritual kinship with its author" (Băncilă, 2008, p. 39).

This critique was also an opportunity to reflect on doubt as the beginning of philosophy or authentic philosophy. It is an exercise in which – beware the nuance – one "succeeds only when one comes to faith again". Again! Yes, because beliefs are the vertebrae and backbone of our spiritual organism. Therefore, the beginning of philosophy occurs when the human being finally leaves the game of existence (i.e., de-socializes, dehumanizes), and the upsurge of success comes when he integrates himself again, "critically and by deep adherence, into the mystery of existence as such", when the socialisation, humanisation or ontologisation of man takes place (1948). And he adds to this last note, some 15 years later (in 1963), conclusively: "Philosophy begins when man comes to doubt. And it ends when he comes to certainty".

*

On 17 April 1948, Băncilă tried to define the triangle: philosophy, science and religion, first of all, by the way they relate to contradiction: the first reduces it to a minimum, the second removes it definitively and the last makes use of it to the highest degree; he then defines them according to object, method, purpose and application, the most important being the way he explains purpose and application in the case of philosophy and religion; both, however, aim at reconciliation with existence, one appealing to divine help, to God or of the idea of God (reference to Nae Ionescu), the other reducing the contradiction as far as possible.

Băncilă's clarification is significant: every metaphysical system has an inner logic based on a contradiction or irrationality, so that the philosophical construction looks, in the end, like an "ideational *reed bed*,[3] floating on an ocean of irrationality, of mystery" (Băncilă, 2008, see pp. 34–36); and as an application: religion offers moral salvation, philosophy – reconciliation with existence based on wisdom.

9.3 The mythical power of philosophy

Vasile Băncilă's worksheets are, basically, the pages of a metaphysical diary, a diary of ideas in which the author exposes his own thoughts or enters into a dialogue (also) with *anonymous* philosophers. In the June 1948 entry, defining philosophy as a whole, the author finds in it "a more or less sublimated anthropomorphism".

We do not know the absolute reality, the Absolute (not the whole), "unless *we have the Absolute in us* and we descend or ascend to it", to our depths. It is here, says Băncilă, that the principle of identity is transferred from logic to metaphysics. As a reflection of the Absolute, man is something sacred, concludes the philosopher. The idea of the Absolute (of the Great One) as the object of philosophical meditation and its echoes in the sphere of the sensible world will be obsessively reiterated in Băncilă's notes, particularly after 1965.

A little later (October 31, 1950) he somewhat categorically enriches the meaning of philosophy: it is knowledge "operated on the basis of the integral experience of humanity (reflected in the consciousness of a specific, original individuality)" and has as its ultimate goal the justification of religion, not the medieval role of philosophy as *ancilla philosophiae*, but a "great role, sufficient to give philosophy a royal legitimacy of existence – an indispensable existence" (Băncilă, 2008, p. 39).

*

On 21 March 1951, when he was no longer a teacher, he wrote a methodical plan on what philosophy is, apparently intending to explain it to an audience. At first, he notes that students and others have difficulty deciphering the idea of totality, of total reality, which is not the same as the universe. For a persuasive description, he devises a five-step definition based on the specific difference between science and philosophy: while the former investigates a small part of reality, the latter does not, "*philosophy is the theoretical discipline that deals with the total reality of existence, considered as a single object*" (Băncilă, 2008, see pp. 40–42); Elsewhere, he will deny philosophy the title of science, calling it super-science because it "does not venture into metaphysical construction until it has scientifically exhausted the world" (Băncilă, 2008, p. 49); and later, in the 1960s, he amends as a *great misery* the idea of some who conceive of philosophy as the induction of facts, because it does indeed start from facts, but then it has to make "the great leap into abstract myth": "And then to have the power of abstract epic fable. And style, literary composition. And, above all, conviction, enthusiasm: to believe in what he says (not to say: this is my metaphysical adventure. But Blaga did not despise *adventure*. That's it!" (idem, 2008, p. 71).

Philosophy detaches itself from facts, thus protecting itself from scepticism or agnosticism. He would later conclude that philosophy is anticipatory, prophetic, just like poetry or religion (December 1964), science merely suggesting ideas to it (but what is prognosis!).

Let's not stray too far from Băncilă's projections of 21 March 1951. Having a strong ontological task, the philosopher, for whom reality is like a *pagoda*, explains it by stacking it, by hierarchizing it into different steps of reality and meaning. He does so by using binomials such as important-nonimportant, essence-appearance, permanent-accident, but not before arriving at the ultimate principle of existence: the philosopher, having a sense of the transcendent, finds the founding basis in the Absolute, in that which transcends concrete, sensible reality in which he sees nothing but its echoes or reflections (the echo/reflection idea is obsessively repeated).

Because of such an ability to decipher reality, the philosopher is sometimes judged to be deformed: he "is a little *demented* to other people, he appears as a lunatic, as the people say: a fussy one" (Băncilă, 2008, p. 41), when, in fact, if he really has a philosophical understanding of the world, he is deeply rooted in its reality. Moreover, it can be seen that the philosopher lives his own theory, transfiguring, in part, his own life and thus attaining a crowning achievement, that is, wisdom.[4]

It was time to reiterate a little Kantian mischief: some philosophers remain on the road to the ultimate goal as simply "*professors of philosophy* or scholars, or artists", interested in careers or other worldly ambitions. He also recalls a subtle joke of Schopenhauer's, who advised a young man that in order to be interested in philosophy one should have an income of several thousand marks.

There are other philosophers who do not attain wisdom because their philosophy is not sound or just; for example, the perverted philosophers, those who "stumble into scepticism, panpsychism and demonism, amoralism, absurdism" (Băncilă, 2008, see pp. 41–42). The difference between the philosopher and other people, Băncilă points out, is one of degree, for most individuals want to have an idea of reality as a whole, and they may even want to be wise.

Vasile Băncilă concluded his didactic plan by setting a theme, perhaps for meditation, namely: philosophy is not only a characteristic human trait, but also "the essence of culture: no one is truly cultured if he does not have a philosophy – and a healthy, noble philosophy, not a negative or bestial one".

*

Some ten days later (31 March 1951), he reiterated something of this definition of philosophy retaining in particular the phrase *total and not general reality*, for the latter can be understood as "reality in *general*, that is to say, not *all*, but the general parts of it". He then emphasised (a gesture which he would repeat; see, for example, the note of 28 March 1952) that such an understanding of philosophy referred to metaphysics (to the *first philosophy*, in the sense of the ancients), whereas he needed a definition which directly included logic, psychology, aesthetics, sociology, pedagogy and ethics.

But what if he admits, added Băncilă (also in March 1951), that philosophy has as its object of study not only total reality, but also "the soul in its main aspects of manifestation"! What about the definition that is necessary to include a single object!

The reference to metaphysics often appears in the philosopher's notes, especially when it comes to the relationship between the relative and the absolute (the latter usually written in capital letters), between phenomenon and essence. As I shall show later, metaphysics studies the knowledge of essences, essences that are linked to the absolute. In philosophy, as Băncilă points out, "every phenomenon acquires an *index of* Absolute, a smaller or larger *square of* Absolute. So: all philosophy is *metaphysics* and ceases to be philosophy if it is no longer metaphysics. In philosophy, all objects have an orientation of meaning towards a single *focus of* light: The Absolute" (Băncilă, 2008, p. 115).

*

These are the perplexities of a reason that exposes, without complexes, the path of analytical and critical thinking, the path of philosophy. Just as they are expressive searches for the act or state of doing philosophy by indicating how philosophers go out of, and re-enter the world; the philosopher begins by becoming self-sufficient under the gnostic relation, by overcoming the phenomenon (does it exist or is it only an appearance? Băncilă wondered) and trusting in the reality of the noumenon, of the essence. A confidence which allows at the same time a wave of distrust (without reaching scepticism) in the power of human thought to encompass everything.

Without this gesture of *cheating*, says Băncilă, it is not possible to create philosophy. That's why, by receiving a philosophical system, "you occasionally come to places where the argument becomes worryingly sparse and you see the author instinctively resort to paralogisms or, in the rare case when he is aware of what is happening, to sophisms" (Băncilă, 2008, p. 44).

But philosophy is, in a certain way, also inhuman, wrote Băncilă, because the philosopher experiences not only a gnostic insensibility, but a complete one, beginning by doubting everything that exists, after which he goes "so far and so completely on the path of going beyond common humanity and common sense" that he becomes "in truth apart from man, inhuman" (Băncilă, 2008, p. 45). Then, in order not to die as a philosopher of infantile mortality, he will have to return – to re-enter – into life, into the world, in order to restore certainty and community (only, Băncilă also said, philosophy ends when you reach certainty; then where is the truth!).

This is how philosophy proves its serious humanism, its anthropologism (almost as strong as religion's; but art also claims the same trait). If it demolishes idols, philosophy does so in order to reach God; if it overcomes illusions, false prejudices and interests, it wants to reach the essences; and if it disturbs and dramatizes, it is out of a desire to find the truth and to promote a *mobile pragmatism* (!), thus helping religion in its mission.

Aided by the role of philosophy (which remains, despite this role, an independent and necessary theoretical discipline), the task of religion alone is to give us the actual truth about the Absolute (minus the idea that the Absolute is spirit and purpose, an idea suggested and symbolized by the architecture of a metaphysical system); once it has reached this high threshold, "philosophy must self-annihilate, abdicate in favour of religion (great pathetic development)"

(Băncilă, 2008, p. 50; I have also reproduced the parenthesis with the author's *indexical* index, a gesture present in many notes).

The note is entitled "Philosophy and Religion". It was not the first time that the metaphysician Vasile Băncilă had such a conjunction in his sights, but now, in a different form, he adds new determinations. He speaks of the knowledge obtained by the two disciplines of the spirit (for philosophy he specifies: metaphysics and ethics) through "super-intellectual, but *human* intuition", on the one hand, and through revelation, on the other, stressing that the exclusively human means of philosophy are, indirectly, "all given by God, because everything is from God", the latter being, in fact, the Absolute or the Great One, as he will say later; reasons for which he formulates a corollary: "*philosophy must reach religion*", otherwise it slips into Luciferism.

*

Another understanding of philosophy was suggested to Băncilă by Florian's fable (Jean Pierre Claris De Florian, of course), "Le chat et le miroir", the first two and last four lines of which could be a *motto* of any philosopher (Feb. 1952). He doesn't quote them, I will (but I reproduce the last six lines, because they are a conclusive whole): "*Philosophes hardis, qui passez votre vie / À vouloir expliquer ce qu'on n'explique pas*"; "*Sans chercher plus longtemps ce qu'il ne peut comprendre, / Il laisse le miroir & retourne aux souris: / Que m'importe, dit-il, de percer ce mystère? / Une chose que notre esprit, / Après un long travail, n'entend ni ne saisit, / Ne nous est jamais nécessaire.*" [5]

This is the moral of the kitten, the one who failed with his meditative exercise in front of a mirror. And Vasile Băncilă draws, in his turn, a metaphysical moral conclusion from this: there is a "biological philosophy here: what we don't need, we don't understand"; and a practical conclusion: if we seek to understand something we don't need, "we kill ourselves – we discover intellectual exercise and ideas that kill us" (Băncilă, 2008, p. 46), for it is fitting that mysteries remain what they are: that is, mysteries – *for our own good*. This is a lesson that religion has understood, which is why its mysteries are codified; Blaga has arrived at this same religious sense and has made philosophy the economy of mystery.

But that's how animals solve the problem – like the kitten in the fable. Man, curious as he is, breaks through the censorship, the barrier, wants to go further and find out what is somehow forbidden to him. A tendency that hides a mixture of the tragic and the sublime: it seeks the absolute in the relative, it creates high culture, an effort of human ingenuity to give solutions to the insoluble. And the history of these clarifications is precisely philosophy.

In many of his notes, Vasile Băncilă veiledly refers to Blagian philosophy on which he offered, in 1938, an essential exegesis. It can be seen how he either expresses his adherence to Blaga's ideas or subtly increases them, except in cases where he departs from them categorically (especially on the question of salvation, religion and the relationship with God).

*

On 28 March 1952, in his *notes on philosophy*, he attributes to philosophy the property of being "a variety of mysticism – or not be at all" (Băncilă, 2008, p. 47). Moreover, in view of the method of expounding truth, he first distinguishes between mystics and rationalists, and then concludes that they are all mystics, the difference between them having more to do with temperament than with truth (he does not abandon the Schopenhauerian grid). The statements derive from the preoccupation of philosophy (more precisely: *metaphysics*) with the Absolute (for this mechanism he refers again to Nae Ionescu). He resorts, as always, to comparisons for the being of the philosopher (different from that of the scientist): he is like a spider that takes its house out of itself (i.e., subjective truth) and weaves it "over the gaps or precipices", thus filling "reality with the subtle geometry of its 'system'". On one condition: the philosopher will be a messenger of reality only if he is an organic soul. Such a dowry of the soul, he would also specify on 28 March 1952, takes the form of complete abstractions, or codifies spiritual beliefs and intuitions.

But Vasile Băncilă is also interested in *aberrative* metaphysics, in "the psychology of the aberrative philosopher" (Băncilă, 2008, see pp. 48–50). Basically, it is a question of the diseases of the spirit: the latter is either crippled, because it lacks (or does not have enough of) "moral, or religious, or ethnic chords", or some other noble feeling; or it is a spirit deformed by tendencies such as exaggerated pride, contradictions, a feeling of revenge or a sickly desire for originality, even erraticism.

This leads to an aberrant philosophy, which includes scepticism in its "delusion and paralysis" phase. And he admits that "sick spirits are discursive: they are intent on doctrine", thus justifying their infirmity, whereas "the great, true geniuses are healthy, moral".[6]

Individualizing the illness of some philosophical creators, Vasile Băncilă calls it metaphysical pathology (from which Schopenhauer, Hegel and others are said to have suffered), "the highest pathology of the spirit in history" (Jan. 1953), an illness that occurs when a thinker "begins to tread like a demiurge, competes with the metaphysical factor and moves towards *Luciferism*".

*

In the note of October 1952, where he presses on the relationship between the absolute and the relative in knowledge (the tragedy of man is that he has "the feeling of the absolute and the intelligence of the relative"), an extremely profound observation appears: political morality *tramples on* all that is most sacred in domestic and metaphysical morality. And if there is no harmony between these three spheres, then 'there will be no morality and man will not find peace'.

Historically speaking, socialist Romania was, at that time, in what Marin Preda well called *the obsessive decade*, an interval with its political-ideological obtuseness, with its morality compromised by the experience of totalitarian evil.

9.4 A philosophical perspective

Around February 1953, a note bearing the title: the philosophical perspective appears among Vasile Băncilă's files. It is the same way of philosophizing, and yet different if we consider that the definition of philosophy now becomes not only the knowledge of the Absolute and its echoes[7] in the sensible world,[8] but also a *unitary* knowledge, encompassing – under the dome of the spirit – every branch of philosophy.

To which are added two theses that Băncilă proposes to develop in the future: first, philosophy – true philosophy – is metaphysics (with gnoseology) and ethics; the branches of philosophy will always be "indebted to philosophy" (Băncilă, 2008, p. 51), even if they become sciences (though not independent, like the positive sciences).

Later, he will make a specific difference between metaphysics and ontology, the latter "concerns *all Existence* in relation to Essence, but metaphysics deals only with essence (see Nae Ionescu)". The object of philosophy is ontology, and metaphysics is its highest part (1964).

Gnoseology will also be individualized as "a child of metaphysics, a metaphysics in disguise or bridging metaphysics and the other branches of philosophy". Understood as "the hygienic function of the philosophical soul", gnoseology was the metaphysics of the nineteenth century (5 April 1967). He recognizes, however, that the meaning of philosophy as gnoseology began in antiquity, with the Sceptics, then became more pronounced in the modern age through Locke, Leibniz and those who followed, so that Kant would be the one who *gnoseologized* philosophy and *Kantianized* philosophical thought in the contemporary period (July 12, 1970).

Defining philosophy in steps, somewhat repetitively, Băncilă says at one point that he is writing the last definition of it: "the discipline called upon to restore the sense of ontological community[9] – this time on a critical basis" (Băncilă, 2008, p. 106); but he does not keep his word (it was probably a relative, not an absolute statement).

Also within the horizon of the perspective of thought is placed the religious concern which mentioned above; a threshold which, if a system of philosophy does not reach, it will be like climbing a mountain with perseverance and determination, and when reaching the top "suffocating for lack of air".

Philosophy will be understood as the critical foundation of religion, as it will be resumed in a note of the beginning of the eighth decade of the last century, stating that, "in our age, *naive religion* no longer works. Today the believer must be a philosopher. Today a *fool or a mediocrity* can no longer believe – or you are no longer sure of them" (Băncilă, 2008, p. 108).

So that, also in the arc of perspective, some philosophical avoidances can now enter in order to put cognitive emphasis on what has been said above. The question is: who can reach the wisdom to explain it more clearly, because there are also individuals who "do philosophy but are neither wise (Bacon?) nor do they even *live* philosophical problems"; and the comparison that comes as a conditioned reflex: they are like "grave diggers that touch the skulls of the dead, but feel nothing" (Băncilă, 2008, p. 52).

The entry is called "*Philosophers 'in the head*'", a name related to what people understand by "girls in the head", i.e., those young women who "threw their bouquets overboard", as the French would say, and "continued bareheaded".

Băncilă returns to the relationship between the absolute and the part, investing the latter with the power of having the whole absolute within it.[10] To say that this is precisely why the absolute is powerful is similar to the meaning of Noica's *Hermes' logic*, where the part, *the holomere*, had the privilege of being raised to the power of the whole (*pars pro toto*, the synecdoche previously mentioned). The absolute is distributed, like light, but it is not divided, it is "at most *reflective*, denser or less dense, purer or less pure" (Băncilă, 2008, p. 53).

However, another novel characterization of philosophy is given – now as "the highest expression of *human consciousness*" (March 1953). But, says Băncilă, even animals (!) have conscience. And there was talk of *la malheur de la conscience*, a subject he himself proposes. Only, in the philosopher, conscience is at the maximum, and this is because he "is most aware of his ego, of his non-ego, of his destiny", even though "it is the higher religiosity that has more conscience than philosophy".

It is unclear what Băncilă meant by higher religiosity. We only know that philosophy leads to religion and that it is obliged at some point to abdicate in favour of it. Later, however, Băncilă put forward an idea in which he expressed a kind of revenge for this abdication: "But we should have the courage to live philosophy as a religion: without the ambition of renovation and originality; for philosophy is made to be lived, and not always deconstructed and remade!" (Băncilă, 2008, p. 66; the emphasis always placed on philosophical *living* came, surely, from Nae Ionescu).

And also, for the first time, Băncilă puts forward the idea of two types of philosophy: a theoretical one, concerned with the existence of an external world, and a practical one, for which the problem to be solved is that of a future world. In the latter, salvation or evil are essential, "for if there were no evil in this world, there would be no search for a future world" (Băncilă, 2008, see pp. 56–57).

*

Nor does Băncilă escape the noise (without fury, if one thinks of a work by Faulkner) of the philosophical currents at the crest of the wave. Existentialism, for example; the reflection is made in April 1955, by which time Jean Paul Sartre, unquoted, had published much of his work. He directs such a current to blow in the sails of other philosophical trends, stating that "all philosophy is existentialist, but it is a matter of measurement".

Why such a strange, unnuanced and approximate inclusion! Philosophy means its connection with man, says Băncilă, a man who is "obsessed with existence, with its drama as such, with its burden, with the concern to understand and to act accordingly, in order to redeem or to reassure and save itself".

And this is how philosophy becomes existentialist in nature and defines itself, in accordance with the meaning of the famous "*Christian* doctor" Paul Tournier, in *Medicine de la personne*, as "the *product of man's spiritual instincts working on the representation of the totality of existence*"; he suggests that the notion of representation could be replaced by that of idea). But when he reads W. Schmidt's *Der Kampf der Weltanschauungen* (1904), he exclaims conclusively-interrogatively-approvingly, "philosophy is a sublimation of instincts?" (Băncilă, 2008, p. 92).

However, he reserves a certain specificity for existentialists: they "exaggerate the sense of the pressure or drama of existence and *make* melodramatic, literary *tapestry*, or, if it is sincere, morbid tapestry" (April 1955, Băncilă, 2008, p. 56). Leaving aside the somewhat sly and ominous stings generated by the *noise* of some philosophers who were not exactly minor (in 1964, the same Sartre would refuse the Nobel Prize), let us be honest: generalities of this kind do not make every philosophy an existentialist one, a construction in which we find, as in other philosophies with identity, a mode of thought with a specific code. However, over the years, a change of emphasis is apparent, with *Sartre's village* being mentioned under the meanings of philosophy: "philosophy as the discipline of the absurd", and also in a parenthesis under "the Luciferian existentialists" (Băncilă, 2008, see pp. 118, 122).

From other notes, however, a nuance can be observed: Băncilă criticizes above all not authentic existentialism, but "a kind of existentialism", the one that does not reach serenity, wisdom, the one that turns into "an art of torturing the soul through ... metaphysical machinations, through ... metaphysical instruments of torture" (Băncilă, 2008, p. 102).

In his notes of June 1956, Băncilă also meditates on instincts in conjunction with conscience: these two are *the pillars of philosophy*, because an instinct, once validated by conscience, becomes a spiritual instinct, and "from here to the elaboration of philosophical principles, postulates and dogmas is only a step".

In other words, once an idea becomes organic, it is instinct converted into a symbol of intelligence. This is why, in order to be a true philosopher, one needs deep instincts and a penetrating consciousness and meaning. However, one cannot be a philosopher if one's instincts are *weak* and do not go beyond the biological, even if one has a certain degree of consciousness (and the idea of the metaphysical instinct will return in later notes). With such a structure, this type of philosopher cannot "attach himself to existence" and remains in the category of those who only make "*ontological exfoliations*".

But I wonder if Băncilă also often attempts various attachments to existence or multiple ontological exfoliations; his laminations are indispensable parts of a metaphysical process of knowing the essence of total reality, of the ontological-metaphysical real (there is only one form of knowledge: the philosophical one; an idea, I believe, vulnerable).

*

It is true that, at other times, Băncilă gets jovially enthusiastic about some deeply banal, to be somewhat oxymoronic, features of philosophy, shouting, for example, "Eureka! Development!" when he comes across a statement proclaiming that philosophy is "one of the factors by which man can be defined". And he does this not when he is young, but well past the age of 60 (Dec. 1960).

He recognizes, on the other hand, that such a definition has the shortcoming of referring only to earthly sciences; moreover, it identifies only one defining characteristic of man along with others, equally important for the essence of man: abstraction, religion, morality, art, disinterested science, laughter, weeping, metaphysical (or other, deeper) ideas, cynicism, sadism, a taste for adventure, madness, perversity, exaggerated or perfidious hatred, arrogance or active imperialism, as the highest form of Luciferism, the spirit of denial (in this string of characters, which indeed expresses human complexity, there are, however, some that can also be found in animals, which Băncilă saw as also endowed with conscience).

9.5 Portrait of the philosopher

Even if, sometimes, he repeats things already said (it is significant, sometimes, if he says the same thing in different historical moments), Vasile Băncilă remains the undisputed master of the philosopher's portrait, of what one essentially needs in order to study philosophy.

He is therefore speaking as a professional, not as one who philosophises at the level of common sense (a trait that distinguishes him from animals). He sums up the conditions in a few notes: to do philosophy, one needs "intelligence of the universal type" (Băncilă, 2008, p. 60) capable of subtly grasping all reality, the ontic whole (not like Spencer, unable to understand Kant), just as one needs strong and integral, complete spiritual instincts.

Philosophy thus becomes the attempt to capture the unity (and correspondence) between existence and soul (or between the human soul and the ontological universe), eliminating the tragedy of loneliness and restoring the connection with the community of existence (an approach that is not confused with the naturalist thesis, since it is about ontological-metaphysical reality).

The philosopher must have, in this process of finding the truth, a kind of *ontological piety*, to behave without pride, to be modest (examples: Plato, Kant, Newton; Schopenhauer and Hegel "played the demigods" – Băncilă, 2008, see pp. 61–62). Human gnosis finally knows something of the Absolute thanks to *the Grace* it needs from God (25 March 1964; these are notes made while reading A. Rivaud, *Histoire de la philosophie*, and J. Chevalier, *Histoire de la pensée*).

A philosopher's vocation is that of one who can "think outside the usual mental structures", an aptitude non-existent in *mytherophagi, scientific* insiders who tell us, for example, that time, space or causal relations come from experience (an approach alien to apriorism which cannot be annulled, a confusion between succession and causality).

And the philosophical vocation also implies an obsession with the Absolute and the ontological totality towards which the authentic philosopher prioritizes everything in terms of value (he is "the greatest architect and the greatest symphonic creator"). The philosopher is unique, and also unique is the reality which he makes the object of his meditation (March 25, 1964), more precisely the intuition that extends even to the threshold of revelation (but does not the privilege of the latter only belong to religion!): "When a man has the great revelation of the meaning and structure of all reality, then he is born a philosopher. A *shepherd and* a *Neolithic man* can have it, and a great modern scientist, a Picomirandolist scientist, cannot have it" (Băncilă, 2008, p. 70; Băncilă had his ... rancorous ironies).

Băncilă would also write some notes about the *revelationism* of philosophy in the summer of 1970, when he was preoccupied with another meaning of philosophy: "*creativity* par excellence". He states, rhetorically, that the Absolute created and continues to create the world, the Absolute degrading itself at the same time (this is the law of metaphysical creation). The Absolute (Archimedes' "fixed point" or Leibniz' "supreme sufficient reason") is "a *Creator*, the only Creator", and the philosopher embodies, in part, "*an intimate of the Creator*", provided, however, that he is "modest, and not insolent and unbalanced" (Băncilă, 2008, p. 110), i.e., that he does not attempt a demonic attitude.

With metaphorical truth, the philosopher proceeds like oysters and religions: "wraps the mystery in a layer of *pearl*, which makes it somewhat transparent and a principle of light" (see July 12, 1970). Through philosophy, however, another meaning of the Absolute is also captured, namely, the way it "penetrates, takes in and architecturises the empire (which would otherwise be *membra disjecta*) of the sensible world.

For the world (reality) is monarchical!" (Băncilă, 2008, pp. 113, 117).

*

For Vasile Băncilă, there is no similarity between *doing philosophy* and *philosophizing*, except when philosophy is understood as philosophizing, as is the case – in Băncilă's examples – with Kant or Nae Ionescu (Keyserling seems to be a counterexample, because "he always vanishes!").

Philosophy presupposes the existence of a fixed general system, principles and methods (hence: "belief-visions"), and is different, I believe, from that form of philosophizing whose adherents protested "against didactic inertia, against the lack of living thought".

Băncilă returns, several times, to the need for philosophy. If he has no philosophy, man is a toad, "worse than an animal", for he has a profound relationship with nature through "the breadth of instinct"; whereas, in the absence of any vision, the human being becomes "a little atom of sensuality and presumption – what terrible filth!" (Jan. 1970, Băncilă, 2008, pp. 104–105).

This statement on the value of philosophy should be contextually linked to another – on the causes of philosophy, written down after Băncilă had attended a lecture given by D. D. Roşca at the Dalles Hall in the capital. The motivation of the thinker from Săliştea Sibiului was, Băncilă believed, a pragmatic philosophy, and not a theoretical philosophy, which sits at its basis and with which it is in a nuanced influence and harmony.

*

Philosophy has its drawbacks, however, "the unadorned thought, which is always rummaging through things, disintegrating everything, like a chariot" (Băncilă, 2008, pp. 90–91). This is how thought becomes both aberration and pathology, how heresies or various forms of scepticism are born (except for genuine scepticism, which is philosophical in its obsession and nostalgia for the Absolute, otherwise, we would not be dealing with sceptical thinkers).

So the question arises: how can we arrive at a doctrine without slipping into dogmatism and tyranny? He invokes the example of Plato's school, which ultimately arrived at that grounded scepticism. Even Marx would have doubted it in the end. Thus, a tragism that dissolves thought may manifest itself. The solution? Let philosophy be put on guard against itself; this is why it must renounce reasoning that goes on forever, and defeat the vanity of thinking.

Philosophy versus philosophy! If it does not stop, thought becomes a killer in itself. From this point of view, religion is superior in its progress: it never returns to something inferior, but reaches towards something better, because it is inspired by the One Above. And also superior to critical culture is folklore, whose philosophical vision is preserved in the same ethos for thousands of years; and if it needs to be replaced, it is done without contradiction or dissolution of soul. The continuity of the spirit is thus saved.

Vasile Băncilă also noticed another deformation of human thought, this time philosophy appearing to him as a piquancy (in which women excel) and piracy of the spirit. The latter, also of pathological extraction, he discovers in many existentialists, in Sestov and Nietzsche, "both full of worldly fripperies, of perfumed essays", "of approximations and entertainments"; in Romania, it would be illustrated by D. D. Roşca and Tudor Vianu (see 5 April 1967, p. 97).[11]

And the assimilation of philosophy has, didactically speaking, its deformations. Vasile Băncilă had spoken at length about the role of philosophy in high school. Now, he is talking about philosophers-pedagogues, the teachers who apply texts/tests of 20 words or so in order to check someone's memory (not the Pisa tests!). A totally irrelevant teaching strategy, because it is possible for a person to have a good memory for some ideas and still not remember more than a few words. And he concludes: "No wonder the *land of tests* is the USA, the land of non-philosophers" (Băncilă, 2008, see pp. 100–101).

*

Discussing the relationship between the Absolute (the Great One) and the Relative, examples of *pure-blooded philosophers* who are close to him are Plato and Kant, whose methods can mature you as a philosopher and make you question your philosophy. It seems fundamental to him to experience (always following Nae Ionescu) religions such as Christianity or Buddhism (the German philosopher would be a "product of the Christian religion" and the Greek thinker an "introducer"), which are significant for the absolute-relative binomial.

Being unable to distinguish the absolute from the relative, *philosophy does not exist for the Communists*, remaining a kind of science characterized only by quantity (August 1956); moreover, it is still the Communists who "sacrifice the world of consciousness ("the best")" and that of the real, while erasing the specific difference between philosophy and science (22 July 1961); Communist philosophy is a "weapon for social progress", its materialism is "*aphilosophic*", substituting a kind of essence for appearance (9 March 1963). Then, in another place, he notes that the spread of Communism is based on a murderous philosophy and generates a spiritual cataclysm: "*Where he settles, the world is deserted*: *a desert* appears, as in the Sahara (...) A much more serious desert: of the soul. In the words of a girl: where Communism spreads, "the world is deserted" (Băncilă, 2008, p. 65).

Vasile Băncilă noted, at the beginning of the seventh decade of the last century, the cracks produced by the totalitarian regime. His testimony is important: "my philosophy fights against the decline of the spirit: today, the values in which I believe, the classical values of man, are in decline, in danger of death; so my philosophy *today* is an *agonistic* philosophy: it fights death" (Băncilă, 2008, p. 65).

But he believed and hoped for a return to our true destiny, when the sovereignty of the spirit would be restored (if he were still alive, he would have enjoyed the validity of his premonition). And almost a decade and a half later, speaking of philosophy as a "social, possibly revolutionary medication" (following Comte), he recalls the birth of that: "new man, the laboratory and blueprint demiurge, the human termite armed with "science", but also a: "new romanticism, not like the literary one of almost 200 years ago, but an *industrial and political romanticism.* When social resentment and ambition came along, Communism was born" (Băncilă, 2008, p. 147).

*

Băncilă was also critical of nineteenth-century philosophy, because it forgot all about the knowledge of the absolute and suddenly became positivist and aggressive, "scientistic", but also a "grammatical or even Talmudic type of philosophy" (he rejects, in fact, most nineteenth-century philosophies). Such a philosophy "has eaten us alive"; the philosophy of Vasile Conta, a thinker of serious aptitude (sometimes underestimated) is, says Băncilă in revolt, a funereal one, because it has missed its purpose and "fallen out of destiny", just as it is a philosophy-reptile, because: "it is a philosophy which has grown too many empirical rhizomes, but no longer has ontological roots" (Băncilă, 2008, p. 58).

Other philosophical tendencies from elsewhere also aroused reservations: "Philosophy as word analysis (semantics) may at best be a method of philosophy (which I also thought of as a student), but not the object of philosophy itself." (Băncilă, 2008, p. 67). An attitude that would later mature with the reading of a text by G. Bachelard (see *Literary Romania*, August 6, 1970). He is put on meditative alert by a thought of the philosopher and founder of modern literary criticism: "Meditating on a word, you can be sure that you come across a philosophical system."

It took Vasile Băncilă just an instant to turn the tables, to nuance his old attitude towards semantics, redefining philosophy as a discipline that meditates on words. In other words, philosophy: "puts order between words, *architectural order, pagodic order,* we would say, going from appearances to essences, from the terrestrial to the celestial" (Băncilă, 2008, p. 111).

But other disciplines of the spirit (grammar, linguistics, sciences) also think about words, on the one hand; and the meaning given to philosophy in this way is plastic and too general, on the other. It remains to be seen from what point of view philosophy meditates on words, along with the truth that "philosophical thought, like all thought, is a great – even indispensable – ally in words (but at other times, it is an adversary: psittacism, hermeticism, verbiage, defiance, exasperation)" (Băncilă, 2008, p. 112).

*

Reading Jacques Chevalier's *History of Thought* in the spring of 1964, Băncilă seems contaminated by the latter's idea of the object of philosophy: *God,* in whom he naturally identifies the Absolute (something he said earlier). But he also emphasises another side of the object of philosophy: it is the One and the way in which all reality participates in it – here is another form of the relationship between t*he one and the many* (April 1964).

Rivaud's reading confronts him with another equality: philosophy as the history of philosophy, a concept that appears to him as contradictory, and this because, "if it were true, philosophy could never have been born" (Băncilă, 2008, see pp. 74–75; doubtful opinion).

He was also interested in other histories of philosophy, as evidenced by the notes in which he invokes Höffding or Fouillée. But one sentence remains axiomatic: "in order to make a history of philosophy, *philosophy must first exist* (in order to have something to historicise). Moreover, no discipline *depends so much on time* as philosophy", even if, according to Nae Ionescu, there is a kind of recurrence (Băncilă, 2008, see pp. 107, 144).

In our country, philosophy as the history of philosophy was illustrated by P. P. Negulescu in ten published works out of his projected fifteen volumes, in which the author understands philosophy "as a philosophical *attitude*: progressive and based on scientific discoveries, first of all". He criticised Negulescu, however, saying that "what he did, he did not do well", alluding to the fact that his approach was not a receptacle that could replace a more profound one, on the one hand; and stating it would turn the public away from reading philosophy in the original, on the other (even if, in a lifetime, one cannot read more than 5–6 authors).

But it recognises the legitimacy of the concept: it is clear that there is a history of philosophical thought, and in this respect, every age has had its own tone of creation; but so much has been written, perhaps too much, that modern philosophy seems a kind of reprint of that of antiquity. He draws out seven misconceptions of philosophy and as many reasons why so much mediocre philosophy exists, concluding that a strange thing was happening: "people are becoming a-philosophers, but philosophy is still being done" (Băncilă, 2008, p. 81).

On the other hand, he considers that the history of philosophy is "the best *introduction to philosophy*"[12], because "without a good introduction to the history of philosophy, we could not even do good philosophy today", thus preventing us from slipping into scepticism (where even Plato's school delved), philologism or artificial collectivism. Vasile Băncilă himself is an example of good initiation, as can be seen from his repeated summaries of the history of philosophy, in order to fix the definition of philosophy as totally and completely as possible.

*

Among the authors Vasile Băncilă (re)reads is Mihai Eminescu. One would have expected him to go to Eminescu's manuscripts and hermeneuticise the philosophical reflections of the thinker who had designed some "stones" for a possible temple. But he is drawn to the poetry, not to the probable portrait of the man who philosophically dreamed of a mathematical idealism.

Under the title "The Quatrain of Philosophy" he subtly and sporadically meditates on the poem "From hundreds of ship masts"; he concludes, among other things, that "two great Moldavians, Eminescu and Enescu[13], examined the problem of destiny very profoundly; Eminescu with resignation, with pity, Enescu with humanization. But both within the same musical spell" (Băncilă, 2008, pp. 77–78).

9.6 Power of the Absolute

I have already spoken about absolutes. With the beginning of 1965, in the notes on the definition of philosophy, this concept (and "its echoes in the sensible world") appears more and more often, invoked along with the irrational, considered slightly dubiously as a sublimation of instincts.

One thing is certain for Vasile Băncilă: you cannot do philosophy without the Absolute. "Are you snickering? But you see how even materialists have the absolute as a concept, though they fight it; for, according to them, matter is the ultimate essence, from eternity, to which all things return. But materialists are devoid of mobility or honesty." How can one not give up another concept, that of the metaphysical: "Communism is either stupid or foolish when it combats metaphysics, although it has its metaphysics too – insofar as it deals with the ultimate reality." (Băncilă, 2008, p. 103)

And the notes on the meanings of philosophy, on the understanding of philosophy and its experience as a way of philosophizing also have a slightly repetitive emphasis. In many of the perspectives outlined, the range of meanings that philosophy has is much the same, only with slight nuances. It is a succession of meanings depending on the dominant philosophical dimension in one era or another (ontological, metaphysical, axiological, etc.), a picture which ends, however, each time with the invocation of the Absolute in the definition.

This is the defining formula that Băncilă arrived at in the summer of 1970, when he characterized the philosophy of law: "the *discipline concerned with the application of the Absolute to the general reality of existence*"; creating the impression that the object of philosophy was twofold: the Absolute and its echoes in the sensible world were thus removed, but at the same time the rank of the Absolute was clearly fixed, viz: "the principle that comes and unifies general reality, transforming it into a *single* object, which is precisely the domain of the philosophical discipline". Reality is converted into a symphonic structure, and the philosopher, obsessed with the Absolute (I will spell it with a capital letter, like the author), becomes "the conductor of the greatest possible symphony: that of existence" (Băncilă, 2008, p. 109), which he discovers and follows step by step.

*

Although he mentions philosophy as anthropology in some of his notes without criticizing it, he does note, in March 1973, under the same title, some thoughts about another kind of contemporary philosophy: the "anthropology of the spirit". In other words, an *inverted philosophy*, one which, instead of dealing with existence in its entirety, is concerned with a certain atom of it.

Vasile Băncilă agrees with this kind of philosophy, on one condition: the human ego "needs to be *framed*: not to believe in an absolute that commands the Universe" (in parenthesis, he jokes about Edmond Rostand's rooster, who "believed that the sun rises because it crows"; this is in the play *Chantecler*, 1910). It is an ontic framing of the self, and its value is given by "how much onticism is in it and how much newness it creates" (Băncilă, 2008, p. 122).

At the same time, he also speaks of a different philosophical anthropology, one "of whims and absolutizations, of frills or bagatelles. Mr "philosopher" wakes up with an idea of his own and launches it to the world, nicely packaged, just let them all know! That's how women do philosophy". Here Băncilă discovered a false and dangerous philosophy, a worldly exercise that absolutized whim.

*

A diachronic understanding of the face or nature of philosophy is also provided by Băncilă in his long meditation of 28 April 1974, a synoptic that begins with the etymological meaning of philosophy and ends, naturally, according to the author, with that of integral reality based on the idea of the Absolute. The bridgeheads between these fit the other meanings of philosophy, most of them taken from previous essays, sometimes with more eloquent expressions.

He invokes, for example, the *thanatic* sense – and not the problem of death – for meditation on the ultimate mystery of man, noting that "the dead have contributed to the creation of philosophy, as well as of religion". Or he recalls the *ponirological* sense (with reference to Shestov), i.e., the preoccupation of philosophy with the problem of "*evil seen on the ontic and moral plane*". Or the sense of *amputation* (invoked: Comte and Spencer), when "*the phenomenon* is the whole of reality", an absolutisation which has generated "either materialism or metaphysicalism (Avenarius, Mach), or rhinocerism, or sadness, or philosophical grammaticism".

Among the 21 variations of the face of philosophy, however, new formulations appear; for example, the rebellious sense of rancour which cultivates pessimism, impotent Luciferian existentialism ("refined undertakers"). The "ones from beyond" are cited: Schopenhauer, Nietzsche, Heidegger, Sartre, Cioran (the latter had published, a year earlier, his seventh book in French: *On the Inconvenience of Being Born*), authors who "struck everywhere at religion and the nation. A huge part of the plague resides in Communism" (wasn't Băncilă a little contaminated, unwittingly, by the nationalist propaganda of the totalitarian regime!).

He re-formulates the meaning of philosophy as effacement or exhibition, illustrated by the sophists and sceptics of antiquity, but also by modern sceptics ("The refined undertakers-wasters of culture. They feel good in existence"). He also dwells on the ludic sense, a philosophy for which intellectual play counts, just as it does in pure art. This is where the authors of maxims come in, those who produce "approximations", "meanings" (perhaps rather sub-meanings), "points of view", "associations, dissociations, mountaineering philosophy", as well as "essays" (Montaigne, A. France).

The meanings mentioned by the thinker are either stylistic nuances or are related to a predisposition (or temperament, as Băncilă himself would say) of the receiver, just as things happen in literary criticism with the so-called aesthetics of the consumer.

In the final part of his note of April 28, 1974, he eliminates improper meanings and builds the true meaning of philosophy on just the legitimate ones. Of course, everything revolves around the Absolute (also an object of meditation for art or religion) and metaphysics (as in "metaphysical sensibility"; Nae Ionescu – "metaphysician par excellence").

The definition he recommends is, as I said at the beginning of the comment: "*Philosophy deals with integral reality on the basis of the idea of the Absolute*". To which he adds the endosmotic relationship between philosophy and the sciences, so that the gnoseology of philosophy captures in it "an Amazon of Gnosticism", a state that expresses the originality and majesty, or kingship, of philosophy. And he concludes with, "Science and *Gospel* (Rivaud)!"

*

For those who might be disturbed by the terms Absolute or sensible, he elaborates appropriate definitions of philosophy, stating that the philosopher is basically obsessed with three ideas: ultimate essence (synonymous with Absolute), the hierarchical view of existence (living organism) and the integralist view (the real as a single whole).

The last two worksheets on the definition of philosophy are dated September 1977 and May 1979. In the first, seemingly significant for the twilight of the philosopher's life, he speaks of *Heaven*, which represented in the history of philosophy "the first cosmological philosopher". Heaven became for man and mankind a "scientific and philosophical teacher", a "fount of religious thought and worship: the sun, the moon (and, by comparison, the earth)" (Băncilă, 2008, see pp. 150–151). And in the other sheet, in only ten lines, he gives for the last time the definition of philosophy: "the explanatory view of the integral reality of existence, through the rational valorisation of a large irrational (element)".

Both the most rational and the most irrational of the disciplines of the spirit, philosophy was, says the octogenarian Vasile Băncilă in his "very old age", "a profession of faith or generalized (determined) perplexity; in very rare cases, a *sanctity* (if philosophy helps). Compared to the dog, which hides its provisions in the ground and forgets them there (rotting)".

That philosophy was, for Vasile Băncilă, a noble aid for his long intellectual exercise, is a fact. I am not so sure, however, whether he reached the threshold of sanctity through the philosophy that he constructed as a potential *system*. Maybe not, apart from a kind of holiness of his literary-philosophical imagination, a stylistic piety towards word, concept and metaphor. This is also the reason why the provisions he left us do not deteriorate, but, on the contrary, are a model of exceptional spiritual nourishment for the philosophy of the Romanian space.

9.7 A system of Philosophy or Transcendent Grace

The definition of philosophy also gives us a picture – admittedly somewhat truncated – of a possible system of philosophy. Not to mention the fact that in the thousands of worksheets or edited texts left by Vasile Băncilă, we have an embodiment of the philosophical system built – but not completed – with scholarly painstakingness by the author.

Let us now take a closer look at what it means, what the philosophical system designed by Vasile Băncilă would mean. Through philosophical systems, the author wrote on 17 April 1948, in our effort to "catch at least a reflection or a thrill of the Absolute", "we manage to breathe metaphysically", systems being "a kind of *spiritual gills*, metaphysical gills" (Băncilă, 2008, pp. 35, 38–39).

At the same time, he says that every philosopher does nothing in his system but "justify his spiritual instincts or his soul interests," which consist of "inclination towards individualism or communitarianism, asceticism or hedonism, mysticism or positivism, optimism or pessimism, ethnicism or cosmopolitanism, moralism or amoralism, etc.". These are the emphases that Vasile Băncilă expressed in one of his first theoretical sketches of a philosophy/book system. It is an architecture with 11 chapters, from fragmentary knowledge to freedom and framing, a certain way of use in which he explains, for each fragment, what it should contain.

For example, in the first chapter, he deals with science, here he plans to deal with the philosophy of science and, equally, of scientists; and in the next – neutral harmony – he deals with the philosophy of art and shows that art has a neutral character if we judge it from the angle of truth or morality; that is, it is neither good nor bad, except for those who consider art to be moral in itself (a thesis with which he disagrees). Philosophical emphases are placed at the level of artistic reality and aesthetics.

Entitled *Perspective of Philosophy*, Chapter III was devoted to the possible and actual meanings of philosophy, which, as noted earlier, described in great detail, in the dozens and hundreds of worksheets written over some four decades of intellectual-metaphysical meditation.

Loneliness and community was the name of the next part of the system of philosophy, a pathetic part because it aimed at solving human loneliness – particularly that of a metaphysical nature, specific only to the human being (the target was "the tragedy of metaphysical loneliness"), but also the psychological causes that produce boredom.

What point could philosophy have in such circumstances? To offer "framing inside the ontological community, to build truthfully this community, to free man from the morass of metaphysical loneliness, to give him supreme plenitude" (referring to Ruskin, Carlyle, Pârvan, Nae Ionescu).

A cornerstone chapter of the system/book was the one on *osmotic knowledge* (the most commented part), where interest is shown not so much for scientific, formal and precise knowledge, but for metaphysical knowledge, which is essentially knowledge *all at once*, together with another feature, also fundamental: "cognitive ontological permeability or osmotism" (which is metaphysical, and which he details in a long history of knowledge scenarios, both pathetic and dramatic).

There are also self-referential confessions that should be taken into account when characterizing Băncilă's philosophy: "I am neither a mystic nor a rationalist (...), but I synthesize mysticism and intelligence". As well as unusual and paradoxical formulations: he combats, in equal measure, Gnostics and agnostics, but proposes: "*understanding agnosticism* (it is obvious that I am inspired by the peasant), *enlightened agnosticism*", a form of knowledge that values "more than all Gnosticism, than the most formal metaphysical systems and than all knowledge based on the weighing scales and the metre". It is a state of enlightened knowledge (as if you permanently lived after Easter, in the *week of enlightenment!*), a principle of knowledge, like osmotism, which is something other than what Blaga means by the potentiation of mystery (he tries to express the specific difference; I am Blaga's friend, but...).

*

Talking about knowledge he also found its central point, the metaphysical factor, God, who gave to the human being not the transcendent censure, but something diametrically opposed, the *transcendent Grace*, the divine help by which man is transformed into something more than he is by nature. Thus appear: the man of nature, the man of spirit, the man of culture. Transcendent Grace, Vasile Băncilă said, could even be the title of his own philosophical system, a splendid reply to Blaga's philosophy.

He indicates from now on the differences (in about seven points) between him and the philosopher of the Mycological space. He draws his inspiration from Lucian Blaga only indirectly, and much more from the peasant (which is what Blaga was). He does not admit Blaga's "*anthropological demiurgism*, but only the person rehabilitated and exalted by Christianity". Through himself, man can do less (not more, as Blaga also suggested) and thus needs God's help.

Vasile Băncilă was in favour of the traditional, Orthodox religion; the author of *the dogmatic Eon* was not. For Băncilă, man is not the result of an ontological mutation, but of a continuity between him and nature, between the human spirit and the Cosmos, not to mention the fact that, as he says, "*I lift up nature*" and consider it "a reality permeated by *nus*, by divine will" (therefore, nature is "little spirit").

Then follows a self-positioning: "I think I am closer to the Christian mystics and *Orthodoxy*, and to the *Romanian* peasant". And if for Blaga the supreme goal of man is creation, for Vasile Băncilă it is salvation. This is the reason why Blaga's philosophical system has a demiurgic-artistic colour, while Băncilă's is more moral-educational. Finally, the osmotism for which he pleads is radically detached from the positive metaphysics-cosmology that Blaga develops in *Divine Differentials*.

Next in the description of the philosophy system are chapters: VI (only a provisional title, with which he was not satisfied: "The moral tide" or, better and perhaps more expressive, "Moral monism", "Moral community" or "Moral framing"); VII – on "Social community", where he was interested in: "Ethnic framing. The community of blood. Ethnic Integralism" (also approximate formulations); VIII – "Religious Transfiguration"; religion gives the best and most effective framing – it provides "*a positive content of (metaphysical-cosmological) ideas, grafted on osmotism*", which means a "*metaphysical solidarity with the cosmos and transfiguration/overcoming through religion*". Therefore, concludes Băncilă, he is "*cosmotheist* – like the Romanian peasant".

The last three parts, quickly dispatched, concern culture or philosophy of culture (IX), metaphysics of education (X) – where he wanted to display his knowledge of pedagogy, in other words, the promotion of education "with an understanding for metaphysical essences and community pedagogy". And in the last chapter (XI), a conclusive chapter of "great guiding pathos" (the directorial indications he proposed), in which he spoke of intimate things such as destiny, sin, death, freedom and framing, as well as history, tragedy, pessimism. In other words: "osmosis and personality".

*

The year is 1942. He had not even finished the script of his philosophy system, or of any book (!), and Vasile Băncilă's attitude already becomes a bit defensive: "If I don't write the complete philosophy system, then I'll write the next studies" (Băncilă, 2008, see pp. 25–26). And he retains about seven titles from the previous chapters, with all sorts of strategic clarifications.

Two other worksheets from the same year speak, presumptively and laconically, of the same thing. A new thought appears: "I want neither the absoluteness of the individual nor the despotism of society (neither anarchy nor dictatorship), but *I want critical community.*" (my emphasis) Then he goes on to illustrate: "the beautiful patriarchal communities in which the critical spirit was weaker but unity greater. See the anarchism of American democracies and their disguised dictatorship."

A 1947 entry bears the title "system of philosophy", but deals with the definition of philosophy, so that in April 1951, challenged by W. Durand's preface to a book on the great philosophers, he writes only a few lines in which he specifies the three parts that a system of philosophy must have: theory of knowledge, metaphysics and ethics.

*

There is a big gap or a long parenthesis until 28 February 1972, during which time he writes only about what philosophy is. The present note, not very long, has about seven specified points, in which he outlines his *adherences to* one philosophical issue or another. Some of them are important, for example, the one in which he admits that he is "an adherent of an *objective idealism*", but not like Schopenhauer's (which is the *word*); nor like C. Rădulescu-Motru's "diffuse and vague personalism", as distinguished from the "monad-force" of Leibniz's system.

But what is, after all, the place of Vasile Băncilă's original attitude? He admits *the original perfection* from whose will the world arose. The reasons? Out of love, amusement, the desire to torment someone or to free himself from loneliness, unless they are all together "absurd" (there is some rhetoric here, of course). But if we are not sure why the world was born, the Absolute knows for certain, an Absolute to which it will once return (a "Platonic-style personalism" is admitted here).

The human being, it is said, can know, but cannot compare with the Absolute, which did not create *human-moles*. Brief indications on psychology, ethics, sociology and pedagogy follow.

9.8 Philosophy and progress

A text such as "The genesis and evolution of philosophy", a 31-page manuscript (written on one side only, in blue ink, with some additions and notes made in pencil) and dated March 1965, gives us the image of the conversion of supposed files, of fragments into a unitary whole, under the integrating action of Vasile Băncilă (Băncilă, 2008, see pp. 153–179).

I started reading this text with a pre-judgment, perhaps naive: it is impossible that the author would not melt into the substance of his discursive thoughts most of the ideas in the circumstantial space of the earlier (1965) sheets. A horizon of expectation that, for the most part, did not deceive us. Nor did I consider Băncilă's attitude towards the history of European philosophy as congruent with the ideas contained in the histories of philosophy elaborated by Eduard Zeller and Heinrich Gomperz for ancient philosophy, Étienne Gilson for the Middle Ages and Harald Höffding for the modern era.

Four main parts structure this philosophical manuscript: 1. the genesis of philosophy; 2–3. the evolution of philosophy (two periods); 4. unity and progress in philosophy. At the outset, Băncilă dwells at length on the founding fathers of universal thought – the Greeks and the Asians, whose philosophy, although it has been the subject of analysis for important studies, is waiting to be fully exploited, particularly by scholars from those communities.

Emerging with man or nation (an idea familiar to Băncilă) and culture, philosophy has its origins in religion and folklore. But let us take this truth *cum grano salis* and not "get lost in pan-philosophy", says Băncilă, for philosophy is not the same as cultural philosophy, as philosophical thought spread throughout a culture. It was not just an *abstract humus* that was the philosophy of the beginnings, but – especially in the East – "a disconcerting chaos, in which mechanical memory and the simple association of ideas played a great part", along with oddities or inconsistencies, "fantasies or orgiastic epics, as in the epics of northern Europe", "obscurities and brightness, lack of symmetry or architectural sense" (Băncilă, 2008. p. 154).

Many of Băncilă's ideas are largely commonplace, but the context in which they were formulated is important. The beginning – or beginnings – of philosophy would, according to many, be placed somewhere in the 6th century BC, in Greek Ionia. The miracle of Greek culture, in philosophy, meant the distillation of Egyptian and Eastern culture in the Greek alembic, a successful historical attempt.

Vasile Băncilă lists here what the Greek advantage in philosophy consisted in, as it was seen in our country in the first half of the seventh decade of the last century. Selection and assimilation, systematic decantation and exposition, literary-philosophical discourse, the unprecedented autonomy of philosophy, by all these they proved their originality in thought and construction, in the creation of an essential fund of ideas (the Jews, however, says Băncilă, the *bearers* of philosophical ideas and with various *services* in this respect, brought nothing of their own to the system, or added unfortunate ideas).

Once formally established, philosophy has, less than religion, undergone a terrible and pathetic adventure of the spirit, a destiny which has passed through two great stages: from its origins to the beginnings of Christian philosophy (2nd and 3rd centuries) and from then to our own time. If in the first period paganism was dominant, despite metaphysical, religious or cosmic efforts, afterwards the atmosphere became Christian, "with resistances, deviations and heresies, but with no fewer spiritual sublimations" (Băncilă, 2008, p. 156). The last centuries, Băncilă points out, could not escape the Christian background, philosophers being indebted to Christian thought even when they criticised religion or Christianity (he quotes Ferdinand Buisson, who said that "we are deeply imbued with the *Gospel*, even when we are free thinkers").

Segmented according to the ages of man, Greek philosophy had, before the 6th century, a happy childhood, with poems in which practical philosophy was subdued, with authors of aphorisms, with the seven sages, with sacred songs and with the first cosmological proses. The genius of the Greeks then produced such names as Hesiod, Solon, Theognis, Onomakrit.

The youth of Greek philosophy – practically speaking, its birth – is that of the well-known thinkers Thales, Anaximander, Anaximenes. For two centuries there was a creative effervescence, a philosophical atmosphere in which various currents of thought clashed. It is a period of time in which most of the problems of philosophy and the horizon in which it was to evolve were conceived. Ionia, with the city of Miletus and a few islands in the Aegean Sea, became the *topos* par excellence of Greek thought, its capital, a place from which many philosophers were to leave for the Greek world.

The full maturity of Greek philosophy followed, with the unmistakable and unrepeatable personality of Socrates, Plato and Aristotle, after which – in the golden age of Antiquity – philosophical directions such as Epicureanism, reworked and accentuated scepticism, Stoicism were consummated again for several hundred years. The twilight phases of Greek philosophy which, before its extinction, still had a "protuberance of genius, nostalgic for the past, but also full of virtualities" (Băncilă, 2008, p. 158) would include the thoughts of Plotinus (3rd century AD), present in Alexandria and Rome. Plotinus's work is in fact the link between the two great periods of development of European philosophy.

Let us not repeat other things that have long since found their way into classic textbooks on the history of philosophy. The philosophical legacy of Socrates, Plato and Aristotle, created over a hundred or more years, was to nourish the dialogue and the substance of thought for some nine centuries. Emperor Justinian's move to abolish the philosophical schools that claimed to be part of this tradition was not entirely lethal. However, even without his order, they no longer had much philosophical power, they had become, says Vasile Băncilă, "more like masks", what naturalists *often* call *faits de survivance.* Christian philosophy was the real commandment of the day.

*

The second period of the development of European philosophy, both pagan and Christian, also has five epochs: patristic, medieval, renaissance, modern and contemporary philosophy. What is interesting is not information that has already entered the boundaries of commonplaces, but some of the emphases that Băncilă places on one aspect or another. He finds curious, for example, the attitude of those who see in the philosophy of the Holy Fathers or even in medieval philosophy "a mere application of ancient philosophy", an extension or an appendix of it, not to mention the gesture of leaving it to theologians or literary historians alone. Of course, if the term "application" is so elastic, then the coefficient of relativity is greatly increased, since many epochs may be, in the end, "echoes of ancient philosophy" (the history of European philosophy being thus called the history of Mediterranean philosophy – Băncilă, 2008, see pp. 159–161).

History cannot be conceived as a succession of applications; European culture, with an undeniable originality, is a *dicotyledonous* one, that is to say, it is intertwined with two major cultures: Greek and Latin, the strength of Greece coming particularly from philosophy. Băncilă insisted more on the identity of patristic thought, its originality and relative autonomy, formulating in this regard eight ideas; some of them reflecting – through re-discovery – his own attitudes of Christian thought.

*

Starting from the endosmotic faith-reason binomial, with the same cognitive and value empathy, Băncilă summarizes the merits of medieval culture and philosophy, scholasticism, in its principles. He does not leave aside the links of the Middle Ages with the East, "through the Crusades, man thus widening the circle of his intuition of universality and seeking, perhaps instinctively, to draw on the ontic sources from which his philosophy had started, to verify it and to verify himself" (Băncilă, 2008, see pp. 164–168).

This is the modernity quotient of medieval culture, a modernity that seems to have surpassed that of the twentieth century. The same Middle Ages made possible the emergence of the European nations, a process in which the Church played a complex and decisive role, beyond the high spirituality it created particularly in the symbolic space of monasteries, places of scientific and spiritual works similar to that of later academies and scientific institutes.

Vasile Băncilă's synthesis of medieval philosophy also pointed out that the false anathemas cast upon it, mostly coming from the aggressive subjectivity of historians and intellectuals, were "at least an ingratitude"; it is strange that there were various insults even from political parties. That it was "a kind of paragraphed penumbra" of ancient philosophical thought, or an age of barbarism and devastating obscurantism.

The negative attitude continued with the Enlightenment, with such an explosion of progress and encyclopaedism being little aware that it owed much to the spiritual combustion of the Middle Ages. It is true that the resistance to the medieval age has subsequently diminished, a revolt, observes Băncilă, "appropriated by the much more compact Marxist resentment that endures to this day" (1965). No wonder that even a historian of philosophy like Emil Bréhier would have failed to see what was right in the substance of medieval thought (! such an observation is surprising).

Leading later to rationalism, medieval philosophy, Vasile Băncilă believes, is important for the subsequent evolution of religion: "Catholicism will approach Orthodoxy, whose vision remained more detached from reason in the strictly scientific sense", a rapprochement that is mutually beneficial.

*

The Renaissance, in its potentialities, in its sketching out of so many projected philosophical themes, will be similar to the segment of Ionian philosophy, "both epochs of youth, of protean activity" (Băncilă, 2008, see pp. 169–170). And the modern period (seventeenth and eighteenth centuries) remains the period of the great philosophical systems: Descartes, Spinoza, Leibniz, Malebranche, Kant, to which German Romanticism is also linked: Fichte, Schelling, Hegel, a manifestation of "the same rich maturation of the European peoples", even if, historically, the Romantic orientation belonged to the nineteenth century.

*

As regards the contemporary period, Vasile Băncilă noted "a great advance in science, a certain decline in philosophy", even though many excellent books were written, "some of them unjustly unmentioned". Other masks, same play: Epicureanism takes the form of Utilitarianism, Scepticism – that of Positivism, while Stoicism no longer satisfies the taste of the age, except perhaps for certain orientations of the philosophy of action and life, in which something of the last phase of Greek Stoicism transpires.

More for the sake of symmetry, Băncilă identifies, even in this old age of European philosophy, a spark, a "special protuberance": the philosophy of Henri Bergson, with its past and its future.

*

After such a "fast forward" film, which attempted a synthetic and rapid overview of the evolution of European philosophical thought, Vasile Băncilă posed a vulnerable question, which is why it is sometimes contested: whether this process of evolution can be characterized by unity and progress. What is needed, first of all, are some criteria to assess such a state. The strategies of the rationalists and progressives seem to him to be inoperative – in what they have rejected or despised – just as he does not adhere to the "ability and universal goodwill" of the eclectics, nor to the position adopted by a Hegel, for example, or by those who promoted a materialist-historical vision, through the decisive pre-eminence of the economic factor (alluding to Marxism).

He is not interested in the formal unity of the evolution of philosophy, but in "an even freer unity of substance" (Băncilă, 2008, see pp. 171–172). And in this respect he finds points of reference in the history of the arts, once philosophy has been declared by some to be an art. What they have in common is a unity of action, one that is deeper and more expressive in philosophy than in art, which allows for "all the variety of possibilities engaged in a life and death struggle of the spirit to see as much as possible of the meaning of existence". And it is the historian of philosophy who can, and knows how "to shape this supreme abstract symphony which is philosophy, spanning centuries and millennia, like lightning that sometimes encompasses the whole sky".

*

As far as the progress of philosophy is concerned, there are some reasons that complicate, in a way, any evaluative attitude. It is difficult to identify a progressive strand, primarily because philosophy is organically linked to the time, place and psychology of a creator. Then, by the way an author relates to the creators who preceded him, philosophy seems like a beginning that keeps repeating itself. You get the feeling that each philosopher, through his work, starts from the beginning, often displaying a negative attitude towards the value of past thinkers. Others, on the contrary, praise the past, even overestimate it. Added to all this is the fact that the fundamental questions, even the branches of philosophy, were formulated long ago, and since then, all that was essential has been said. *Déjà vu*, or *déjà dit* hovers over any philosophical discourse; or, in the words of the Ecclesiastes "what has been will be, what is has been, for there is nothing new under the sun".

In philosophy, there seems to be no progress: why should a philosophy created at this moment be superior to that of the past, especially when we believe that in the past, all quasi-complete truths would have already been said! Vasile Băncilă states that he does not have "the naivety and presumption of progesism"; moreover, he would be overjoyed if the complete and absolute truth had been revealed one day.

And if things are different, some justification is needed. He risibly compares progress in philosophy with that in science, the latter having a "stalagmitic character" (Băncilă, 2008, p. 174), whereas in philosophy new ideas count for not much more than a "drop" that would be added to a potential column. Not to mention the quantitative significance of progress in science (except when it comes to radical changes: a Newton or an Einstein does not appear every day), without any correlative metamorphosis of perspective or vision, i.e., in the absence of qualitative progress, as in the case of philosophy. Science and philosophy are not productively comparable in terms of novelty quotient either.

The state of progress, in the end, is more complicated than the appearance of limited spirits. Being bound up with time, space and person, philosophy's answers to man's place and purpose in the world can mean progress, at least through the pathos and drama of human destiny. Philosophical meditation is not, however, an endless repetition of the beginning. Every philosopher carefully reads what has been written before him and, however much we may disagree, carries forward the process of thought.

One could invoke Albert Camus who said that he called truth *what goes on*. The history of philosophy, the uninterrupted succession of meditations on more or less the same problems, but in a different context, undoubtedly signifies a continuation through relative truth towards the unattainable goal of absolute truth.

Vasile Băncilă also answers other puzzles related to the same progress of philosophy. Without being tempted by passivism, it seems unquestionable to him that the great cultures of philosophy are in the past, as in literature or art (a symphony, he exemplifies, has its climax long before its end). Which does not make the idea of progress, of a higher value stage in relation to a previous one, superfluous. And to the usual retort: everything has been said, there is nothing new under the sun, he invokes Bergson's attitude: "everything is new under the sun".

Organically speaking, any stage of evolution is an inevitable mixture of old and new. Especially if we are dealing with a vital era, this necessarily indicates a significant coefficient of novelty, which includes the contribution of philosophy. Even if some of the ideas of the past are taken up again, the philosophical atmosphere – as Mircea Vulcănescu says – is different, the context resamplifying, amplifying the nuances and expressive intensity (the resemblance to art is unmistakable here).

But even if we do not agree with what has been said so far, progress in philosophy is based on the phenomena of deepening meditation, of its critical sense and of organization. There is a deepening of the meaning of concepts in which various problems are formulated, together with the stimulation of positive sciences.

Critical thinking is perhaps the most important. We cannot avoid the heights reached in this respect in Germany by the philosophy of Immanuel

Kant, who made a kind of mutation in the history of European philosophy, a not only epistemological incision. Critical sense, Vasile Băncilă observes, presupposes subtlety, fairness and limitation, aspects through which the history of philosophy is, in retrospect, otherwise re-dimensioned in relation to what some philosophers have thought in relation to the creation of others. It is thus clear to see, as C. Rădulescu-Motru says, that all philosophical concepts are organised and structured in the process of history. "Philosophy," Băncilă completes, "thus becomes a world of intuitions, in which the depth of meaning competes with the most refined critical spirit and the inner freedom of combination, in the firmness of serving the truth" (Băncilă, 2008, p. 177).

It is true, the philosopher also observes, that historical eras are uneven, sterile or misdirected (let us recall Maiorescu's reaction in the second half of the nineteenth century: *le stupide XIX-e siècle*). And our thoughts can also be rightly directed not only towards the past of philosophy, but also towards its future (a problem that has long preoccupied Blaga: see "On the future of Romanian philosophy", *Saeculum*, 1943, no. 1, January-February).

Vasile Băncilă wondered, in 1965, what philosophy would become. It will evolve, of course, it will develop, despite the fact that it may never reach the level of the past peaks, or it will experience, why not, various cataclysms.

The latter, Vasile Băncilă believes, were provoked by those who were then, *in some places* (to be understood as the Romanian space!), in power; by "elementary people", those who – following the statements of a footnote – "throughout past history they have worn the muzzle, and if they have bitten, they have done so exceptionally, whereas now they claim to make laws for all of us" (Băncilă, 2008, p. 178).

The Communists, because the story is about them, do not have – the thinker specifies – a philosophy, "at most they have science"; and if all that they have can be called philosophy, then "the *third period of* philosophy will begin, completely de-Christianized and de-metaphysicized – which is, after all, a kind of *zoology of the second degree*" (my emphasis). The fourth period will follow, when the spirit will triumph, for otherwise "the *human* history of man will end, and man will become even worse than the animal (for he is not Lucipherian)".

Those elementary people, mentioned by the philosopher Băncilă, were individuals lacking "metaphysical and moral sensibility" who wanted to build – supported by technique and skill – "a way of life copied from that of the termite", a genus of ant-like insects without religion or philosophy. And the future of philosophy "will be determined by whether man will remain man or become a kind of super-termite" (an ending in which, in a *postscript*, Băncilă annotated his sentences with a clarification: "to replace it with a more discreet one"; a useless substitution, since the meanings or intentions were still revealed by the context).

9.9 The polytropy value of philosophy

Now another manuscript needs to be considered, slightly longer than the previous one at 35 pages, also with additions and notes made in pencil, dated September 11, 1965. So half a year after the previous text, Vasile Băncilă does not escape from his obsession with philosophy, being encouraged to think about its "value or advantages" (Băncilă, 2008, see pp. 181–207) by its "power of progress". He deals with it in six parts: philosophy and the development of the sciences; philosophy and the other disciplines of the spirit; philosophy as the embellishment of life; philosophy and pragmatic utility; philosophy and the ideal of knowledge; philosophy and culture.

*

Here too can be seen the reworking, in slightly changed and recapitulatory forms, of ideas from the previous worksheets. For example, the deep correlation between philosophy and science, with Băncilă observing that, as the latter becomes increasingly and excessively specialised, it also moves away from philosophy and turns scientists into "craftsmen". This process is also felt by philosophers, who can no longer master the avalanche of scientific knowledge; but this forces them to intensify the systematisation of scientific discoveries. Ultimately, the role of philosophy is to give science "anticipations, problems and exhortations" (Băncilă, 2008, p. 187).

The same happens when Băncilă exposes the relationship between philosophy and other disciplines of the spirit, such as art and literature, morality and religion, or the relationship with the language of a cultural space. The longevity and profundity of some artistic creations, especially masterpieces – in sculpture and painting, in music and literature – is due to the philosophical spirit that underlies them. It is not "a discursive philosophy and even less a didactic one, but a philosophy of the signification of the real", embedded in a work that makes the receiver discover the idea of the real in it.

Philosophical morality, Vasile Băncilă observed, ran the risk of being based on wrong ideas, yet that is "infinitely preferable to the simple morality of sentiment or habits". But even the latter are distorted by modern civilisation, which requires a much deeper philosophical reflection on the part of contemporary society in order to decipher the way of correctly applying a moral norm. Hence the great duty of philosophers to provide us with "moral ideas"; otherwise, through pernicious meditation, they can cause "crises or deficiencies in the moral life".

The indissoluble link between philosophy and religion, more precisely, the incorporation of a philosophy into the latter, is very important when it comes to man's adherence to one religious belief or another. There are many and varied faiths, some better than others. But if one does not assimilate a higher religion, then it is preferable to have one founded predominantly on "bigotry and superstition, on fear and conformity". Why? Because such an attitude can activate in the believer's soul "purely religious possibilities" that would otherwise be wasted. And if he turns to philosophy, it can sublimate, or in some cases defend, his faith. Except in vulnerable situations, when the religious man "risks being bitten from all sides by the *thousand-headed dragon of atheism*" (Băncilă, 2008, see pp. 184–185; my emphasis), a situation in which a critical, philosophical spirit is of real use.

What essential connections can be detected between philosophy and history? There cannot be a great historian who has not had an underlying philosophical thought in his work, apart from some false philosophy of history, some misinterpretation of history, such as the adventurous historical materialism, instead of which it is better to value an honest and banal account of the facts in a "naive chronicle".

*

Philosophy seems to have a very special role in its very special relationship with language, with the idiom of a spiritual space (Băncilă resignifies his attitude towards semantics). Philosophy has imbued language with subtlety and suppleness, a sense of depth and nuance, of synthetic and totalising comprehension. There cannot be a people with a high philosophy that does not also have a language that is proportionate, differentiated and rich in meaning and sense, one that can express metaphysical thought, ontic and ontological thought – to limit ourselves to these potentialities.

As said, the Greek language was refined by the Sophists, even if Plato uses in his dialogues the language of the street, the language of the tannery and the charioteers. And in our country, a Blaga or a Noica could only appear after an essential metamorphosis, after an in-depth alliance with the Romanian philosophical spirit, with the language spoken in the hamlets and villages.

Vasile Băncilă, on the other hand, also pointed out the global degradation of the language through the harmful invasion of a technical lexicon. "Today's language seems to have the ambition to be spoken by a robot. It is becoming Esperantized as a spirit by itself and is, in this sense, a reflection of the simplification or impoverishment of philosophical thought." (Băncilă, 2008, pp. 187–188)

That is what happens to people who use three or four hundred words or less. Moreover, the crisis into which language is entering at a given moment, beyond the ills brought about by internationalisation, by expansive civilisation, is also produced by the "partial dilution of ethnicities", of the ethos which initially generated a certain philosophical vision.

*

In a short fragment, Băncilă discusses the life-enhancing function of philosophy. Through articles, essays, maxims or conferences (in other words, an *en détail* offering), an "ornamentation", an "exaltation of life" is also achieved at the same time as the communication of ideas. It is as if, through a "graceful or at least suggestive phosphorescence", one "puts a kind of 'sequins' on the often grey body of existence: without it, life would be uglier".

This aesthetic effect was achieved by the works of great thinkers, writers or moralists, who were sought after for the beauty and temptation of their ideas; the same purpose was served, in all high-spirited societies, by the cenaculums (in patriarchal societies: séances), the various forms of symposia, schools (the Greek ones in particular) or other forms of meeting (such as, for example, the Capșa Café in Bucharest).[14]

The idea of embellishing life through the intelligence of the philosophical elite is a profound and extremely generous thesis. A surprisingly pragmatic thesis in a discipline as general and abstract as philosophy. But this discipline is also practical – in the sphere of education, human knowledge, social reform and the existential values that guide human conduct.

*

It can be said that the "pragmatic usefulness" of philosophy (Băncilă, 2008, see pp. 188–194) means, first of all, the usefulness that one of its branches, namely psychology, brings to education, since man can no longer rely so much on intuition and instinct. And alongside psychology, the same process includes pedagogy, "a kind of orthopaedics".

The transformation of a society or, in other words, social reform is not a product of chance and is not carried out by ordinary people. It is one of the most important and complex episodes of history, its actors rarely appear on the historical scene and, apart from some less common personality traits, they must have a deep and just vision of the future and of human nature.

It is enough to recall, says Băncilă, names such as Pericles, Caesar, Charles the Great, Napoleon or Stephen the Great, to see that this "intuitive, practical philosophical genius" distinguishes them, philosophically speaking, from "ordinary politicians, octopuses, political swindlers and all the exasperated public exasperators". Such chosen spirits exercise a kind of *providentialism* that incorporates itself into things with their will and help, sometimes independently of their will, but not without their acceptance, because they are aware that they are "instruments of history".[15]

But if a society lacks saviours, great politicians, reformers or even political geniuses, such an absence – believes Băncilă – is made up for by the existence of philosophy, whose purpose is the careful study of human nature. That there is a need for such a discipline of the spirit is evident if we consider the fate of ideologies, theories and practices that balance between social good and social evil.

Băncilă also invokes the extraordinary role of ideas in the process of history, a fact accepted even by the Communists (see "progressive" ideas). Especially philosophical ideas, encapsulated in various ideologies and used as a theoretical and practical platform for reforming a society. This does not mean that the philosopher has to be a politician with a special soul structure (Plato provides a counter-example of the symbiosis between a great philosopher and a mediocre politician).

It is clear that the philosopher provides ideas to the one at the helm of the reform, ideas with which he structures his own philosophy. However, this does not suffice for building a more effective personal conduct, which requires knowledge of others, of one's own self, of life's values. Psychology, then, is necessary for those who aspire to change society. "Ordinary people," says Băncilă, "conduct themselves, after all, partly zoologically, partly ethnographically, but even in them there is a remainder or an excess that is theirs alone".

What matters a lot is the insights of these ordinary people and the force of the analogy they put to work: "Two crooks get along immediately, and even two simpletons get along wonderfully". But life is complex and complicated, so a lot of critical thinking and psychology is needed to empirically build a psychological typology, which sometimes proves ineffective when one is mistaken, when a "new type, or one that presented itself differently than it really is" appears.

But self-knowledge is also deficient even if man has the necessary power to achieve the descent into himself, if it were not for the opacity that his own subjectivity manifests. And the appeal to philosophy arises again, one that can be saving. "Know thyself" means not only revealing the good side of the human being, but also unformed knowledge, such as it is, for wrong views of the self can lead to insurmountable practical complications. The fun-loving boorishness of the human being is also taken into account, an attitude sometimes appropriate for gaining some courage in confronting life and history. The secret, however, is the measure in everything: "in small doses, even poisons can be medicines".

Philosophy can also be the archetypal point when the question of knowing the values of our existence arises, especially when life is lived in an atmosphere of axiological confusion. A proper conduct for success in action is one based on wisdom (but let us not overlook the exceptions: some philosophers have not been wise at all, and others have been downright lunatics). For this, Băncilă had a personal judgement: like holiness, wisdom depends on predestination, on an "innate balance, on a hereditary structure" that is difficult to discover.

Therefore, one must have a *calling* to be wise, although wisdom can also be acquired through intense personal exercise, except in the situation "when greater folly is not born" (the idea of infinity can lead to wisdom even for those with a wandering mind). And in common people, the state of wisdom may come more from instinct, and from the preservation of trust in truly inspired philosophers and in a better organised society.

*

This leads Băncilă to a problem that he deals with at great length; namely, the conjunction between philosophy and the ideal of knowledge, more precisely: ideal knowledge (Băncilă, 2008, see pp. 195–205). The latter means knowledge of reality as such, without practical connections or fragmentation of any kind. "The single human subject stood before the single object", wanting to know it "without any deviation from its meaning in itself and without any diminution by breaking it up into isolated aspects"; in other words, the human mind, "in its fundamental and unaltered gnostic reaction, wants to know existence unmultiplied and undivided, total existence, undenatured by utilitarian interests and, we would say, torn from the deep meaning that pervades "all that lives and sings'".

In time, after the osmosis between spirit and existence has been consummated, man has transformed himself from object to subject, aspiring to reach "knowledge as such, disinterested but dramatic and bewitched knowledge", because, with this, man will become "the tireless and often tragic disciple of this need for knowledge".

Such knowledge in itself, which "encompasses everything in a unicity", has a name: philosophy, and its author, the philosopher, embodies "the authenticity, the originality, the ideality of knowledge, which is characteristic of the full degree of the human being". A being that does not forget itself, on the contrary, it is concerned with its own destiny, with the meaning of life and existence as a whole. Just as it is interested in practical knowledge that ensures its existential comfort. Specialisation thus appears as a necessity, but also as an inevitability, dictated by didactic needs or the conversion of means into ends ("perversion of the spirit"), when research is completely isolated from real life.

But neither scientific nor practical knowledge corresponds to the gnostic ideal specific to the human spirit; only philosophy can reach the vision of a totality. Thus, for Vasile Băncilă, for the umpteenth time, the idea of the Absolute emerges, for it is the ultimate essence of all that exists; it "marks the unity of this *membra disjecta* of general reality, transforming a boundless plurality into a single being". He arrives, in short, at the supreme conjunction of the *one* and *the many*, at the *raison d'être* of our existence.

*

Vasile Băncilă also stopped at a few corollaries or consequences arising from the fact that philosophy studies total and general reality, based on the idea of the Absolute. He thus takes up again a theme that had been dealt with in his previous worksheets: the preservation of a philosopher's vision of reality (some small variations and new foundations appear later); the endosmotic relationship between part and whole (which is the Absolute); knowing the truth in its essence from the beginning, philosophy "offers a *terminus*, which is also a spiritual rest, preserving the unexpected".

The philosopher thus appears to us as the image of "sovereignty, but accompanied by modesty, of a sense of peace, but also of a permanent actuality". A picture of determination that cannot be found in science, where research is practically endless, in contrast to the peace of the philosopher. The scientist "can speak at best of trophies, or of the fatigue of the fighter who has been too long in the arena".

But science, at some point, "became a kind of serious sleep aid, which confiscated the ultimate thought, the metaphysical thought" ("ontological or metaphysical sleep aid"), with the scientist being satisfied with a secondary reality, a kind of greenhouse of reality that can be put "in test tubes, telescopes, turbines, documents and formulas".

Cut off from first-order, deepest reality, the researcher is transformed into a *non-ontic being*. This impasse can also be overcome with the help of philosophy, through a genuine metaphysical education.

Another corollary, drawn from the understanding of philosophy as the study of general reality based on the idea of the Absolute, is that it is not a passive discipline, or one that man can do without. Even the most ordinary people have a tendency to look at reality in general and to think for a few moments about their own destiny and the purpose of all that exists. Goblot is quoted as observing that non-specialists do not master the terms of the sciences, whereas "no one can avoid the special language of philosophy", the philosopher being considered a "specialist in the sense that he deals specifically with matters about which everyone talks" (*apud* Băncilă, 2008, p. 203).

These are things that come to people's attention episodically, especially when they feel that things have something ultimate in them; which is not the case, for example, with their need to know "the temperature at which minerals melt", "the number of eggs a worm lays", "the tongue of a maggot" or "the spread of birds' nests in New York City", as Băncilă jovially jokes.

And the last consequence: of all the disciplines dealing with knowledge, philosophy is the hardest. Băncilă speaks of the duality of philosophy: it is human, in that it attracts people, but it is also superhuman, because it is very difficult to access. Religion, however, is easier, since it is essentially created somewhat directly by God.

However, there have been philosophers who have sometimes been inspired by the Absolute, but they have mostly spoken as humans. Their power of knowledge measured up to that of the gods, thus justifying Aristotle's statement about *something divine which characterises philosophy*.

*

The last section of the manuscript "The Value of Philosophy" deals with the links between philosophy and culture. Culture understood not only on the level of individuals, but also as the environment of peoples or nations. It is inconceivable that a culture can exist without philosophy, which gives it its own vision of life and the world. The same is true of a scientist or a theologian, who cannot be considered cultured if they have not assimilated some philosophy.

Some ideas are mentioned in passing, on the grounds that they will be dealt with in other chapters (!), but it is not said where. As is the case with the specificity of philosophy, which structures a culture and imbues it, even platonically, with its own form of wisdom. Moreover, such a state can be conducive to an "act of formal and lucid religious adherence" (Băncilă, 2008, p. 206), when the philosopher ultimately becomes a *pilgrim*.

Vasile Băncilă draws attention to the meaning of philosophy especially if it contributes to the constitution of a culture. He departs from a somewhat broad understanding, namely, when philosophy is linked to instinct and habit: "Man does not have philosophy as the bee has the science of life". The blame is cast on philosophy for everyone, for the masses, as the Communists "manufactured" it "zealously and tyrannically"; only "everyone has more common sense now..." (Băncilă, 2008, p. 207).

However, Băncilă also referred to philosophy considered as metaphysics (as access to essences), because, through philosophy, metaphysics penetrates history and somehow transforms it into a supra-history. Only in this way does it "acquire a depth beyond the world, the ineffable depth", which can sometimes disturb us, but which constantly gives us "the sense of the greatness of existence, the quiet joy of broad meanings" and gives us the tonicity of an existence in "the underlying reason of things".

This is how Vasile Băncilă's manuscript on the value of philosophy ended, somehow in suspension, with promises of further meditations; and this at a time when Romanian culture had been, for years, invaded and amputated by the political-ideological factor.

Notes

[1] We don't know if it is an allusion or simply a coincidence: in the same year, 1940, Cioran printed his *Twilight of Thoughts*; the philosopher from Rășinari is not much mentioned in Băncilă's notes, on the contrary, he distances himself from Cioran's *existentialism*.

[2] Infinitely more than birth, it is *death* that "gives a real sense of reality and opens up the world of problems that make the human soul a fragrant flower, coming from afar and returning there after a tourist's walk through the phenomenon" (April 1, 1973; Băncilă, 2008, see pp. 122–123).

[3] *Plaurid – reed bed* is a compact aquatic formation made up of roots, reed fragments and various organic and mineral elements that floats on the surface of the water.

[4] In August 1951, he notes the apt German terms *Weltweisheit* (world wisdom or world knowledge) and *Weltanschauung* (worldview) – see Băncilă, 2008, p. 45. And also at that time he referred to the doctoral thesis of E. Sperantia: *The Definition and Prehistory of Philosophy*, Bucharest, 1912 (reprinted 1942; may be a comparative source for Vasile Băncilă's approach).

[5] *"You bold philosophers, who spend your lives / Trying to explain what is not explainable"*; *"Without looking too hard for what he does not understand, / He leaves the mirror and returns to the mice: / What does it matter, he says, to penetrate this mystery? / A thing which our minds, / After long effort, neither hear nor perceive, / Is not necessary to us."*

[6] We are referred to the historian of philosophy and Plato specialist Henri Joly (1927–1988) with his book on *Génie sains et génies malsaines*.

[7] A term with an uncertain semantics, as he will admit, interrogatively, in his note of April 1954: "But isn't the idea of "echo" vague? Isn't there an "echo" in science too? A matter of degree? But by what measure?" (Băncilă, 2008, p. 55)

[8] In order to remove any ambiguity about the meaning of echoes in the sensible world (which "occupy most of the philosophical horizon, though they are not essential"), he will state, in a note on *what philosophy is*, that in order "to be able to speak at length of the *Absolute*, as philosophers almost always do, we must mix or confront it with the world here, with the *relative*, with the *phenomenon* seen within it" (12 July 1970, Băncilă, 2008, p. 109; my emphasis).

[9] As we shall see later, under the heading of *ontological community*, Băncilă will meditate at length on *existence as being*.

[10] To illustrate, a quotation from Ecclesiastes is given: "If you have faith as a mustard seed, you will tell the mountain to move, and it will move" (*Matthew* 17:20).

[11] Vianu, T. (1898–1964). Romanian aesthetician, literary critic and historian, philosopher of culture, translator. Among his writings: *The Dualism of Art* (1925), *The Art of the Romanian Playwrights* (1932), *Aesthetics* (2 vols., 1934–1936), *Introduction to the Theory of Values* (1942), *Philosophy of Culture* (1945), *F.M. Dostoevsky* (1957), *The Ideas of Stendhal* (1959).

[12] "The Germans, in particular," said Băncilă, "have filled the world with philosophical *Einleitungen*, conceived on the basis of the history of philosophy"; and in our country "Mr. Florian has published *Guidelines in Philosophy*, which is simply a manual of the history of philosophy". Motru observes, however, that "the history of philosophy can lead students to negativism" (14 Oct. 1976, Băncilă, 2008, p. 147), which is not true of religion.

[13] Enescu, G. (1881–1955). Considered the most important and complete Romanian musician. Among his compositions: *Romanian Rhapsodies* (No.1 and No.2, 1901), *Orchestral Suites* (1903, 1915), *Oedipus* (1910–1931; premiere: 1936), *Cello Sonatas* (1898, 1935).

[14] *Capșa* was a famous café (founded in 1891) which was part of the largest firm of restaurants and confectioners in Bucharest, known in many European centres. It was a meeting place for the fashionable people of the day, intellectuals, writers, journalists, politicians etc., a place to express witty words, to utter comic and satirical appreciations that became memorable, but where there reigned also an atmosphere of *cancan*.

[15] A footnote written here by Băncilă: "If Napoleon said that destiny must be replaced by politics, it is because it is in the politics of great men that destiny manifests itself." (Băncilă, 2008, p. 189)

Chapter 10

Existence, reality and metaphysics

10.1 A spiritualist metaphysics

Vasile Băncilă's meditations on metaphysics are also important. There are about 107 worksheets on this subject, with various ideas captured in the period 1936–1979, in which one feels the "provisionality of notation", as Dora Mezdrea also observes; this does not do too much harm to the fibre of sapiential thought. The notes have various titles, some of them expressly formulated: metaphysics or my metaphysics, but there are many with the syntagms: metaphysical attitude and philosophical maxims.

I suspect that the author intended to draw up a treatise on metaphysics, as he briefly noted in December 1964, a corpus that would have an "almost geometrical" unity (see Băncilă, 2009) in its three parts: the metaphysics of knowledge, of reality and of conduct (on 30 September 1964, he speaks not of conduct but of *action*).

Finding in spirit the essence of the world, the metaphysics of reality is a spiritualist one, founded on a gnoseology of the same nature, one that "values the integralism of knowledge and especially Gnostic isomerism: man is ontological and reality is anthropomorphic, so *spirit* is the common part" (Băncilă, 2009, p. 68).

It is a spiritualist and universal monism (individuals make up a single monad, manifest in all people), a view that determines morality and thus makes moral motive, concern or moral conduct possible. A world in which there is no progress, but no regress either; a static world, different from the modern vision and allowing for relative progress, even if, in essence, "nothing changes"; it has occurred "only as *a displacement of ontological consciousness towards man*; a coagulation or provisional confinement of it in man" (Băncilă, 2009, p. 11). As I have noted, Băncilă expresses himself, not just once, antinomically – or adopts the strategy of a speculative logic in which opposites (not contradictions!) can coincide.

In fact, the first entry (January 1936) refers to the very need for a metaphysics in order to constitute a morality and, equally, for the moral attitude to function. Admitting the idea of the transcendent, the world is, for the young Băncilă, morally ordered by means of two principles: of Good and Evil, as in Persian thought, a necessary vision for moral technique in any space.

It is fitting to see what determinations Vasile Băncilă subsumes to metaphysics, on the one hand, and to his own metaphysics, on the other, noting, if necessary, the specific difference between them. The distinction is more difficult to make, however, because the same ideas often move from one thematic register to another.

I will follow the notes as far as possible chronologically (as they are arranged by the editor in the volume) and thus observing the redefinitions, the additions, all the nuances that have occurred subsequently, but also the similarities between *metaphysics* and *my metaphysics*. I will proceed, as before, by favouring quotations over paraphrases, for two reasons: Băncilă's writings are not widely circulated, being little known, and there are sentences or phrases which, through interpretation, lose some of their original meaning (but also their metaphorical charge).

*

In September 1964, Vasile Băncilă writes: "Metaphysics is not all of philosophy, but it is the condition of its existence" (Băncilă, 2009, p. 59). At the same time, he observes a flaw – he wonders if it is fatal – of all metaphysicians, who include in the ultimate factor, the metaphysical factor, i.e., in the first cause or myth, most of what they do not understand about the world, believing instead that this explains everything.

Băncilă adheres to the Kantian position: metaphysics can only constitute a framework, a direction, a grid that must be filled by religion; or, metaphysics is also "the attempt to displace the incomprehensible and absurd from the immediate world into the intelligible world", an operation that apparently "reconciles logic". Metaphysics thus becomes a philosophy of religion; an idea also present in another note of the same year, but under the title "my metaphysics": "The best metaphysics is religion, and the noblest and ultimate function of philosophy is to introduce one to religion: the oldness of religion" (Băncilă, 2009, p. 11). It was also stated that this is a preparatory chapter for the one on philosophy of religion.

But metaphysics must not be separated from psychology, for it is, as he later says, the abstract projection of our whole soul (February 1963). To understand a man's metaphysics, one needs the armoury of his psychology. In another meditation, it is Blaga who, in *Differentials divine:* "does metaphysics with the discipline of the game, of the artist" (Băncilă, 2009, p. 14). Metaphysics, if it is a system attitude, needs a certain fanaticism, but the power of individual or even collective suggestion must be paramount (in Blagian metaphysics, should this effect not be fully felt!). On the other hand, he thinks that Blaga would go too far with his metaphysics, in that he explains too much: "It is an indiscretion and it seems sacrilegious to try and explain these ultimate mysteries, which are the privilege of the Absolute."

Metaphysics doesn't give us details (that's why we have religion), but the truth given by the direction, by the meaning of the Absolute. It is enough, Băncilă thinks, to say, for example, that "the Absolute is a diffuse and vigorous providentialism" (Băncilă, 2009, p. 15). Otherwise, metaphysics becomes a kind of *prestigious fairy tale, transcendental elucubration,* or an artistic game, through details borrowed from the empirical sphere. This does not prevent the expressive Băncilă from noticing the help that history gives to metaphysics, through tradition, collective suggestion, childhood memories and so on.

Here, too, is formulated again that principle of philosophy or the logic of holomerism, *pars pro toto:* "The unity of life: everywhere in existence there is intelligence somehow, life..., *in every part there is everything*" (Băncilă, 2009, p. 10; my emphasis.). Or is this, in Băncilă, seen as a spiritualist principle – that spirit is, like light, whole in every part that exists (it distributes, but does not divide).

*

What, after all, does a system of metaphysics mean for Băncilă? He never doubted the need for metaphysics, for metaphysical knowledge, something he got from Nae Ionescu. He leaves aside scientific metaphysics or other easy, naive variants, such as a simple spiritual game produced mainly by art, or an attitude resulting from an immense collective suggestion.

But he also gives us an approximation by comparison: the system of metaphysics is something real which organically links us to reality, "as it links the plant to reality, without being able to say that the form of the plant has copied reality" (Băncilă, 2009, p. 13). The metaphysical attitude is immanent to the structure of any healthy, organic culture.

He returns, in the same year, 1940, with some suggestions on the relationship between a system of metaphysics and experience: the latter cannot verify metaphysics, but it would be enough not to contradict it (as Blaga says). It follows that a system of metaphysics is likely to be untrue, for experience is one, while metaphysics is plural (he refers us to Nae Ionescu).

Every system of metaphysics has a point of departure or support: an idea, an intuition, a revelation that imposes itself on the whole spirit and acquires a particular expression. Băncilă is convinced that the fundamental theme of his philosophical synthesis does not lie in some sophism, or in a "pragmatic postulate, an act of faith or even an act of mystical knowledge" (Băncilă, 2009, p. 17), but in the fact that general reality constitutes *an order* and that it also has *a purpose*, he is thus interested in knowing what the world is made of, what is its beginning and its end (the banal metaphysical questions). And in the service of such a starting point he proposes osmosis, a form of organic knowledge, a kind of original, diffuse but profound perception, without accepting anything mystical in it (he is far from admitting any real form of mysticism).

In another entry (September 1942), he even puts forward what one might call a preformist perspective, something like the oak tree in the acorn: being congruent with an author's attitude to life, his metaphysical system exists in an anticipatory way ("as a virtual, vague, profound personal truth"), and only then does he explore its intellectual foundation and formal expression. And at the end of the same year (1942), he wrote radically, terrifically and exclusively: "Metaphysics is the most sumptuous and sublime impossibility. There is no possible metaphysics. There is only one acceptable one: religion" (Băncilă, 2009, p. 18).

The last sentence is more than acceptable to the Christian thinker Vasile Băncilă. It is certain that the metaphysics which he was certainly dreaming of shaping into a system, that unscientific metaphysics, had a solid Christian basis: "Christianity: this is what we admit (because it admits both good and deep evil, is combative and not passive, as is belief, and metaphysical)"; and then added: "let us fight for the salvation of *the nation*, not only of the individual". And he stated in a long argumentative parenthesis that there is no contradiction between Christianity, which is metaphysical, and the nation, which is historical. But with a codicil: "religion should be subordinate to history, to ethnicity", in order to avoid "the mistake of A. C. Cuza and the French Action" (Băncilă, 2009, p. 19).

Here again, he emphasized that metaphysics implies a spiritual and profound struggle, and throughout the ages such a struggle has had other solutions besides Christianity: Mazdeism (which gives man too great a role) and progressivism, evolutionism, meliorism (*ametaphysical*, not validated by history – the sociologist Dimitrie Gusti is quoted with *The Problem of Happiness*).

*

Two years later, in 1945, he also speaks of Christianity, more precisely of the problem of evil. He quotes from the *Gospel of Matthew* (10:1) the episode of the sending of the twelve apostles, to whom, says the biblical text, Jesus "… gave them power to *cast out unclean spirits* and to cure every kind of sickness and every kind of disease" (my emphasis). From which Băncilă draws a conclusion: "it is not concrete, empirical evil that must be combated, but its principle, the funciary, metaphysical evil" (Băncilă, 2009, p. 19). Compared to metaphysicians who proceeded in this way, he noted a bizarre reporting of ordinary people, whose revolt is aimed at the evil of everyday existence, not evil itself as a principle.

In other metaphysical attitudes, he is also obsessed by evil, with its different kinds of being (public evil and private evil), which expresses the *foolishness* inherent in the world (November 1948), or evil as a principle (1948), where he quotes again from the Evangelist Matthew (4, 1), the passage in which Jesus "was led by the Spirit into the wilderness to be tempted by the devil". It was a moment that preceded the preaching, which means, notes Băncilă, "*that before doing good, before fighting evil – he had to show that he could defeat evil* as a principle – the demon – that he was *immune from evil* itself, that he was above it!" (Băncilă, 2009, p. 23). Even if there was no need to be tested, the parable of the Saviour is telling for every man: before defeating the evils in the world, the principle of evil must be defeated – at least in yourself, says Băncilă.

Evil cannot disappear from the world; it has a *metaphysical existence*, so that its essence remains untouched, even if it is sometimes removed in "some people (by transfiguration)" (Băncilă, 2009, p. 27). Therefore, our happiness is not complete here on earth, which is why, says Băncilă, infinite progress is not a valid idea.

Paradise cannot be realized in a mundane, profane existence. Ordinary man: "cannot live like a saint: it gives rise to morbid complexes or even greater immorality when it gets out of control" (Băncilă, 2009, p. 26). Băncilă refers us to Pascal's words: "*Qui veut faire l'ange, fait la bête*" – "Who wants to pass as an angel turns out to be a beast". But evil coexists with good, a cardinal value that has always been associated with truth and beauty. A triad in which each term, different in experience, involves the other, is in correlation with it, not in fusion (see Plato, Cousin). Alongside these abstract values, Băncilă places three other values ("foci"), this time concrete: God, the social or ethnic community and man, as suggested by a hierarchy: the divine, the moral, the ethnic.

Băncilă makes here a metaphysical eulogy to the human being: "Man is *divine* (and, in the Pauline sense, a son of God). (...); do not take revenge, also love your enemies. The *metaphysical ego in man is that ecceitas which makes the unity of the psyche*: psychology cannot be separated from metaphysics" (Băncilă, 2009, see pp. 22–24). And the pedagogical spirit in it certainly points to subsequent forms of pedagogy: religious, moral, communitary, humane, supported by the heroic element, realistic. Like the Christian religion, which is "spiritualist, antinomian, polyphonic, real and salvationist".

Contrary to A. Comte, Lasserre or D. D. Roşca, man, Băncilă believes, has the strength to somehow know something of the metaphysical mystery, and this because "*he cannot give up the metaphysical absolute and put something else in its place*". Otherwise, this will absolutize what is relative, as the excesses of nineteenth-century positivism showed.

Man is a metaphysical being, and that happens "either because *from the beginning* God put in him a breath, a reflection of Himself, or because *slowly*, in the course of evolution, the metaphysics of general reality, the Absolute, concentrated by growing in man" (October 1949). An analogy that makes him think of the way plants use light: the same happens with man who captures the metaphysical light of reality, the source of spiritual creation (here is a confirmation, says Băncilă, of the fact that humans are sons of God).

*

It is increasingly clear to us that the metaphysics preferred by Vasile Băncilă was a *spiritualist* and *providentialist* one. The metaphysical spirit of things "enters the historical world and gives reflections from it and fixes destinies in the way that a central or abyssal fire would penetrate with its rays through a sieve: the rays pass through the sieve and enter the historical world... In every being such a ray enters, stronger or weaker..." (Băncilă, 2009, see pp. 25–27). So a spiritualist metaphysics (or a metaphysical spiritualism!), whereby "we must put at the basis of reality the spirit (as all that we know deeper) or something higher than it (a super-spirit)". And also in 1951, he wrote in a quasi-Aristotelian manner: "Everything is a tendency towards form in existence. Reality itself – the Absolute? – is something formative."

In the Cosmos, in biology or in history, life orders forms, even after catastrophes. It is life that creates, alone and unaided, even against death. The formative energy is in things, in the *"pulp of existence"*. Reality is not something blind, nor is it pure matter, but "an ordering principle, therefore intelligible, therefore spiritual". Here I sense an Aristotelian trace: *form* as an active factor, immanent to all that is in the world.

Băncilă formulates some fundamental metaphysical themes through theses that call materialism into question: "If matter generates spirit, matter is no longer matter"; instead: "Spirit can generate matter" (Băncilă, 2009, p. 30); as he doubts hylozoism or some monists, unable to explain the emergence of spirit; he adheres, however, to a hypothesis, congruent with his metaphysical vision: the judicious thesis that "matter is *densified spirit*", which would justify the fact that, at some point, life would have arisen ("Matter un-blackened and let the soul free, and densified"; December 1952). A formulation that relies on expressiveness, on metaphor even, for elsewhere it is frustrating and categorical: "Through evolution, the spirit cannot emerge from matter" (Băncilă, 2009, p. 31), after which he invokes two arguments, one typically spiritualist, the other offered by ancient hylosaicism.

These statements were uttered by Vasile Băncilă, a thinker whose metaphysical self refused to be a prisoner of the phenomenon, just as he refused to see how the spirit has the rank of an epiphenomenon, given that the universe, he says, "is all spirit! This universe suddenly becomes alien to me, and my ego becomes an orphan, wandering through the universe like a comet or nebula, with its irregular gait" (Băncilă, 2009, p. 20). There are many notes, moreover, which reiterate and reformulate the thesis that spirit is the essence of existence.

*

As I have pointed out so far, Vasile Băncilă's spiritualist metaphysics is Christian in nature. For him, spiritually speaking, God means everything, he is something transcendent (Băncilă, 2009, see pp. 28-29); he is, as it is said in *Genesis*, the Spirit who floated over the waters and who breathed life into chaos; he is the one who "made the universe somewhat as he made man", so that, "in a way, the universe too is the Son of God – but only in a way" (October 1953).

Transcendence is also perceived in finalism, and this is because, first of all, the complex and profound order which it presupposes could not have come from the universe, but was received from somewhere outside of it; then the universe cannot be said to formulate its own purpose, because it is not, like man, a being, and again we have transcendence involved here.

*

This is how, with the passage of time, the spiritualist metaphysical vision (with substantialist accents) becomes, for Băncilă, more and more evident. The essence of reality (Băncilă, 2009, see pp. 32–33) is given, on the one hand, by the metaphysical spirit: God and the angels embody the good spirit, while the devil represents the evil spirit; on the other hand, the same essence of reality is constituted by the spirit of phenomena: matter illustrates the lethargic spirit (with the trait of uniformity), plants – the diffuse spirit (this is how individuality takes shape), animals – an accumulated or concentrated spirit (with them, locomotion appears); finally, man represents the super concentrated spirit (with him, consciousness appears).

Băncilă also writes about the duality of the essence of reality in the sheet of 19 October 1962 (Băncilă, 2009, see pp. 33–34). With advantages and disadvantages, he puts forward two theses: either that God made the world out of nothing, or that he created it out of something, i.e. spirit. Each of us is free to choose the version that suits him. Even the Church, says Băncilă, affirms the creation of the world either from nothing or from something.

However, it does subject the two theses to closer scrutiny to see if they are not too close to each other. Without disregarding the phenomenon, he admits the existence of cause in the world (which science also states) and that in making the world, the creator gave it something of his power.

Although both hypotheses form a more complex thesis, it is appropriate to keep both, says Băncilă, because in this way, we save the supreme power or greatness of God, and we also *rationally* understand the genesis of the world. But the creation of the world from nothing or from something else is, for him, the *same thing*.

It must be said, however, that, with regard to all this, Băncilă only affirms something, he plays a majestic speculative logical game, but much of his reasoning lacks the rational argumentative backbone. He himself feels a certain insufficiency of persuasion, which is why he often repeats the same idea in a slightly changed form.

For example, the two theses on creation are also the subject of the meditations of 11 and 12 November 1963 (Băncilă, 2009, see pp. 38–40) and April 1964, except that he now has some nuances and arguments in addition: he refers to Nae Ionescu (with an essay on "Creation and Sin"), to Blaga's Great Anonymous, to Max Weber. Admittedly, in the end, the demonstration is rounded up and convincing for the most part.

Also, variations on the same theme are the critical metaphysical attitudes towards materialism of March 1964 (Băncilă, 2009, pp. 41–42) and June 14, 1964, where empiricism or naive realism is now the workhorse. Let us dwell for a moment on Băncilă's statements, which also accuse ideas of a false philosophy of history.

*

Materialism is naive realism. It is guilty of the logical error called *petitio principii* or vicious circle. Whoever does not doubt, in Cartesian manner, the external world and does not try to overcome such a hypostasis, places himself in pre-philosophy. He thus disqualifies Marxist philosophy: "Communists are the greatest monument to pre-philosophical hollowness, yet they insist on doing "'philosophy' (presumptuous fallacy)", ensconced, in other words, in empiricism, like D. Hume.

Other cracks in materialism: it cannot explain order (because it preaches chaos), nor the birth of spirit (because it practices *the mystery of* organic matter, which generates spirit when it reaches a high threshold of evolution). And he returns to Communism, with its fundamental contradiction ("it will die of contradiction: like an ox strangling itself"): the concept of matter is contradictory and absurd, because either "matter is unconscious, and then it cannot produce spirit, or it produces it, and then it is no longer matter, but at most philosophy".

Even the ideas that Communists believe in, especially those that are considered progressive, are an obvious and naive contradiction, because matter becomes determined by the idea. This, says Băncilă, is no more materialism than it was when Stalin abolished the linguistic theory of Nicolai Yakovlevich Marr.

The June 14, 1964 entry, longer than usual and less metaphysical, goes on to criticize historical voluntarism ("about Mussolini, Hitler, and especially the Communists"), which makes a case for the primacy of the human psyche. Communists practice a kind of *immense ideological Janissarism* or *psychological Janissarism*. They want to destroy ideological opponents and spread their ideas. In the latter sense, one of Băncilă's theses, which he proposed to develop on another occasion, found in Communism something "congenitally pedagogical: it is a propagandist (because it is, originally, mostly Semitic; see how even at the trials they sought to propagandize: "from the accused, accusers")" (Băncilă, 2009, p. 47).

Nor did historical materialism escape the anathema of the thinker Băncilă. This is not materialism, but economism and psychism, or if it is – it represents the vulgar meaning of the term. Thus, when Communists fight vulgar materialism, they criticize themselves. Moreover, for fear that history might contradict it, the same Communism has resorted to a successful swindle: the philosophy of history would have as its motivation and goal material factors. Hence Băncilă's acid reaction: "Bizarre, strange theory, a great lie, a shameless philosophical lie, accepted by many half-witted people, clamoured and vented by the opportunistic retarded crowd". Finally, after a sustained critical shot, the question arose: if materialism is both false and nefarious, then why is it adopted by Communists? Destructive action is the ultimate goal, as Communism has a negative, anti-human, demonic, Luciferic essence; it is: "the most tenacious and stupid expression of the anti-Christ, the revenge and offensive of the thug in history" (Băncilă, 2009, p. 48; he set out to investigate the relationship between materialism and thuggery).

Băncilă therefore categorically rejects dialectical materialism and historical materialism, accepting only the formulation: metaphysical dialectical materialism and historical dialectical materialism, as well as putting critical and subtle-ironic accents on naive realism. Marxist philosophy (called *Mordechaist*[1] – after Mordechai, Karl Marx's real name) is completely devoid of arguments, it is in the air, and when it wants to convince, it ends up being tempted by metaphysics: "To condemn metaphysics, you have to do metaphysics" (Băncilă, 2009, p. 32). When they end up combining species and altering them, Communists show a *lack of ontological piety* (see Băncilă, 2009, p. 50), just as the Japanese are tempted to create dwarf trees, or others want to change heredity.

In another entry, Communism is declared simply to be objective idealism (November 1964). Băncilă's views are, for once, paradoxical. The concept of matter is not a physical one, because spirit cannot emerge from it, but a metaphysical *matter*. The Communists' homage to matter turns it into a kind of deity, an ontological Demiurge. In another context, when they affirm the endless progress of knowledge, the same Communists are subjective idealists, agnostics. Their expressions are ambiguous, contradictory, they "juggle incorrectly and unintelligently with an equivocal concept of matter" (Băncilă, 2009, see pp. 76, 81–83). Băncilă also constantly criticizes materialism and builds arguments in favour of metaphysical spiritualism, while also evoking the drawbacks of a non-spiritualist metaphysics.

*

If in his early writings, Băncilă logically approaches the relationship between science and philosophy; in his later notes, he derides the "scientists in philosophy", those who admit that man has spirit, reason and so on, but without questioning their origin. According to them, the spirit is born in man through a kind of spontaneous generation, which sounds like a mystery or mysticism, a trait that he also sees in evolutionists who have also become, in some cases, anti-evolutionists (when they admit the emergence of a new quality).

Băncilă speaks, moreover, of the "mysteryophagy of science and scientific philosophy", those which "cover the mysteries with 'wax' – the wax of simplicity and presumption –and move on" (Băncilă, 2009, p. 30). Some entries, such as the one mentioned above, are more about philosophy and less about metaphysics.

Many reflections with the title "philosophical maxim" try to resignify philosophical ideas, dragging some of them, when appropriate, towards metaphysics. He considers objective idealism (July 1964) as a genuine philosophy on the good side: Plato, Kant, Bergson, the first two being "the greatest thinkers of the human race" (Băncilă, 2009, see pp. 49–50).

Being concerned with arguments for spiritualism (24 August 1964), the Stoics or Tertullian are seen as spiritualists (peasant-like), such an orientation of philosophical thought having certain moral and destiny benefits, while materialism reduces man to zoology and abolishes his spiritual life. Even the Ionians were not physicists, but metaphysicists, because they wanted to know the ultimate essence. And Augustine, by his magnificent work, *definitively enthroned* the spiritualist view (only in patristics? the thinker wondered).

*

Spiritualist arguments also concern a "maximal philosophical plan" outlined by Băncilă in his syllogisms of 16 September 1964 (Băncilă, 2009, see pp. 51–55). It has six paragraphs: introduction, classical arguments for proving the spiritualist thesis, the configuration of spirit, the dialectic of spirit, the meaning of reality, philosophy and religion (meditation reprinted, for arguments, on 8 October 1964.

Besides reiterating ideas confirming that spirit is the essence of reality, the first three parts have a predominantly critical role. They set out their next themes; they aim to discuss and combat: monism, Spinoza, Taine, Ostwald; dualism (except for the *Old Testament*, inevitably dualistic); pluralism (a philosophical heresy); pantheism (which is self-affirming, and when it comes to peoples – it is a false pantheism, as in the Romanian peasantry); immanentism and transcendentalism (rejecting pantheism, the same fate befalls immanentism; and God can only be transcendental, not something "drowned in things"); panentheism (things are all in God; but we wonder what happens to the problem of evil, of the infinity of the supreme creator; here we come up against a *mystery that is incontrovertible* for philosophy); finally, deism (a contradiction in terms; it can disprove spiritualism and facilitate unbelief, like the Reformation).

In the paragraph on the "dialectic of spirit", he would like to discuss and criticize successive creationism and evolutionism. In both, there would also be some truth. But he rejects Cuvier's term of *catastrophism*, just as he does not accept Heraclitean cycles or metempsychosis (a kind of resurrection positivism, in which women in particular are interested), nor does he agree with the use of Darwinism in metaphysics.

He elaborates a little on the thesis that the world has experienced an *original perfection* and is now moving towards *ultimate perfection*. Interestingly, however, is a certain prediction, also spiritualistic: "Man began by being an idea in the Metaphysical Factor and then became a historical, imperfect person;

and will end by being a transfigured, perfect person – like the whole universe."
(Băncilă, 2009, p. 54)

As for the meaning of reality, it is spiritual only for those who are willing and able to see it. In particular, he would like to develop the idea of the pluralistic universe, according to which, simply put, everything that exists forms a whole community, more precisely: an *ontological family*; in other words, existence has rationality and, in equal measure, purpose; there is, without doubt, a meaning to things.

Therefore, existence is neither absurd nor at the mercy of chance, nor is it the despair promoted by some existentialists - he wants to analyse Kierkegaard and confirm, in the "religious maxim", that authentic existentialism is Christian.

Up to this point, Băncilă said, it was philosophy. From here on, the "torch of knowledge" utters the word; religion, which brings to metaphysics "formal, somewhat concrete precision", and this because it possesses the right means: revelation, faith, worship, pedagogy, even superior political justification (we are curious what he would say about the latter).

He veridically annotates A. Comte with the three phases: theological, metaphysical and positive, saying that they have always characterized the world, even in prehistory. The three are stages of knowledge, perfected by theological knowledge, more precisely: mystical knowledge, because theology is a part of religion. Finally, he takes up an idea and re-emphasizes the role of philosophy: *to lead to religion.*

10.2 Metaphysics of reality

Vasile Băncilă lacked everything, except ideas and plans. Two weeks after the project discussed above, he wrote another one, an outline in which he would combine in one book all that he had written in "philosophical maxims" and "religious maxims", with the name: metaphysics of reality or existence. In fact, he aspired to a trilogy, as this was joined by two other volumes on: the metaphysics of knowledge and the metaphysics of action (simulating, I believe, a Blagian model).

Reworking ideas from the past and adding more. It would begin with: spirit – essence of reality; and then in Part IV, it would address the rationality of existence with three chapters: freedom and fatality, the pathos of evil, loneliness and death. And the last section, the fifth, he wanted to call resignation and transfiguration, or perhaps the divine spirit. It was intended to show what philosophical attitudes we can have towards evil, which meant, in essence, an approach from the perspective of the philosophy of religion.

Such a project was important, so he takes it up and develops it after only a week. He now insists on the problem of evil, on the relationship between freedom and fatality or between loneliness and death, makes arguments in favour of the rationality of existence and calls into question the (positive) way in which religion resolves these questions, the religion towards which philosophy is heading.

The Christian thinker Vasile Băncilă does just that, namely, tries to show in a separate chapter that all evidence is valid *if there is faith in God* (if there is faith like a grain of mustard seed, according to the Evangelist Matthew, when you tell the mountain to move, it will move). In this way, philosophy ends up in apologetics (yes, in a way, as *ancilla religiae*).

*

It must be said that the metaphysics of reality preoccupied Băncilă more and more intensely in the last 3–4 months of 1964, but also in the following period, when he wrote more notes and fragments. And from the period 1973–1977, there are about 5 or 6 philosophical or metaphysical notes. He speaks of *metaphysical surrogates* in those who no longer believe in God and find a kind of narcotic in the "drunkenness of instinct" (Băncilă, 2009, p. 84); or briefly analyses the paralogical basis of metaphysical systems.

The last worksheet is on *sublime death* (April 1977). It refers to Aristotle, who would not have had a pathetic conscience, thus not being able to rise, spiritually, to the level of the legend of Socrates, even Plato, who made possible the legend of his main character in the *Dialogues*. Of course, another motive of the Socratic story was the way the philosopher died, an attitude thanks to which people characterized him as divine (along with Plato).

In volume VII of Vasile Băncilă's works, Dora Mezdrea includes, next to the chapter devoted to metaphysics proper, the metaphysics the thinker wrote on a very privileged topos: the space of the Bărăgan. I will talk about this being somehow on a par with Blaga's Mioritic space in another metaphysical context.

10.3 Existence as being

Under the title "ontological community", Vasile Băncilă meditates for almost four decades (1940–1979), interrogating himself, in fact, like any authentic thinker, on the question *of being* or *becoming*. He has a double ontological perspective: on the one hand, he is interested in the determinations of being as existence (for which there are only fragmentary notes), on the other hand, he wants to investigate, as Mircea Vulcănescu would say, the *Romanian dimension of existence*, or, what is the same thing, *Romanian existence* (for which there are notes and finished texts – see Băncilă, 2015).

The view of being refers us to the way ontology was thought of by classical Greek antiquity: what *it is*, but also what *it is not*, i.e., being and non-being. And Romanian existence, as Dora Mezdrea also observed, is conceived congruently with the way C. Rădulescu-Motru, Nae Ionescu, Mircea Vulcănescu or Constantin Noica reflected on the Romanian spirit; to whom we should add, through some of his writings, Lucian Blaga in whom Vasile Băncilă, his first exegete, discovered a Romanian energy.

So with a few exceptions but covering some three decades (1940–1968), Băncilă's sheets on being bear the title of ontological community (in metaphysics, as seen earlier, he spoke of ontological family). The perspective on the relationship between the individual and the community is the traditional, Christian one, man being included in the community together with all the existing kingdoms: with animals, with plants, with mineral life.

Such an ontological community specific to the Christian peasant (December 1940), in which heaven takes part in what happens on earth, is finally substituted by the Cosmos (here are signs of the cosmic Christianity of which Mircea Eliade will speak), so that reality as a whole is, I repeat: for the peasant, essentially communitarian and subject to a logic of the same principle called *pars pro toto*: "each fragment participates in the Whole, and the Whole signifies each part" (Băncilă, 2015, p. 11; it is, I repeat, what Noica would call, when Băncilă was no longer alive, the logic of Hermes, that of the privileged *holomere*).

However, since we are talking about *participation*, we have here the properties of a primitive mentality (the latter term has nothing pejorative in it), as described by Lucien Lévy-Bruhl in 1922 (not so positively received by Băncilă). It is a structure in which the identity of the individual is absorbed/dissolved by or in the community, thus merging with it.

A vision, of course, in contrast with that of the modern spirit, with its individualistic-contractual acceptance, modern man, says Băncilă, expressing a kind of *ontological orphanism* (7 January 1952) for he feels cut off from reality, is lonely and sceptical, lives more from illusions. But it was the task of philosophy to restore to man the feeling of ontological comfort, of an intimate, familiar existence, a kind of *sacred wedding* with it, one that would give him the very spirit of celebration (here Băncilă finds the positive meaning of *philosophical festivism*, "the maximal result of philosophy". (Băncilă, 2015, see pp. 11–12)

Instead of an energetic personalism, as Motru conceived it, we are dealing with an ontological one. The individual is not isolated from the community or the Universe, on the contrary, and his higher feelings are *"echoes of the absolute in us"* (July 1953).

*

Băncilă's notes have a predominantly conceptual content. And are also enunciative. He formulates concepts, gives them minimal determinations and then makes some judgements. In speaking of existence as being, he often makes an underground connection with his metaphysical (providentialist or theistic) vision, sometimes using terms or ideas specific to the latter. In this sense, he tries to nuance the distinction between ontology and metaphysics: the former would deal "with all that exists, but in relation to *essence*", while the latter "is a part of ontology". (Băncilă, 2015, p. 21)

It should be noted that, according to Băncilă, the ontological community is dualistic, i.e., it accepts that matter and spirit are both part of the one reality of existence. This is what he calls the adventure of ontology, comparable to the isolation, in gnoseology, of reason from intuition. Neither did the people, the thinker points out, ever separate spirit from matter in an absolute way. The matter-spirit relationship is more complex: the spirit is primordial, it can generate material things through its *lethargy* (a recurring idea), and "matter, through sublimation, can release the spirit deposited in it through "objectification" (Băncilă, 2015, p. 26). These are theses which, says Băncilă, we can also find in materialism, because otherwise it would not be possible to explain life, the psyche, the spirit, which are generated by matter. We must "rehabilitate matter", because it has "a kind of life potency in it: it is *lethargic spirit*".

The matter-spirit binomial is often approached by Băncilă, with many perspectives, sometimes antinomic, but the conclusion is always spiritualist, the spirit being something transcendent and allowing the demands of a speculative logic. But it often problematizes the matter-spirit relationship. He cannot understand, rhetorically, of course, how spirit can emerge from matter, but neither vice versa, unless we accept that "the virtuality of matter was contained in spirit, and vice versa" (Băncilă, 2015, p. 41), only in this way do we end up with hylozoism.

The world was born from spirit, matter being, as mentioned above, the result of the lethargy of spirit, even if Băncilă's hypothesis implies a form of *degradation* and is a possible drawback of the thesis that the world was not born from nothing (but Plato's world is also born through degradation). He thus senses a mismatch between degradation and original perfection.

Băncilă seems to be only partly against materialism, which he declares at one point to be "clearly metaphysical!". This is because he is fighting against spiritualist metaphysics or spiritualist mysticism, not metaphysics. Although, in another interstice of reflection, he sees in materialism "the most extensive, tenacious and "scientific" scam in the history of human thought", "the expression of simplism (a-philosophical or pre-philosophical), or of rancour"; in the latter form is hidden, in fact, *ideological gangsterism.*

*

In order to familiarize us with the theory of ontological community, Băncilă also gives a brief bibliography, with 38 entries, of authors (foreign and Romanian) and books (philosophy, metaphysics, mysticism, theology, including some "Communist books"; Băncilă, 2015, see pp. 18–19). These are sources to which he himself resorts, challenged to a critique of ideas exposed by his notes (among the sources are some of the magazines he used to read: *Literary Romania, The contemporary, The philosophical review,* etc.).

Băncilă saw community as a structure organized in four concentric layers: the ontological, moral, social, destiny and cultural community, all vertebrated by the idea of a dramatic and disturbing human destiny. The supreme ontological community, however, is God, at whose level there is no destiny and culture, which are specific to man alone. In May 1963, however, he also invokes a fifth community: the *focus of personality.* And religion is the last chapter of the ontological community.

At the same time, it also stratifies the community-personality binomial: individuality (specific to the biological sphere), personhood (characteristic of the social-legal one) and personality (found in the spirit world). The historical goal of mankind is personality (the reference to Goethe is clear), while "the metaphysical goal remains salvation" (leaving one wondering what Faust is all about!).

The idea of concentric community circles seems to him beneficial for what he calls ontological realism (see also Mircea Florian, received without much sympathy), by which he detaches himself from subjective idealism, with all the forms it took since D. Hume (if, in metaphysics, he identified an objective idealism in Communism, he now classifies it, contradictorily, as subjective idealism).

By opting for ontological realism, a philosopher basically accepts the existence of a reality independent of human thought. With Băncilă, the meaning is somewhat changed. For him, matter is an idea of ours (and not the substance of reality), in endosmosis with spirit. Not once does Băncilă critically refer to English empiricism or scepticism, the former suffering from *ontological blindness,* a consequence of a kind of "metaphysical poeticism". And scepticism "must either be rejected altogether or must be carried to the end, that is, to total scepticism".

Instead, he accepts apriorism because it confirms the ontologism of man, in that it is *"the extension of reality in us"* (Băncilă, 2015, see pp. 21, 43). It is apriorism that gives human specificity, but also "our nobility as a species"; Kant was a "colossal (unique) philosopher" in the way he analysed its forms: "intellectual, aesthetic and pragmatic (moral and religious)". Without apriorism, we would remain devoid of spontaneity in the production of ultimate concepts, and the denial of any apriorism is akin to *remaining in the air* (as Nae Ionescu put it). In this respect, he is fruitfully obsessed by the phrase ontologism of man or ontological man, in which he sees a synonym of ontological community, a phrase put in conjunction with the anthropomorphism of reality (or anthropomorphic reality, as has already been seen).

The ontological argument seems to him not at all illusory, as Kant, Ruyssen and others have said, but the most important proof for apologetics and genealogy. Where would man get the idea of the perfect "if there were not something perfect or absolute in the substance of things"? Man is thus *ontological in essence*, and anyone who disagrees with this truth denies apologetics and the possibility of gnoseological knowledge, for you cannot "reject the existence of God and still believe in knowledge" (Băncilă, 2015, see pp. 25–26). Such an ontologism of man was, moreover, advocated by Hegel and, paradoxically, "is naively and aggressively implied by Communism". The conclusion of the Christian thinker Vasile Băncilă was to be expected: "he who renounces God renounces everything" (December 1967).

*

The ontologism of man is, after all, the identity of the human being and vice versa, identity being a given of the human body. Băncilă brings into question the situation of similar scientific discoveries made in different places and times, in the absence of communication between their authors. If it were not a human constant, it would be in vain that the same problems would be put before the human being. We are told, somewhat forcibly, that even "animals sometimes think like man – though the form of the body is different"; or that "if there are superior beings on other planets, entirely different in biological form, they must have the same kind of reason or gnosis".

There is a kind of isomorphism between human identity and reality: "it is impossible to know reality unless there is some identity between it and us. We know as much as the identical is in us: ontic identical and anthropomorphic ontic" (Băncilă, 2015, p. 40). It's a thought provoked by an author, Gonzague

Truc. If we don't believe in these truths, we are naive realists, or, in the case of Communism, it is "dogmatic and despotic" naive realism. Then he ends his note with an allusion to the apostle Paul: "Whoever believes otherwise 'does not know what it means to know'".

Speaking of the ontologism of man, the idea that reality cannot but be *anthropomorphic* was also stressed, because, says Hegel (quoted in French), "things do not come from the self" (Băncilă, 2015, see pp. 42, 39); moreover, the ontological in man is the presence of the divine in him: "Poets, philosophers (Plato, etc.), who create under divine inspiration, emphasize precisely the ontology of man." It is what psychologism or demythologizing, which drive the ontology out of man and predispose him to illusionism, do to subjective idealism (this was what the critic Adrian Marino did not know, notes Băncilă, "in his doctrinal article" entitled "The Rationality of Creation" – see *Literary Romania*, 30 July 1970).

*

Talking about human knowledge, Băncilă indexed two enormities as evidence of *Gnostic Luciferism*: that the Universe would have a limit, for which purpose radio telescopes penetrating up to 12 billion light years have been invented; and that the number of atoms or particles of the Universe would have a limit. Just as, in another entry, he ironizes the strange combination of strict determinism and absurdity that we find in various cosmogonies (November 1971).

And a distortion of knowledge was also coming, in Băncilă's view, from existentialism, with Jean P. Sartre being targeted in particular (March 1972). No work by the French philosopher is named, but it seems to refer, in subtext, to *Being and Nothingness* (1943) or *Critique of Dialectical Reason* (1960), two of Sartre's most important writings. He agrees with the way in which this school of thought conceives of existence, but rejects the primordial thesis: existence precedes essence; existence, says Băncilă, "is that which the Romanians call *Fire*, the Germans call *Dasein*, and the French: *L'Être*" (Băncilă, 2015, p. 122; I will not comment on Băncilă's statement, it is a theme on which treatises have been written).

*

Numerous entries problematize the beginning of the world, especially from a logical point of view. The ideas of the ancients, the moderns and scientists (with whom he is often in dispute, from physicists to genetic biologists) are invoked; all of which together, Băncilă believes, do not prove anything, do not find sufficient reason.

Christian metaphysics remains the only valid one, God "has in truth sufficient reason in himself" (Băncilă, 2015, p. 32). He created the word out of nothing, and through it he created the world: "But the word (the logos of the apostle John) is the idea. And the idea was "from the beginning", that is, from eternity; therefore, God's idea created the world, and the idea is from eternity, that is, *uncreated*.

The Uncreated created the world!" (Băncilă, 2015, see pp. 30, 40, 44).

Or the note in which Băncilă asks whether the spirit is lucid from the beginning, or not at all: "God is either clear Providence or He is not. But he is!" A vision, at its core, Christian, with platonic overtones. Metaphysicians, says Băncilă (August 1970), differentiate among themselves according to where they locate perfection: at the beginning or at the end. Spiritualists place it at the beginning ("original perfection"), as in Plato, Plotinus or Christianity, the latter also conceiving "final perfection" in the form of an Eden, but different from the initial one, because it will be "*lucid and unalterable*".

Plato and Plotinus also refer us to the relationship between the whole (or perfect) and the part, where, ontologically speaking, the explanation starts from the first term to the other, and not vice versa (between the whole, or Whole, and the part is, however, a one-to-one relationship which the thinker discusses in another context).

For Băncilă, the idea of original *perfection*, not at all novel, works with the force of intuition, being an argument in support of the fact that the world could not have arisen from matter or chaos. As he himself defined his *Weltanschauung*, his conception is "a precise ontic personalism", "a transcendent, eternal, original perfection that creates a diffuse providentialism in the universe, in struggle with a demonism (or in struggle with a historical demonism) in the created world, partly tolerated, partly abused (autonomized), and in which man realizes his personality and salvation" (Băncilă, 2015, p. 75).

Băncilă pointed out a serious dilemma to those who were interested in cosmogony or, in general, in metaphysics. They all ended up with two options: either they took as their starting point the idea of matter or chaos, which meant admitting creation out of nothing; or "they transposed the present or subsequent essences of the world to an imaginary principle or object, which encompasses them all as potentiality or virtuality" (Băncilă, 2015, p. 50; Motru's metaphysical personalism, Spinoza's substance, Schopenhauer's will, Hegel's Absolute Idea, Plato's Ideas were indicated). Băncilă's choice was for the second alternative, credited by religion and seemingly more rational. Why agree that matter has always existed, from which everything would then have arisen (by *ex nihilo nihil*), and "not admit that spirit is eternal and from it everything was born"?

Chaos, with its vicious theory, has tempted many: scientists, philosophers, poets. It is a mixture of philosophy and poetry taken to extremes, Băncilă thinks, of existentialism, for which he refers to Spencer (!), a thinker "more *integral* than one thinks", but he also quotes, just as surprisingly, the critic Ov. Drimba[2] with *Blaga's Philosophy*.

This chaos theory was completely contradictory: if we are dealing with absolute chaos, there is nothing to legitimize its transition to another form (he proposed to quote from one of Eminescu's *Letters*, certainly from the first satire).

And the shift from the homogeneous to the heterogeneous seems illegitimate. Why does existence pass from one form to another! Perhaps a deeper law justifies the phenomenon, similar, for example, to that which Heraclitus invoked when he spoke of the existence of cycles in the world (he now tacitly adheres to the vision of the Ephesian thinker).

*

But the "scientists" (Băncilă's friends!) were also interested in the beginning of the Universe, and they emitted a series of *"cosmological absurdities"* (Băncilă, 2015, see pp. 51, 54). They speak of antimatter, which, says Băncilă, can only be matter (unless it is spirit!), just as, in the third decade of the twentieth century, they spoke of energy as the ultimate reality (it could also be spirit, according to Băncilă). Or they were looking for the ultimate expression of the so-called small infinite, at a time when knowledge of the structure of the atom was expanding without limit.

But the way *scientists*, secular philosophers and poets explain the emergence of the cosmos from chaos is no more scientific or rational than the biblical way in which *Genesis* explains the same phenomenon. Except that the biblical text is "more picturesque and plastic – and more morally grounded".

*

Many of Vasile Băncilă's ontological notes have a metaphysical content. This is natural, because metaphysics is a part of ontology and is concerned with answering questions such as what, how and when the world was born, what is its purpose or essence. He is, in fact, troubled by the decisive arguments supporting a spiritualist metaphysics; he introduces them in various logical justifications, reworks them tautologically and induces new nuances. Just as he does with the hypotheses of the creation of the world: from nothing or from spirit, a constant of countless writings.

Risking partial reiteration of some ideas, let us follow his logical strategies. The first hypothesis of the creation of the world – out of nothing, which is the true creation, "agrees with the greatness" of God, "but we do not understand how anything can be made out of nothing" (Băncilă, 2015, see pp. 55, 61, 70).

Ex nihilo nihil! Logic is instead saved if the world is made by objectifying the spirit, i.e., it came out of something. Only here too, says Băncilă, a misunderstanding arises: how is the spirit objectified, how is it exteriorized? All that remains is the *basic* understanding of this phenomenon. But there is something else: we don't agree with the complete lack of causality, because we don't understand and cannot accept nothingness. And "complete lack of causality would mean that something can be born out of nothing, out of nothingness". Băncilă is even more categorical: "*Absolute nothingness has never existed and never will.*". Accepting it makes it impossible for the world to be born, just as nothingness cannot arise from something.

Băncilă then problematizes the hypotheses by invoking the cause: if the world came out of nothing, it means that it had no cause to determine it; *causa sui* seems to him an absurd expression: "what is without cause cannot be a cause"; and yet, Băncilă antinomically concludes, if the world was created out of nothing, this implies that: "it was created out of something: because of it" (Băncilă, 2015, p. 56).

One inevitably asks oneself: why does Băncilă almost obsessively invoke these hypotheses, those of the making of the world, when, in fact, he so often accepts, as absolute truths, the *original Perfection* (a *Deus*), or the idea that the essence of reality is of the nature of spirit, or (diffuse) providentialism!

As an answer, one can invoke his cognitive interest: to bring the two theses closer together, to link them until they are conflated: creation from nothing and creation from something. Which is possible only through the use of a speculative logic in which the opposites coincide, as things happen in the sphere of transcendence (transcendentalism – or the positive spiritual Absolute, i.e., God – being another of Băncilă's cognitive aims). In other words, the mechanism of this speculative logic is specific to spiritualist metaphysics, the foundation of the ontological community.

It is curious, however, that in none of the ontological notes is the philosophical and religious concept of *coincidentia oppositorum* mentioned, even if it is partially implied. He admits, for example, a "*unitary ontic plurality*" and another "*unitary gnostic plurality*", which make up Existence, thus eliminating the contradiction between the relative and the absolute, between rationalists and irrationalists. These contradictions are, however, specific to Existence, a particular concept of world or Universe (which can only be taken symbolically as Existence).

It does not explicitly refer to the coincidence of opposites, but speaks of antinomy as a maximal gnostic category: "Any superior value is antinomical: so is the Real! Antinomy is the most complex and appropriate gnostic category." (Băncilă, 2015, p. 73) At the same time, for the community of destiny, he invokes "the incidence (the engagement, the encounter) of opposites", or, for the community of culture, "the harmonism of opposites".

*

Another constant in Băncilă's comments is the "ontological family", i.e., the Real, which includes plant and animal species. He admits the becoming of human existence, speaking, in this sense, of existence as form, for which he provides three proofs: the mineral order (it is the astronomical one and the one specific to physicists and chemists); the plasticity of evolution in plants and animals (their evolution follows a "*line of plasticity*, and not anarchy or diffusion, or randomness": Băncilă, 2015, p. 60); the finalism of instincts, in other words, an evident teleologism of life (science, however deterministically it conceives of the world, accepts finalism, final causality).

There are three of the four forms of spirit here: the lethargic spirit (mineral), the sensitive spirit (plants), the instinctive spirit (animals) and the lucid spirit (humans). Băncilă proposed a comparison with Aristotle's metaphysics or with Hegel's phenomenology of the spirit (but he does not like the term phenomenology, because it refers to phenomenon, to appearance; how can he not see that it is a superficial meaning, which ignores the Hegelian one!).

And in the final perfection state, in Paradise, people will not have "physiological functions", but a spiritual body; there, says Băncilă jokingly, no one marries, no one burns, as Christ and the apostle Paul said. There will be no more demons, evil will disappear from the world. Even if he doesn't understand the process, the hypothesis would make it easier to understand how spirit produces matter, at least at the level of principle.

In another entry, he glosses dubitatively: "The final Paradise will be quasi-perfection; or shall we say it will be in God, in the Absolute? But does the Absolute need this?" (Băncilă, 2015, see pp. 78–82)

*

From the perspective of its spiritualist and providentialist metaphysics, it is not only the old materialism, from Democritus and Epicurus onwards, that is criticised; but especially the materialism used by Communism (which I have also discussed elsewhere). In this respect, an avalanche of extremely corrosive accusations are also to be found in an (unpublished) reply to an article which appeared in the journal *The contemporary* under the title: "The Universe – an infinite cybernetic system" (June 7, 1974).

He formulates, one after the other, retorts to the "truths" expressed by this amputated naive realism, whose science and philosophy represent "just a *translation of aspects*. The Communists have plundered the culture of the world (taken away all its great concepts and discoveries), but they have not lived up to these concepts: they are therefore perfect cabotines (with added resentment and presumption)."

Communist ontological materialism is a "philosophical scam, i.e. a philosophy of bribes, fed in pustules, with intellectual deficiency (and a lack of philosophical spirit)". Communists, it says elsewhere, "want to be both chicken and egg" (Băncilă, 2015, see pp. 88, 91, 86), making a mixtum compositum of materialism and spiritualism.

His more thoughtful retorts continue in later notes (1974 and, for the most part, 1975), where he reiterates the view that, underneath the surface, such materialism creates arguments for philosophical spiritualism: "introducing the Trojan horse into materialist philosophy", matter living with a "spiritualist subconscious" (see "Oaths in the Communist Regime", Băncilă, 2015, p. 105). And the poets of the Communist regimes took to worshipping matter "as if it were alive, as if it were the Lady of Life, as if it were *Providence*".

These are opportunities for Băncilă to constantly specify how he conceived the world from an ontological point of view. A vision, it must be said, in which the data of sciences about the universe also find their place, as "philosophical auxiliaries" that deserve to be interpreted thoughtfully and rationally. In mathematics, for example, he finds "the most strained *apriorism*", a proof that "between the human mind and the Real there is a *correspondence*" (Băncilă, 2015, see pp. 91, 105, 126). He admits some truths of science, without, of course, renouncing its principles, first of all the Absolute, the ultimate essence: "In matter I am not lost, but in God I am. God is the great and only sufficient reason". Because: "The world is created by the will of God, so it cannot be said to have come into being out of nothing".

*

The period between 1975 and 1979 is that of the *densification of spiritualism*, of the recapitulation of the elementary, invariable constants of a spiritualist metaphysics. Among the many syllogisms, we choose one: "Spirit has been from eternity both in and out of matter. Analogous to Jesus Christ incarnate; therefore, He also, as man, could be perfect.

This is the only solution to the metaphysical problem" (Băncilă, 2015, see pp. 106, 116, 117, 178).

There will be countless variations on the same themes:

- about the illusion or truth of understanding matter (the evidence of science is increasingly leading to the disappearance of the boundary between matter and spirit);
- about the essence of the Real and the rationality of the world;
- about the false philosophies produced by the twentieth century (in which he detects a "demiurgism of Luciferian manikins"; many of which are opportunist ideologies (in line with the "Bonzes of Mordechaist philosophy", i.e., Marxist;
- about the positive arguments made by biology (for the order and finalism of the Real, the uncreated and eternal, in solidarity with apriorism);
- about the idea of God, without which the Real becomes inexplicable;
- about the creation of the world out of nothing, but not without a cause; about the epic of the phrase "nature takes care";
- about old concepts in new clothes ("linguistic toilet");
- about Spinoza's substantialist philosophy (often invoked);
- on Schopenhauer's Blind Will (also often mentioned);
- about philosophy as *ancilla of* religion;
- about the domestication of the idea of infinity and nothingness that existentialists fear (Heidegger, Camus);
- about the various forms of materialism, with its limits and absurdities, criticized from many angles;
- about the non-existence of a materialistic tradition in Romania (even if, apparently, there are traces of peasant materialism);
- about the mystery of man's emergence (an *insoluble* problem, like the problem of evil and the essence of the Real);
- about his dog, Dianu, who has some "judgments" to offer;
- about direct and indirect returns to spiritualism (confirmed by cybernetics and genetics), monism, providentialism;

- finally, about the most controversial problem of knowledge: the Universe (whose laws can be reduced to attraction and repulsion – these are the vectors that the aesthetic man obeys).

*

The stacks of sheets written by Vasile Băncilă should not be left to *the provisionality of the provisional*, to use his own expression. After the systematisation (what a Sapphic operation!) carried out by the editor Dora Mezdrea, the crates of notes must be interpreted (another Sapphic operation!) in their intrinsic organicity, in their ideational architecture and in their cognitive finality. Especially since, often, whoever reads some of the notes is puzzled or unconvinced by various syllogisms. And rightly so! It is clear, however, that just as in the principle of communicating vessels, in the archipelago of notes (i.e., of parts), the sense of a possible whole, of an organicity of the whole, circles just under the surface. Whoever reads Vasile Băncilă's work can reach the wholeness of this meaning, in which breathes the organic thought of a *private philosopher*, or, as he puts it, of *housebound Anchorite*.

Beyond his comparisons with great suggestive power, basically metaphors, as Aristotle would say, Băncilă operates with contrary statements (not contradictions!), which harmonize, I repeat, only inside a speculative logic. The thinker reasons with *autological supercategories* (the phrase is Alexandru Surdu's),[3] which have the property of *self-production*, such as the Absolute, an *abstract myth* (Băncilă, 2015, see pp. 142–143) that any philosophical system arrives at; categories that belong to the transcendent (*beyond* the world of our possible experience), where the usual principles of thought no longer function. In such a structure, reasoning can mean something other than understanding, as in traditional logic. And it happens this way because of the method, that is, thanks to *speculation* and *the philosophy of antinomy*, which Băncilă accepts and makes use of – and sometimes abuses.

*

Vasile Băncilă was, is and remains a *spiritualist*. He has always been so in accordance with his temperament and faith, and the obtuseness and absurd utopia of Communism, through the *wonders of* matter, led him to reach the Logos as soon as possible and, through the cultural insufficiency of an inhuman oligarchic system, to believe: "in *spirit as the ultimate ontic factor*, for the salvation of man" (Băncilă, 2015, p. 181, we underline).

He is a spiritualist who looks at the same phenomena that we all look at, but through speculative intuition, sees something different from each of us. He makes almost excessive use of *antinomy* (which, he thinks, Kant would not have understood), a legitimate strategy in the sphere of metaphysics (but also of religion), for otherwise "it would mean to *impoverish* the Real, to understand it unilaterally" (idem, 2015, p. 134). A Real whose essences are equally abstract and plastic, in the manner of the art of Brâncuşi.

The last entries under the title *ontological community* conclude with the thinker's somewhat Kantian reliance on intuition and reason: "Reason is not possible without very intimate (deep) intuitions, and intuition is not possible without also very intimate or behind-the-scenes judgments." (Băncilă, 2015, see pp. 193–194) Above all, we find "*love* from a moral point of view, and a kind of infinite limit"; in other words: "God, who is infinite, but is also, for our consciousness, something in which we lose ourselves; we know through him, we gain something out of his infinity."

Notes

[1] I didn't quite understand the meaning of this codification or substitution, especially since Băncilă has countless direct, unencrypted references to Communism and Communists (i.e., Marxist philosophy). It is rather an ironic, small linguistic fad, an attitude that does not, however, make him immune to possible censorship, as his editor Dora Mezdrea believes.

[2] Drimba, O. (1919–2015). Romanian literary historian. Other writings: *Pages on European Culture* (1945), *Don Quixote, the Meaning of the Hero and the Significance of the Work* (1955), *The Beginnings of Cultic Narrative Prose* (1961), *Rabelais* (1963), *French Symbolism - Style of Culture* (1966)

[3] Surdu, A. (1938–2020). Romanian university professor, philosopher, disciple of Constantin Noica, the most representative Romanian thinker of the last century after Lucian Blaga. Among his writings: *Elements of intuitional logic* (1976), *The actuality of the thinking-language relationship. Theory of Prejudicial Forms* (1989), *Modern Philosophy* (2002), *Contemporary Philosophy* (2003), *Pentadic Philosophy* (4 vols., 2007–2020).

Chapter 11

Romanian existence

11.1 Transylvania – differential ethnic psychology

Starting frames. The editor Dora Mezdrea has brought together, under the title *Romanian Existence*, pages written by Vasile Băncilă between 1940 and 1979, some of which are finished texts; others, perhaps most of them, are still in the form of worksheets.

I will start with the first ones, largely following the chronological criterion. The manuscript "Transylvanian dimensions" seems to be, according to the date and place indicated on the first page, a conference presented at the Romanian Athenaeum (February 22, 1944). The context of this writing cannot be ignored, especially the events of the *second* Vienna *arbitration* (August 30, 1940), when Romania was forced to cede almost half of the Transylvanian territory (43,492 km²) to Horthy's Hungary (until October 1944). And, perhaps most importantly, the Second World War had not yet ended.

There are three parts that structure Băncilă's essay: introduction, spiritual dimensions of Transylvania (the most important segment) and final considerations. He was interested in the knowledge of the individual or collective soul of the Romanians, an aspect that scientific disciplines such as the psychology of peoples, sociology or philosophy of culture have investigated. He noted, not surprisingly, that the self-awareness of the Romanian was in a certain crisis, the average Romanian being, until the war that had not yet ended, more interested in political quarrels inside the country and in what was happening in Europe ("what Europe will say"). And for ordinary Romanians, their gaze was directed from near to far, from the county to the capital and from there to other capitals, especially Paris.

In spite of the questions that have been asked since Bălcescu about the soul of the Romanian people, neither the atmosphere nor the method have been suitable for a steady and systematic research,[1] the opportunity arose immediately after 1918 when, beyond the somewhat idyllic ethnographic approach, a double orientation began to take shape: one of Europeanization or "universalization", the other of capitalizing on the native potential. Both must be seen as attempts to highlight and impose the potential of the Romanian nation, our meaning and role as a people among the peoples of Europe.

There was no lack of methods for getting closer to our national being, from those proposed by C. Rădulescu-Motru, D. Gusti or Tr. Brăileanu, to those used by L. Blaga, Nae Ionescu or N. Iorga. The method of the latter, that of direct intuition, complementary to the others, required, however, a "very ethnic construction" on the part of the person applying it and, on top of that, a specific approach: first of all, the "soul" of the provinces (Băncilă, 2015, p. 197) had to be investigated, so that an overall understanding of Romanian existence, of the organic Romanian, could be developed (I believe the monographic method of the sociologist Dimitrie Gusti partially achieved this objective).

Through the grid of a differential ethnic psychology, Băncilă chooses and proposes to inaugurate the research with the province of Transylvania, a large part of our ethnic trunk. The reasons were manifold, ranging from its particular psychology or local cultural tradition to pragmatic-political ones, which "fall under the category of the sacred": Transylvania, partly under Hungarian occupation, was waiting for the moment when it would be "politically reunited with the Dacian area of Romanian rule" (Băncilă, 2015, see pp. 198–200).

Spiritual dimensions of Transylvania. Vasile Băncilă's perspective was not far from his spiritualist metaphysics. Without accepting, *ab initio,* negative differences between the Romanian provinces, he saw in them "encapsulations of creative absolutes", with their unique virtualities.

But what individualized Transylvania, a topos in which he was tempted to include all the regions and Romanians from the Carpathian arc to the Tisa River? He breaks down the soul chemistry of a spiritual Transylvania into 19 elements that form a unitary whole. First of all, he reveals the idea of the original form, of an original element in the form of the energy of the Transylvanian, manifested in three moments of our history: when the Romans and the Dacians formed the Romanian people (a process that took place mainly in Transylvania), at the time of the foundation of the Romanian principalities and in the cultural renaissance of our country. In all three of these "foundations", the Transylvanian ethnic vein was involved. There is a philosophical reason for calling Transylvania our "mother country", an expression attributed mainly to the Old Kingdom.[2]

He also notes, at the same time, the ardent nature of the Transylvanian, not only revealed by literature, but as it manifests itself in everyday life. Such an attitude needs to be especially appreciated, as it belongs to those who, living under the Hungarians, neither know nor accept the old proverb "the sword does not cut off the bowed head". This is what they did in 1848, when they did not want to accept Hungarian freedom because, as Simion Bărnuțiu said, "freedom without nationality is death". And the Transylvanian has another trait: unlike other Romanians who forget and are forgiving, he is different: he does not forget, his memory is kept alive, and he is brave.

This structure of order and culture characterizes the area of Transylvania, where the Latinity of the Romanians[3] seems to be more pronounced than in the regions situated to the East of the Daco-Roman island. The attitude of the Transylvanians towards history is also noted by Băncilă. Unlike the French, Russians, Spaniards or Jews, the Romanian people, he believes, are not revolutionary. They do not have a volcanic temperament, but rather show "historical tolerance, if not historical absenteeism" (Băncilă, 2015, see pp. 203–204); which does not mean that, at certain historical moments, they would not be *fit for a revolution*. One can, however, speak of a Transylvanian revolutionarism, a "*moral and national"* one.

Transylvania has not stood, during history, with its hands in its pockets; its life, says Băncilă, meant not only the revolutions of Horia or Avram Iancu,[4] but a great number of other revolts too, so that the idea of revolution manifested itself here as an *endemic factor*. The aim of the Transylvanian people was not only social justice, but also national justice, based on morality and on a logic of Romanian spirituality, Transylvania harmonising suffering with dignity and conscience. The Romanianism and revolutionaryism of the people of Transylvania are exemplary: "They realized the archetype of the Romanian revolution: Ion Ursu Horia and the Archangel type: Avram Iancu" (Băncilă, 2015, p. 206).

*

The physiognomy of revolutionary Transylvanianism is not complete without another tendency, namely, *legalism*, the Transylvanian legal spirit, from Simion Bărnuțiu to Iuliu Maniu, slightly exacerbated in the latter. Statistics show that, before the Great Union, the specific professional choices of young people in Transylvania were: teacher, priest and lawyer. Vasile Băncilă points out that the people of Transylvania do not have a fetish for the law, as is the case with others, because they did not want to codify privileges. Their attitude to law originated in the legal spirit, which, in turn, was based on "the sense of natural right, in the metaphysical vision of the Romanian people, in the Dacian substratum, in the Latin substratum and in the influence of Christianity" (Băncilă, 2015, see pp. 208, 210). Eventually, the Romanian idea of law came to have, like the revolutionary character, a dual nature, being in equal measure moral and national.

The inhabitant of the Old Kingdom was also interested in the idea of justice; only the peasant here has a kind of idealistic nostalgia, he "presses the metaphysical pedal and resigns himself more easily". Băncilă reminds us of Blaga, who invoked the *withdrawal of* our people *from history* in the medieval period in order to save their national being. A reaction that the peasantry of the Old Kingdom also had, in order to preserve the Romanian nation: "But he no longer retreats into mountains and forests, but into a sort of metaphysical Carpathians". It takes refuge in a transcendent or righteous occlusion within itself, where it is intangible and has spiritual power over those who oppose it.

The Romanians in Transylvania are somehow far from this somewhat passive form. They live history with determination and have concrete reactions to injustice. They exercise the attitude of revolt or revolution, which has often led to a kind of social-political historicism. The Transylvanian went from the formality of law, in peacetime, to revolt or revolution – without much difficulty.

*

Another dimension of Transylvania is the spirit of messianic expansion and historical activism. The first part, about messianism, is captured by Băncilă slightly ambiguously, with adjectival formulations whose related meanings we do not know. Messianism means man's belief in the divine Saviour of the world, as portrayed by the Christian religion. The Romanians (not only the people of Transylvania), says the lecturer, are not characterized by any proud or morbid messianism. They do not have a collective messianism, but show individualism, which sometimes takes on the appearance of a sickly messianic attitude (to what deviations does he refer, perhaps to a zealous, fanatical messianism!).

The Transylvanians are similar to other Romanians, but even without going beyond the sphere of law they have a little more missionary spirit. In this way, Transylvania: "has more historical initiative, fights more against 'fate', creates its destiny more voluntarily" (Băncilă, 2015, see pp. 212–213).

We can speak, says Băncilă, of a kind of expansionism, as in the case of those who went to America or of those who travelled with their flocks of sheep to the shores of the Caspian Sea (this is a form of expansionism in disguise, one, admittedly, economically motivated).

But such deeds do not hide the messianic spirit. Băncilă discovers it "in those monks with the souls of shepherds and the knowledge of Benedictines, who were the heads of the so-called 'Transylvanian school', in whose Hussarism we must see not merely an industry of excessive philosophers and historians, but rather the activity of a monastic order, without written canons, but with the mission of saving the nation through language and history".

In the Şincai-Maior-Micu trinity[5] there may be a cultural correlation specific to another trinity: Horia-Cloşca-Crişan.[6] It is true that those shepherds spread throughout Ukraine or Southern Russia, who helped the Romanians of Bessarabia with gold enabling them to continue their national struggle in 1917–1918, also had a messianic spirit and an ethnic sense (Professor Onisifor Ghibu is remembered for his efforts in this regard).

Economic life. From what has been said so far to the economic skills of the people of Transylvania there is only one step. Their harsh life and often harsher conditions of cohabitation with economically skilled minorities led to the development of specific skills, to a "good old-fashioned *economicism*" (Băncilă, 2015, see pp. 214–215). The banks, the shepherding industry and the merchants supported the formation of a national bourgeoisie, which our arrivistic spirit did not preserve. But, added Băncilă, this economic spirit had, at that historical moment, real chances to flourish in the small bourgeoisie and in the towns and cities of the Old Kingdom.

Closely related to the economicism or economic spirit of the people of Transylvania, Băncilă situates their healthy opportunism, completely foreign to the attitude of "*pilfering*" or sick opportunism, of cowardice or petty scruples. Having gone through so much hardship, the Transylvanian has become accustomed to fighting on the ground of political efficiency. Hence his solid opportunism, his tactical spirit and his biological intuitions, all congruent with his determination and power to confront concrete history. The Transylvanian has, to simplify things, two norms of historical conduct: one is the political opportunism of Andrei Şaguna[7] (the result: a state for the Transylvanian Romanians); the other is given by the attitude of Horia or Avram Iancu. It is a somewhat personal, specific opportunism, with features "of the style of the species itself".

*

In spite of the somewhat limited environment in which the people of Transylvania lived, nothing prevented them, including the intellectuals, from being very close to the people, an attitude that Băncilă likened to that of the Danes or the Finns. The morale of the Transylvanians is of a different nature: *the plague of landed gentry* is not so vigorous over the mountains. Not to mention the fact that the Transylvanian peasant is more emancipated, has some bourgeois tastes, is not frightened of lords and cannot see them, as the peasant of the Old Kingdom does, as pharaohs. This puts him in the right position: he is close to both the intellectual and his fellow peasant, a relationship that also forms a fruitful, organic harmony. The teenager from Transylvania can sometimes pass as: "a peasant cub dressed in German clothes and who, by some miracle, speaks Latin"; and the peasant plays the role of an "intellectual who has left his city clothes and has put his hand, still stout, on the scythe or the hoe. This is the *popular character* of the Transylvanian structure" (Băncilă, 2015, p. 216).

The Transylvanians and Romanians in general. Through his insights into the people of Transylvania, especially the peasants, Băncilă presents his views on the Romanians in general. He does so not in an essentialist way, but by deconstructing carefully observed scenes of life. Along with other inter-war writers (Cioran in particular), he too observes that the Romanian "loves the novel, and because of this does not have much science" (!); he is enthusiastic, he is ingenuous, but after a short time he is fed up with what he has done and gives up for good; this is how we come to see: "so many works begun and soon left in the stage and poetry of the frontispiece"; "too many foundations, noisily inaugurated, too few "foundation stones" and too few buildings. The country is full of unfinished palaces, as if we were the land of recent heavens" (Băncilă, 2015, p. 217).

How does Băncilă explain this phenomenon of the Romanian as a perpetual beginner? His suppositions are too fine to be untrue: perhaps there is an intuition, similar to the evangelical one, of the futility of all that exists; or perhaps there is a sudden constitutional fatigue.

But no such miracles happen to the people of Transylvania. They are persistent beings, a persistence that comes perhaps from education, perhaps under the influence of a somewhat hostile environment, as well as a temperamental trait (among many other examples, Băncilă gives that of the Transylvanians who colonised part of the Bărăgan, where they imposed a model agriculture).

This is an attitude towards work, through which something else also shines through: methodism and organisation, pragmatism and pedagogical value. The reactions of the Transylvanian have a maximum of economy in them, they are carried out methodically, according to a well-thought-out form of organisation from which the spirit of improvisation and superficiality is completely absent. Only in such a space could monuments of perseverance such as Diaconovici Loga's Encyclopaedia[8] or Sextil Pușcariu's[9] *Atlas of the Romanian Language* emerge.

Facts and positive things are essential for a Transylvanian. This explains his pragmatism, totally different from the reflexes of the Romanian of the Old Kingdom, tempted more by theoretical adventure, sometimes combined with some practicality. Such a pragmatic soul background leads, naturally, to a pedagogical spirit, *pedagogism*, which is not meant in a pejorative sense, but is understood as an aptitude that positively and intensely values the change of reality through education and school.

The latter, the school, developed out of national and religious spirit, but also because of practical concerns. This is how a "rich and glorious phalanx of national pedagogues" (Băncilă, 2015, see pp. 220–222) emerged, who then spread throughout Romania; and how the education of the Transylvanian people achieved its deserved prestige. Transylvania, says Băncilă, produced not only shepherds, merchants and settlers, but also teachers.

*

Closely linked to the spirit of the school is another determination of Transylvania: its epic aptitude. Of the factors that can decide the choice of a literary genre, Băncilă stops at the arguments offered by the psychology of people, about which Professor C. Rădulescu-Motru also wrote.

From the angle of ethnic psychology, Romanians are inclined towards the "lyrical-dialectical direction". Lyricism also characterises our epic, whether popular or cultured, and is also specific to the novel, after much effort invested in its birth and after its formula has undergone numerous ambiguities. The reasons for the long gestation of the Romanian novel are situated, by Băncilă, in Romanian psychology, just as the specificity of the various provinces is also involved in explaining this process. Such was the particular emphasis of the Transylvanian epic, even though "the Romanian across the mountains is increasingly lyrical". This explains, says Băncilă, the purity of Liviu Rebreanu's or Pavel Dan's epic purity, different from that found in writers from over the mountains.

The epics of the two areas, Transylvania and the Old Kingdom, differ more in *expressive intensity* and less in terms of composition or narrative strategy. Băncilă justifies this epic disposition by ethnic factors, but also leaves the alternatives of external influences open to question: "the Transylvanian epic is an expression of a more objective, vigorous and somewhat more anonymous discipline in presenting the pathos and flowing miracle of life" (Băncilă, 2015, p. 223).

*

Perhaps nowhere else in Romania has the spirit of association been more pronounced than in Transylvania. The psychology of the collective has here a certain applicative object, either with communitarian or with individualistic motivations, in a positive sense. This is why the peasants of Transylvania associate – because they understand the purpose of communitarianism, but also because they have a high perception of their own interests. The geography of associations is varied. Transylvania, says Băncilă, has been and remains a "*city*, not only in the physical sense, but also in the moral, and *especially* moral, sense" (Băncilă, 2015, see pp. 224–226), geography blending harmoniously with spirit. If the geographer George Vâlsan saw in Transylvania a *fortress of mountains*, it can just as subtly be called a *fortress of soul*.

If, up to this point, the features discussed by Băncilă had a definite Transylvanian imprint, the next one seems to characterize most Romanians: the idea or intuition of the autochthonous spirit, *autochthony*. It is a magnetic force of a centripetal nature, one that held Romanians together; alongside which "religion, the idea of the nation and belief in the metaphysical justice of the world" can also be named.

However, Băncilă also finds other characteristics of the Transylvanian region. The sense of autochthony is more lucid in Transylvania, and "minorities are bodies that retain their entire shell, dystonic to the majority element, even if they would not have to prove anything"; this is why "the natives see that they are something else and deepen their self-consciousness". What the poet Octavian Goga demanded of the river Olt, namely "let's move to another country", is a metaphor, because the people of Transylvania cannot ever conceive leaving their Romanian land.

The intuition of the autochthony of the Transylvanian peasantry was the fiercest danger for the Hungarian domination. And in order to annihilate it, the Hungarians devised various methods, from stealing land and falsifying the past, to the psychology of "Transylvanianism", which would justify the autonomy of Transylvania (a utopia which, even today, has not been abandoned by propaganda). A theory equal to "political slyness, woven with white thread; for some naive few, it may be a simple poetry of the native place, which is not grafted on, and is not valued by the substrate, a seriousness, (...) of the autochthonous feeling, as it is in the Transylvanian Romanian and only in him" (Băncilă, 2015, see pp. 227–228).

Major spirit. Inspired, perhaps, by Blaga's philosophy of culture, Băncilă discovers in the Transylvanian area *the form or major spirit*. However, not at all in the Blagian spirit, he draws out some determinations of the major and minor spirit in a culture, with some connections between them. The former has *monumentality* as its stylistic hallmark, the latter opts for "the cult of the diminutive and the graceful, the mundane and the biblical".

In our country, the peasant and peasant culture have a certain major spirit, "in its hieraticism and in the experience of the great moral, metaphysical and cosmic mysteries", despite "the diminutive nature of folk poetry" (Băncilă, 2015, p. 229). He gives a valuable boost to the peasant from the Bărăgan, sometimes also to the mountain peasant, but also to the Besssarabian spirit.

The Romanians of Transylvania, peasants or townspeople, have a more unified major spirit, "different at first sight from the virtues of the Lilliputian culture and the bored Levantinism served in Western flasks". The line of monumental (not colossal) becoming is preserved, with specific characteristics (see the type of the woman, "feisty, manly and social"). Băncilă's discourse becomes, on this segment of the exposition, less convincing.

The soul of the Romanian from Transylvania is also imbued with optimism; a dimension which, fused with the previous ones, leads to a deep *experience* of reality, a fundamental mental structure for the perspective of the philosophy of culture. For it is not "the strictly intellectual and aesthetic aptitude which decides the production and value of a culture, but the substratum of mental pathos, seriousness or levity" (Băncilă, 2015, see pp. 231–232), which decides how reality is experienced. Culture is a somewhat antinomic construction; it is both a playful attitude and a confrontation with an existential space – with destiny, ultimately.

*

Băncilă invokes, I don't know how significantly, the Transylvanian humour, similar to the Romanian one everywhere, but with a certain specificity. The Transylvanian has, like the orphans, a certain restraint when he laughs, as well as an energetic, vital laugh, like that of a "strong lad"; or, at other times, "in his laughter he has gleams of wholesome satire; or has Pan's flames in his eyes".

He quotes Coriolan Gheție, who is said to have stated that there is much that is tragic and sacred in the humour of Transylvania, something similar to that of Don Quixote, characterised by Ortega y Gasset as a kind of sad parody of Christ. He reproduces a long quotation where he talks about Gheorghe Șincai, and about the Transylvanian school, but does not have much faith in the exaggerations projected by the author.

Much more important, however, is Băncilă's observation that the Transylvanian does not have, or very rarely has, "the carefree, sterile banter, the 'devil may care' irony, the gratuitousness of irresponsible and edible laughter".

And then, he asks himself, where does the Transylvanian's difficulty to laugh come from, and why does his humour have particular accents? The explanation lies precisely in experiencing reality so profoundly; laughter, as Bergson says, having deeper, even metaphysical motivations.

Comic, in the people of Transylvania, takes the face of humour, of a: "sovereign and discreet smile, full of meaning, on a deep and balanced soulful background". There is a peasant humour, "a flower of lively and rare wisdom, contrasting with the cheap laughter, tending towards banter or carelessness, characteristic for certain categories of intellectuals or townspeople – a humour of ethnic definition, found as such in the Transylvanian Romanians; it does not invalidate the deep experience of reality, but confirms it" (Băncilă, 2015, see pp. 233–234; I get the impression that Băncilă sometimes substitutes I. L. Caragiale's trademark *irony* with *gossip*).

*

The 18 Transylvanian dimensions analysed so far form a syncretic whole, which is, in fact, the so-called *soul integralism*. We have, also through the viewpoint of ethnic psychology, a relative understanding of the underlined phrase: "the Transylvanian is more harmoniously endowed than the other Romanians, he is the most integral Romanian, without understanding by this that the Romanian as such is a model of integralism".

Băncilă also supports his assertion with a series of arguments: literature in Transylvania, philosophy, the epic of the sheepfold, the organization of the school, the church, the banks, the revolutionary energy the people of Transylvania have. And again: Transylvanian spirituality.

Băncilă reiterates a number of features discussed earlier, in order to gain the strongest possible support for his allegations. In addition, he mentions medicine in Transylvania (he mentions Cluj), without eluding the figure of the *exceptional* Transylvanian, characterised by "the same soulful equilibrium in its depths, the same mental integrity, but in a continuous movement of translation towards the plane of the spirit" (Băncilă, 2015, see pp. 236–237).

Interval conclusion. Vasile Băncilă's conference ended with a series of final considerations. After the praise of Transylvania, perhaps deserved, after the cavalcade of special features, the question arose, just as naturally – did the Transylvanian spirit have no flaw at all! Or did the qualities listed have an admirable pairing in the Old Kingdom!

Not only was there no indication of a flaw, but there was also a meritorious dimension of the Transylvanians: the religiousness of the Transylvanian Romanians, for which they fought seriously. In the Old Kingdom, this was never the case, not to mention a certain "lightness of religion, an air of frivolous paganism"; even if here too there are some aspects (see the metaphysical nuance of bravery) which raise the inhabitant of the Old Kingdom a little above the Transylvanian. Băncilă brings to the fore the intrinsic features of religious life in Transylvania, its secular and somewhat political role, and the Western influences it suffered over time.

Transylvania, concludes Băncilă, has given a splendid lesson, one that can enhance the entirety of Romanianism, the culture of our space, the configuration of the public spirit of the Old Kingdom. All this expressed the definite relevance Transylvania has for the philosophy of Romanian destiny, for the physical and spiritual existence of our nation. Băncilă saw in Transylvania the cornerstone of Romanian existence, "the main buttress of Romanianism and, without the Transylvanians, our whole ethnic edifice would crumble" (Băncilă, 2015, p. 240).

Paradigm escapes. The radiography made by the lecturer held under the magnifying glass mainly the Transylvanian peasantry before 1918, without excluding, in a way, the intellectuals. Precisely in view of such an ethnic heritage, it would be a pity, says Băncilă, if the spirit of Transylvania were betrayed by some of the Transylvanian or the Romanians of the region. As far as the former are concerned, one could, however, speak of some insignificant sporadic gestures that occurred in the period after the Great Union (1918).

Băncilă also begins to list the cases of escape from the boundaries of the demanding spirit of the Transylvanian. This was, first of all, the case of some intellectuals who promoted a kind of positivism combined ("aggregated") with elements of scepticism and pessimism, along the lines of the *decadent aestheticians* from Iași or the capital. He recommended that the people in question should take up philology or history, or try their hand at major naive philosophy, detaching themselves from that "cultural parvenitism" (alien to the Transylvanian tradition), from those "minor aesthetes and philosophers without valid ethos, living off the decay of culture and draping themselves in precious schisms to take the eyes of the galaxy" (Băncilă, 2015, see pp. 241–243).

We don't know the names of the people of Transylvania targeted by Băncilă's critical tirade. He then mentions, also anonymously, some literary critics in training, or intellectuals who "have the ambition to become Westernized roosters", who innocently adhere to the ideology of historical synchronicity, who make art for art's sake or philosophy for philosophy's sake, ignoring the fact that Western thought is increasingly approaching the religious or social-political phenomenon (our interwar synchronicity is mainly linked to the name of Eugen Lovinescu but, beyond its ethereal autochthonism, the generation of Mircea Eliade is also worth mentioning).

Băncilă also places slightly resentful accents on the silhouettes of those who used neologisms and "Frenchified formulas in their language, while on the soles of their shoes they still have dirt from their parents' garden". He casts anathemas on those who live in the capital on the cheap (including at the expense of cultural subsidies), frequenting the Capşa café or other restaurants; or others, of the older generation, tempted by the benefits of politics or capital accumulation; or those who, dismantling the organic link between the national and the social which is typical of Transylvania, eagerly promote various social extremisms; finally, in the chain of these crimes or betrayals of the Transylvanian spirit there are also those few individuals, starting from the bottom and quickly becoming wealthy, who live life with "an outburst of Dionysian epicurean epicureanism that is almost frightening and very different from the usual Transylvanian sobriety".

Even if he mentions the existence of some deviations in the Old Kingdom too, but without details, Băncilă is interested, as a teacher, in the fact that the Transylvanian spiritual model is not sufficiently studied by the intellectuals of the Old Kingdom. His project of differential ethnic psychology should be extended to all the Romanian provinces in order to finally determine the ideal Romanian spirit. Each Romanian province can make up a kind of school, and from all of them, through organic connections between them, the specific essences of Romanianism can be shaped (the *essentialist* strategy has its shortcomings).

If before 1918 there was talk of salvation through the Transylvanian people, in 1944, it was time to critically rethink a solution to save all the Romanians. Despite some deviations, Transylvania represented the essence of Romanianism with "profound and majestic fidelity"; which requires from us, concluded Băncilă, "the same ample and devoted fidelity" (Băncilă, 2015, p. 246) to the Transylvanian spirit.

From Avram Iancu to Iuliu Maniu. A year or so later, in August 1945, the paradigm of the Transylvanian spirit returned to the memory of Vasile Băncilă. He writes then only about the legal spirit or Transylvanian *juridicism*, one of the features identified in the conference analysed above (whether or not it was ever held in that form). The ideas of the Transylvanian juridical spirit, from Avram Iancu and Simion Bărnuţiu to Iuliu Maniu, were taken up and developed.[10]

The first was remembered for the way in which he put the revolution and the law at the service of the nation, this being, says Băncilă, the result of an apparent contradiction. This is also a superficial mismatch for the French area, but, as far as the Transylvanians are concerned, it is obvious that the same goal is achieved if we look more closely at (only) the legal conception or the idea of law in this Romanian area.

After showing what is not juridical in the Transylvanians, Băncilă creates a phenomenology of the idea of law for the Romanians, showing that justice had not only ontological foundations, but also a religious vision. Especially in Transylvania, Romanians gathered around the church, which was transformed *ad hoc* into a "religious, moral, administrative and political centre" (Băncilă, 2015, see pp. 249–250).

Through this kind of politics, the transcendent, as Blaga would say, descended into the everyday life of the village, becoming something accessible and prestigious. It is not insignificant, notes Băncilă, that some of the revolts in the Transylvanian Middle Ages were led by churchmen, and in time a kind of Romanian theocracy was imposed.

Moreover, the concept of Roman law seems to have worked in the legal subconscious of the particular Transylvanian spirit, after this form of justice had also known the customs of the Dacian spirit. Such a Romanian law, supported also by our fundamental Christianity, was to evolve and become strengthened in relation to the dangers brought by history, giving rise in the consciousness of the Romanians to a "style of social decency", which remained unaltered until the Western threats of the nineteenth century and the one that followed. This is how the idea of Romanian *humanity* took shape, a constant that remained intact until the middle of the last century.

Băncilă underlines the decisive role that the idea of struggle played for the Transylvanians, their firm involvement in history, unlike other Romanians who took refuge in the metaphysical. It is the *retreat from history* that Lucian Blaga spoke of for the Middle Ages, a phenomenon that, Băncilă added, continued, in a way, for the areas of Wallachia and Moldavia. Here, the peasants and some intellectuals turn their backs on history and wait for justice to come from above.

Therefore, Romanians lived with the idea of a law "with metaphysical, religious justifications, with Daco-Roman roots and with a harmony of customs or traditions of the land, which constituted a kind of art of social life", and in the face of historical dangers, they gave this idea of law a *national* dimension, "felt even when the doctrine of the national principle had not yet appeared" (Băncilă, 2015, see pp. 253–254).

Unlike in the West, the people of Transylvania fought in the revolution for the rights of the community, one in which the individual was organically included. Herein lies the secret of the *revolutionary* spirit *of the* Transylvanians, with its component – not at all contradictory – called legal spirit or *legalism*, a binomial for which the lawyer Avram Iancu so legitimately advocated (he speaks of the "weapon of the law", a phrase in which the revolutionary and the legal are osmotically combined). It is clear, says Băncilă, that "the revolution is the continuation of the legal order, of a more proper legal order, but with other means, just as the better legal order is a kind of revolution in the substance of things".

In fact, not two months after these notes, Vasile Băncilă was drafting a text of his own on the *revolutionary-juridicalism endo*smosis among the Romanians in Transylvania, so that, a year later, in September 1946, he drafted another study, this time on revolutionaryism in Transylvania (see Băncilă, 2015, pp. 256–263).

11.2 The stylistic mark of other provinces

Pale reflections of differential ethnic psychology also emerge from the brief notes on the significance of other Romanian provinces. In Wallachia, for example, he discovers *excess*, that is political romanticism, an area that has missed its literary priority and is not unified because of the variety of its regions and the people who have come here from all over the world. That is why it seems natural for Băncilă to speak of a multiple personality: the man from the Bărăgan, the man from the Danube and the marshes, the man from Bucharest, the man from the hills and the mountains, the man from Prahova, the man from Argeș, the man from Vlașca and Teleorman, the slum dweller from Ilfov. They all have one factor in common: *political excess*.

Characteriological records of these human types are largely missing. Perhaps also because "the provincial type is not fixed and because there is a lot of *wind* on the plains"; he now draws only a few lines of the man of the Bărăgan: a "contemplative psychology, alternating with terrible outbursts" (Băncilă, 2015, p. 339).

However, the cultural significance of Șerban Cantacuzino's cultural work is retained and enhanced[11] by the architectural style of C. Brâncoveanu[12] and the importance of the reign of Mihai Viteazul,[13] "a romantic, an excessive", the one who made "the greatest political gesture in the history of the Voievodate" by uniting Wallachia, Moldavia and Transylvania in 1600 (Băncilă, 2015, p. 385).

*

As far as Dobrogea is concerned, Băncilă places it between the presence of the past and the call of the future, in a present that seems to disappear. The first dimension is a mixture of geology and prehistory, with its *spiky* mountains, its

Turkish legends, its ancient Roman vestiges: Romanians, Scythians, Ovid, Dobrotici, Mircea the Elder, Romanian fishermen.

Alongside this historical archaeology ("all of Dobrogea is a museum!") we discover the *thalassic* significance, the horizon of the sea that links it to the world, to the universe, to ancient legends ("Liquid gateway to the universal and infinite and living landscape"); as we discover the harbours or the historic bridge at Cernavodă, as well as its *antinomic* nature: watery borders (90%), and inside them – stone, white dust. The people who live here, in a present crushed between past and future, "seem to be dry beings, accommodated to live without water: human tamarixes!" (Băncilă, 2015, p. 384).

How could Băncilă have forgotten another determination of Dobrogea, the *Ovidian* one, contemporary with the poet Ovid: "The Scythians, at the end of their world of banishment... The dramatic, tragic repetition of its theme through the Channel of the road of the slaves (what was the Leningrad-White Sea Channel for them was the Danube-Black Sea canal for us)."

*

For Moldavia, 19 traits are indicated, some of them common to Romanians in general. Specific are, for example, historical and cultural dimensions: the Voivodal tradition (Stephen the Great), universalism (Cantemir, Milescu, Conta, Eminescu, Iorga, Enescu), populism and organicism, coldness, a multitude of monasteries, the taste and prestige of books, anarchy; as defects: individualism, dissimulation, hypocrisy, arrivism, intellectuals with Left-wing doctrines, the genesis of nationalism.

Moldavia represents, for Romanian existence, its *aristocratic* side; it is a narcissistic, tolerant province. In fact, it is a dimension that Băncilă develops more when he writes about aristocratic traditions in this region of Romania. He reformulates the above features: seven types or classes of *Moldavian traditions:* the Voivodal tradition, the monastic tradition (the printing school at Neamț Monastery; Petru Movilă, who gave the doctrine of Orthodoxy), the tradition of culture and art (chroniclers, Milescu, Cantemir, Conta, Xenopol; here "our somewhat modern culture first sprang up"), the traditions of hospitality, politeness, superior citizenship (civic pride), of a *well-dressed* house and of good cuisine.

In short, the Moldavian claims to be the best Romanian: nobler than the others, with spiritual nobility, with an organicism of spirit, but also a traditionalist ("who sighs after his native place"). And on the streets of downtown Iași "there seems to be an air of a *salon* (which cannot be found in Bucharest)".

However, the universalism of Moldavia is emphasized especially through the personality of Stephen the Great, "a brave and a complex and balanced diplomat", which means "*the complex and harmonious fulfilment of the idea of the Lord*"; on top of that, he is the ruler who "gave a style of *art* and gave *religious stamp* and *transcendence* (he built 40 churches) to his policy". It is true that the ruler Mircea the Elder was also "a great diplomat (in Western style) and a great military man", "and a great ruler (a small Charles the Great)" (Băncilă, 2015, p. 385).

*

Vasile Băncilă also expresses himself, briefly, on Oltenia, where he sees a nervous, *fickle* will against a background of gnostic realism or positivism. Then: mercantilism (Motru is a "businessman", but also the author of a philosophical system), pragmatism, justiciarism and a certain shrewdness (T. Vladimirescu, Popa Şapcă, Iancu Jianu), emigrationism (they go to Romania and come back home), the church tradition, the fortified house (*cula*), no moral and religious scruples, pride (the Bănia tradition), folklore music, commercialism, lack of contemplation, no great literary talent (!).

The Oltenian is a picturesque figure, "a great trickster, an ace of tricks, *une lime fine (un fin limie)*", has no moral doubts, but has a "quick temper for both good and evil" (see the song "My mother made me an Oltenian"), which gives him "resourceful and vital *ability*"; and the Oltenian peasant, who travelled to Cernăuți, made, like the Transylvanian, the leap from the bourgeois state directly to the spirit of trade (Băncilă, 2015, pp. 386–387).

Above all the provinces, however, the guardian figures of the Romanian space remain: the greatest revolutionary: Nicolae Bălcescu, the greatest Romanian politician: M. Kogălniceanu, together with the Brătianu family and Andrei Şaguna. At the same time, Băncilă observes that the Romanian provinces are similar in their qualities, only that "their fruitfulness, their monumental *excellence*, moves from one province to another", which is fruitful for the life of a nation (Băncilă, 2015, p. 383).

11.3 Transcendental and Empirical Romanianism

Starting frames. Speaking of Romanian existence, Vasile Băncilă meditates not only on the spirit of the Transylvanian region or the one locked up in other provinces, but also on other permanencies of our space and time. As early as March 1940, he thought of the Romanian spirit as having a predominantly *bivalent* nature and a *mission*, ideas to which he returned episodically. He then identifies a transcendental Romanianism and an empirical Romanianism, in a rather thick plan of study which would have stretched over 16 chapters, with ideas that are sporadically obsessive for Băncilă's meditation.

On the other hand, he always recapitulates and enriches the binomial of these Romanian values. Here is a taxonomy written later, on May 9, 1955, from which the following doublets can be deduced:

- individualism and communitarianism (for which he refers us to the conference of the same title held in 1936 at the Royal Foundations);

- transcendentalism and empiricism (where he points towards a metaphysics of a Platonic nature, an ontological empiricism, with the "depth and pervasiveness of the Absolute", the latter with the determinations of Aristotelian *form*);

- intellectualism and lyricism, through which transpire rationalism ("sweetened by feeling, by inspiration, by intuition") and mysticism ("orderly, quiet, merging into a vision of serene contemplation, almost classical"), the Romanian being neither one nor the other, but synthetic, something with a double character, a being with two gills; in intellectualism and lyricism he sees the necessary conditions for the dialectical spirit, which he does not find in Motru, Mehedinți, Blaga etc. (but it is present in Nae Ionescu, Iorga – "affective dialectics", A. C. Cuza, Maiorescu), so that he wonders if such a form of spirit is actually Romanian;

- dogmatism and relativism, i.e., a form of relativism on a dogmatic background, the code of authentic culture, because people without the "refined *paste* of the Romanian" are either dogmatists or relativists and thus degenerate into fanaticism or scepticism (unless they become dogmatists in the sphere of the relative and relativists in that of the Absolute);

- struggle and resignation: the Romanian does not fight the windmills, like Don Quixote, and he resigns himself through metaphysics;

- moralism and aestheticism, a somewhat unnatural association, but in our country beauty coexists with the moral factor.

All these bivalences make up a spiritual *harmony*, with complexity, variation and dynamism: "The Romanian people never leave the harmonious complex, because they are healthy, balanced, classical, because they use culture for life and salvation, and not for exhibitions. For the people, philosophy is not an exercise in excess (see Noica), but an exercise in equalization, in harmonization (even if it is eclectic), in the capture of opposites in a golden net of wisdom" (Băncilă, 2015, p. 381).

Until 1958, said Băncilă, there was no philosopher who had made the most of Romanian transcendentalism and, equally, of our quiet, luminous mysticism; just as Romania did not have a serious religious philosophy, which Nae Ionescu would have created if he were still alive (and yet, today there exists a deep religious reflection of the theologian Nae Ionescu).[14]

Vasile Băncilă perceived the dissociation of ethnographic harmony in critical culture, a process that made possible the positivism of P. P. Negulescu, the Orthodoxy of Nae Ionescu, the cosmic personalism of Motru, the dogmatic knowledge and the cosmic transfiguration of Blaga.

Romanian ways: a raccourci. It is important to state what Vasile Băncilă's intention was. He was not hoping to get to the *essence of* the Romanian attitude (it would be a metaphysical peak too high to climb), but to some behavioural modes or meanings, in other words, to "Romanian *compliments* or *attributes*". He even aspires to a book with the title *Romanian modes*, an approach to the psychology of Romanians, "but also a voluntary critical limitation of the subject, accompanied by a kind of piety and artistic-philosophical melancholy towards the complexity of the subject" (Băncilă, 2015, p. 344). He extends the Romanian way even to our way of naming plants, which shows intimacy with nature, ontological piety or religiosity, delicacy or meekness.

From Romanian music, especially from folklore, the most representative and beautiful composition seems to be: *The lark*, "a folk symphony, a symphony of nature, *fluid, colourful, windy, delicate and pure* (of great spiritual tenacity)". Moreover, this melody conceals Romanian *cosmicism*, it is "a musical poem of existence in the living Cosmos, full of harmony, piety, novelty, ingenuity, freedom, order" (Băncilă, 2015, p. 389).

Romanians have specific names for plants (maybe even for animals), but it is a trait that is also found in other peoples, so invoking ethnicity in such a context seems slightly exaggerated. On the other hand, Vasile Băncilă's cultural-spiritual perception is distorted when he sees a *Romanian way* in, for example, Petrache Lupu from Maglavit (1935). We are well aware of the media campaign of the phenomenon generated by a personage who was considered, especially by the press, to be somewhere between a madman and a saint, appreciated by Carol II and Ion Antonescu, and cautiously received by the Church.

Vasile Băncilă found in Petrache Lupu a "nervous, elitist type, able to capture, to perceive effluvia and meanings that are non-existent for other people" (Băncilă, 2015, p. 355). More than that, he is a "simple peasant", as the King called him, but who "makes of himself the existential *centre* wherever he is: *he is the boss of the place!* "*He* has a "certainty of *tropisms*", he is "permanently *ingenuous*", "in the face of the world he prays (even improvises): he does not embarrass himself. He is like Gandhi"; above all, Petrache Lupu had "*the intuition of the man in front of him*: he knows when he has a special man in front of him", just as he had "something prophetic in him". In 1937 or 1939, in Brăila, on the banks of the Danube, he told people to face the East, from where he saw a great fire coming towards the country.

Among the Romanian modes, Băncilă does not forget to place the *Aromanians*, with such soul traits as: "energy, quick temperament, practicality, business and industrial spirit, politiciansm, sometimes business-like, opportunism, great talent for diplomacy (see: Șaguna), a romantic-mystical heroism and political realism, coupled with a long-term vision" (Băncilă, 2015, p. 358). But their great significance is "the struggle with destiny and destruction. They did not close themselves off, like the Basques, nor did they myelinate themselves with a national religion (in the Diaspora) like the Jews".

Nor does he forget the history and tragedy of the Aromanians, who in 1859 "were about a third of the population of Moldavia and Wallachia combined". A history that maintained them, thanks to transhumance, as long as the Ottoman Empire was present; later, all through the states that inherited them from the Turks, the Aromanians were crushed "like large or small boulders, or macerated".

A Romanian bivalence. The worksheets written by Băncilă after 1940 are, many of them, ideational sketches for later studies. Ideas are briefly specified; some syllogisms are made or some bibliographical references are given. He continued to make observations on the psychology of the Romanian people, as he had projects of differential ethnic psychology, as he had done for the spirit of the Transylvanians.

A finished text, conceived in 1964, "A Romanian Bivalence", takes up and develops the bipolar structure of the Romanian soul: on the one hand, communitarianism, on the other, individualism. In relation to the first dimension, he explores what the Romanian people mean by family community, village (social) community and ontological community.

We should not overlook the context of these notes. In 1962, our agriculture was entirely cooperativised, except for some hill and mountain areas where natural conditions did not allow such a transformation. Left without land and without the necessary implements to work in the fields, some peasants became agricultural labourers, others worked, more or less skilled, on building sites. The phenomenon of commuting was in full bloom, the exodus towards the cities was beginning. The structures of the Romanian village slowly began to deteriorate, the traditional mentality entered into a shadow, its values were gradually affected by superficiality, improvisation and kitsch.

Nothing else of this tragic scenario emerges in Băncilă's manuscript, apart from some vague connectors that might indicate a certain change: the Romanian family "still has", or the lack of children was "until recently", or "in the city it begins to disappear". For the rest, he meditates imperturbably on the presence and destiny of the Romanian soul, leaving us, by a kind of ricochet, to pick out the implicitness of certain ideas.

It is a patriarchal family ethos or mentality, the solidarity of three generations: grandparents, parents and grandchildren. In other words, o*ne big family*. Hence the sincere respect for elders, for older people, as well as kinship relations (by blood or by marriage) up to the tenth generation.

The important status of nephews (this is where Romanian nepotism originated) or first cousins, but also the status of a brother-in-law, godfather or godchild ("the root of the clientelistic phenomenon?"), all these were not unimportant for the mentality of the Romanian peasant.

In accordance with his own creed, Băncilă emphasizes the role of children in a family (he sees in them the first and most important *posterity*, more precious than *the work*). For peasants, "the *purpose of life was children* (the mentality of "this kinder bores me"! did not exist)"; and that's because once they were born, "*man gave up on himself*" (Băncilă, 2015, see pp. 265–266).

But no less significant was the village community, which began with the seemingly banal belief that the neighbour's fence should not be too high. Here Băncilă invokes the difference from the Saxon spirit of Transylvania, where isolation functioned through house-towns or wall-fences, forms by which people "seem to turn their backs on the village".

The need for public space or celebration is indicated by the way parties were organised at weddings and christenings. The poet George Coşbuc is quoted with "Zamfira's wedding", an event that would not have happened if it had been a "personal affair, with 2–3 pints of beer and schnapps". The village (not the commune!), says Băncilă, thus appears as an ontological centre, it is the world of the peasant, one who does not travel much, but concentrates the whole of *reality* in the space and time of the village community. The mentality of the city dweller, or more precisely of modern man, is situated at the antipode: his days are identical, "space is shanghaied", the spirit is degraded.

The unity of the village is given by blood, by various alliances or kinships, by the same celebrations or customs. The village is a fortress of spirit, a kind of uninsulated burgh, a hierarchically organised structure coagulated around the church (see the primary role of the priest).

But the Romanian village or peasant is part of an ontological community (about which Băncilă spoke in his notes on ontology). Peasants are in touch with the Cosmos, they have some intuition of astronomy, some knowledge of zoology and botany, they feel close to animals. The peasant's vision is Ptolemaic: the earth is the centre of the world, even the sky has a certain fixed position.

The Cosmos-Transcendent endosmosis is identified by a certain intimacy with God, which Orthodoxy preaches, and with heaven; but it is doubled by hieraticism and hierarchy: "*Discipline and freedom* at the same time: this is the cosmic, organic-cosmic, ontological vision of the Romanian peasant" (Băncilă, 2015, p. 268).

It is the structure in which they discover naturalism and Platonism, a family or that ontological community. From one end to the other – a splendid eulogy to the Romanian peasant. This is Băncilă's belief in the pantheism, monism and dualism specific to the ontological vision of the Romanian peasant, a conception that places "God at the top, like Plato's Idea of Ideas".

*

However, individualism is also part of the Romanian peasant's soul. Although biologically strong, the peasant has moments of falling, of neglect in various forms: "His business!", or "What do I care!" Or he refuses to associate, for example, to organise a choir, as in Transylvania or Banat (choirs, not *folk ensembles* as in Communism!). And this individualism, Băncilă believes, expresses the lyrical and satirical-didactic character of our folk poetry, unlike in other areas where the naked and sometimes cruel narrative dominates.

Băncilă does not tell us if some features are sporadic and what their weight is in the structure of the peasant soul, not to mention the fact that our fairy tales have a narrative plot, which does not lack any vital episodes. And the late emergence of the Romanian novel, as I pointed out elsewhere, is due to a not so simple causal nexus, proof that it was first developed in the Transylvanian area.

The approximations at the end of the manuscript, communitarianism and individualism, are not entirely convincing either: the Romanian peasant and especially the intellectual act in the spirit of social revolt, they are *critics*, but also suffer from metaphysical resignation. This is why "the peasant goes serenely to war", he is a brave soldier, only "he is not a man of revolution" (Băncilă, 2015, p. 269), he is not a revolutionary (! less so the Transylvanian).

In addition to this moral or social individualism, there is also a metaphysical one. Reality is accused of being irrational, absurd, with only one point of support: the individual, transformed into the centre, the absolute. The reasoning seems simple: the individual's renunciation of his own self in favour of the communitarian spirit, his martyrdom, could be futile, gratuitous, because it is possible to sacrifice "precisely what is real in favour of a fiction" (Băncilă, 2015, p. 323).

Such a way of thinking, according to Băncilă, is invalid, because we are dealing with an a-metaphysical individualism, which amounts to a bankruptcy of metaphysics (so does scepticism). It is precisely reality itself that is ignored and replaced by the individual. It would be different if individualism were to say that it is everything and that reality is an illusion or its own creation – which "is crazy".

*

I mentioned at the beginning of the paragraph the plan of a theme about transcendental Romanianism and empirical Romanianism. Băncilă was interested in the historical truth of how the real *Romanian nationalism* and, at the same time, "the idea of a Romanian mission" appeared. For this, we need to know what we are, what are the qualities and defects of the Romanians, their essences and their accidents. To which we must add the path, the *method* we follow in educating and fulfilling ourselves. This is precisely the relationship between the transcendental and the empirical, a conjunction that Băncilă wanted to explore more deeply.

He was attempting to fructify an idea of the philosophy of history in the German area, namely that a people "has a *deep*, I would say transcendental *soul*, and that its deeds, its culture are only something external and symbolic" (Băncilă, 2015, p. 356). He wanted to reach what is deep and, in a way, permanent in a human community, something close to the idea of the original phenomenon in Blaga or Goethe.

The same binomial – of the relationship between the transcendental and the empirical in the sphere of Romanianism – was the pretext for a reflection in May 1941. Should the Romanian space be saved biologically, through heredity and adaptation to the environment? The example is given of the allogeneic people who, having come here, married Romanian women, but because they had no descendants, their families died out. And the "more serious case is that of the *foreign blood that has entered the peasant's dough* [...], through the bailiffs who abused the peasants and the servants" (Băncilă, 2015, see pp. 323–324; my emphasis).

And the Slavs were, in a way, alien. In the first centuries after Jesus, they invaded Central and South-Eastern Europe, a successful invasion, says Băncilă. But the Slavs "were denationalized by the Romanians, Illyrians, Greeks, etc.". That Romanians will ever be "swallowed up by the Slavs"? It seems to him a morbid, even guilty or superficial psychology. And if such a phenomenon is to occur, it is necessary: "to *die fighting*. And to create according to your genius, until the last moment, as a flower near propinquity blossoms until it falls into the abyss".

With the invasion of the Russians, it was a different story; they were stopped by the Germans and by us, because the role of the Romanian nation is similar to the one it had 1000, 1500 years ago: "Great merit! First we absorbed the glorious poison like that coal that doctors give you to absorb toxins from the body; and now we simply refuse it".

It is clear that Băncilă was in the lineage of those who reflected on the psychology of the Romanian people, from Drăghicescu and Motru onwards, but also of those who wanted to build the *Romanian dimension of existence*, to use Mircea Vulcănescu's phrase, in particular Lucian Blaga. Besides, as well as the names already mentioned, he adds Nichifor Crainic, Camil Petrescu, Mihai Ralea (also received negatively), Luchian.

Mixtum compositum. These listed qualities of the Romanian are to be found in many authors. At one point, Băncilă proposes to include relevant quotations from foreign travellers in his approach, or makes references to Iorga and Pârvan, but also to the prose writer Pavel Dan. He only states ideas, without developing them, not even briefly; here are the titles of chapters (March 1940): upstartism (on which he meditates in three or four sentences in 1943); energetic personalism (Motru, registered trademark); politicianism (also Motru); the culture of the Pekingese (and their internationalism); Judaism; the great man; a new generation (about which Băncilă wrote in *Thought*, 1936); the *metecs* in Romanian culture; Westernism-Orientalism-autochthonism.

Other possible section titles also have some extensions. For example, the one on *inferiority complexes:*

- self-denigration (the distinction between pedagogical criticism and that which promotes the decline of a people);
- we are a small people and we cannot have a big mission (comparison with the elites); we cannot exclude such an inferiority complex – being part of a small people, which is why some (Noica, Bazil Munteanu, etc.) thought of exile (Noica, however, believed, as far as we know, the opposite); it invokes international prestige:

> Panait Istrati is superior to Sadoveanu, although not more talented,
> Ion Petrovici is known in Paris, but not Motru or Blaga; that is why
> the Transylvanian school exalts our Roman roots;

- we are geographically poorly situated; a small, poorly situated people, "where mountains meet head to head"; but we have rich soil, as well as other advantages: "great complexity, the confluence of East and West" (Băncilă, 2015, see pp. 307-309);

- we have lagged behind the West in civilization and culture; Romanian students are depressed when they arrive in the West; let's not forget one advantage: "we have not yet worn ourselves out", but what a pity, for "we are both primitive, backward, and old: one of the oldest peoples of Europe"; the influence of forms without fundament and the role of Romanian Orthodoxy (matters paraded in the interwar period – see Nae Ionescu, N. Crainic and *Thought*, Mircea Eliade's generation).

And other chapters designed in March 1940 also have novel touches: for example, the autochthonization of language; whoever avoids that language runs away from Romanianism; or whoever speaks badly does not love the Romanian nation – he gives as an example the way a Romanian sportsman expresses himself; or the need for a "clean intimate life", in other words: "Romanian language and non-sexuality"; the harmony between intimate life and public life.

The last chapter of the syllabus was about the *Romanian revolution*, not about the general idea of revolution but about its national character. At that time, in March 1940, Băncilă's thoughts were still on the revolution of the Romanian Right, which had been strangled in 1938 by the dictatorship of King Carol II (a footnote states: "and what followed afterwards was the 'whores' revolution'"). Băncilă wondered what the features of a future victorious Romanian revolution would have been at that historical moment.

*

A synoptic map of Romanian qualities (17, with many ramifications) and defects (32, also with various arteries) is traced in the notes of 22 and 23 August 1944 (Băncilă, 2015, see pp. 335–338). Among the qualities that were never formulated are: non-revenge (recalling Mircea Vulcănescu's exemplary attitude: "Do not avenge us!"), a talent for languages, something sickly (we tire quickly, scepticism of twilight, preventive or retreating scepticism; sceptical elegance), élan and power of improvisation (hence the *communal work* in Romanians, those who also write essays and journalism), we cannot be anti-Semitic (!), individual, not collective bravery.

Among the new defects: collective kleptomania, betrayal (in the many), betrayal (in the few; the psychology of "selling out"), licentiousness, lack of tragedy and moral drama, superficial eroticism, a mixture of childishness and senility (sad things for culture and the public spirit), rank boorishness, parvenitism, lack of political will, disunity, anthropological non-unification of an ethnic type (despite ethnic unity of soul and language), some fatalism, inertia.

*

Cognitively speaking, many of the existential reflections have, in Băncilă, the mark of *folk psychology* (*Völkerpsychologie*), as applied since W. Wundt, with its epistemological (detection of alleged psycho-sociological essences) and methodological (exclusive focus on the past) over-emphasis. Moreover, Băncilă reveals a series of impediments in deciphering Romanian psychology. First of all, it is difficult to determine what is related to the Romanian essence and what is related to the cultural state or to the degree of historical evolution. It is also difficult to determine what belongs to us and what comes from the influences of the Romanian area. Thirdly, there may be a cultural obstacle, because we do not have "a long tradition of culture, i.e., a long-standing written, critical culture", philosophers, poets, artists, theologians, etc., or creators who have created specific paradigms.

It would seem that we have a chance in ethnic psychology, where we can draw on the peasant; only that this apparently particular character also represents (like the woman) an international reality.

And yet, Băncilă believes that we can determine what is *ours* in culture by orienting ourselves according to its depth and duration (in history, says Fernand Braudel, *long durations* count, including in the history of a culture). And influence can be neglected when it has been assimilated and transformed into something organic.

Only empiricists and comparatists hold unilaterally to influence. Every feature of the Romanians cannot be superficially identified, claiming that they have it from this or that community, which would have once enriched us. By eliminating them one by one, one is surprised to find that nothing remains of the essence of the Romanian people (similar, says Băncilă, to one of Nastratin Hodja's pranks: when he boiled beans, he threw out of the pot, one by one, all the beans that came to the surface).

Romanianism: the specific difference. The specificity of a people, according to Băncilă, "is not so much each note in itself (which can also be in another people), but their *constellation* and their *coefficients*" (my emphasis). It is a truth stated differently, but eloquently and forcefully, by Blaga through the stylistic matrix of the culture and civilisation of a space; in fact, Băncilă's notes from 1943–1946 implicitly refer us to Blaga's thought, because these are the years when the philosopher Blaga assembles his essays in the three trilogies: of knowledge (1943), of culture (1944) and of values (1946). The Cosmological Trilogy remained an incomplete project, of which he only published *Divine Differentials* (1940).

The Romanian people (one species in one specimen) means, in the end, the history of the Romanians, with all that it has had congruent with the spirit of each era. It is precisely in relation to this spirit of the times that Băncilă, so to speak, depicts the syncretic hypostases of the *historical Romanian:*

- pre-Roman (Thracians, Dacians, Romans) or in search of (national) identity;

- the original Romanians (the Middle Ages and the founding of the Principalities) or Slavic septicaemia;

- the Voivodal Romanian or historical protuberance;

- Eastern Romanians (Vasile Lupu, Matei Basarab, Brîncoveanu, Şerban Cantacuzino, translation of the Bible from Greek);

- Romanian Fanariots or Fanariot eczema;

- Western Romanian or Latin insemination (second half of the nineteenth century) and

- the national Romanian or autochthonization (those who anticipated: Bălcescu, Kogălniceanu, Eminescu; those who initiated: Coşbuc, Al. Vlahuță and *Hearth*; those who realized: Iorga, Pârvan, Vâslan, Mehedinți, Nae Ionescu, *Thought, Word*).

There is often an emphasis on the autochthonization of our philosophy and written culture, along with Băncilă, Eminescu, Haşdeu, Blaga, Pârvan, Mehedinți, Motru, Nae Ionescu, Puşcariu, Iorga (with his revolt for the Romanian language – see the conferences of 12 and 13 March 1906).

Băncilă's criticism is not to be expected: "Who knew that a new revolutionarism was bestowed upon us: the worst, the Ivan and the Communist and 'beyondist', which have shaken many consciences. Lovinescu, Ibrăileanu, Ralea and the Communist types have spoiled much of the Romanian vocation" (Băncilă, 2015, p. 423). At the end of this historical typology, the thesis is advanced that: "the imperial thread, in us, was broken by barbarians and septicaemia, and the Voivodal thread, by the Turkish curtain; otherwise, we would be far away now" (Băncilă, 2015, see pp. 356–357).

And the Romanian destiny was shaped by two *synthetic myths: the* Latin myth and the Dacian myth, but without taking into account the patriotic, nationalistic exaltations that often inflate the historical discourse. A destiny that was also born from the privilege of Romanian miracles: our endurance over two millennia, the preservation of ethnic unity (thanks to folklore and religion, transhumance and the ecclesiastical books that circulated – Badea Cârțan[15] is a unique character, perhaps not only in our country) and the preservation of the Romanian soul, with its harmony, with "the ethics of our spirit, the serene-idyllic aspect, without the pessimism of Hindus, without the tragedies of presumptuous Westerners" (Băncilă, 2015, p. 360).

The Romanian spirit is antinomic. Thus, the bivalence of Romanian destiny has the status of an archetype for Vasile Băncilă's thought. He seems to return obsessively to it, identifying some polar features through the grid of what would be called today *cognitivism* or *cognitive philosophy*, aggregated with observations of popular psychology or psychology of peoples, with ideas of cultural anthropology. In 1942, he notes that Romanians have an antinomic nature, they have two *foci*, two antinomies (mentioned elsewhere) representing not an invalidity of reason, but "a creative factor in individuals and especially in peoples" (Băncilă, 2015, p. 327). Such a dual structure, he believes, is revealed to us by other spaces: the Germans manifest theorism and practicality, moralism and amoralism, metaphysicalism and are positive analysts of facts; the English: idealism and realism in morality, and the Jews: mystical transcendentalism and sensualism.

The essence of the Romanian soul is therefore made up of opposites, "every great, ultimate reality is antinomic" (Băncilă, 2015, p. 375), even if some Romanian traits do not have their antinomic symmetry (e.g., humanity, ethicism, aestheticism, lyricism, theorism; opposites can be found for some of them, therefore, I believe the idea is somewhat overrated).

In June 1945, Băncilă also meditated on an organic binomial when he detected, on the one hand, a double layer of knowledge (rationalism, lucidity, intellectualism and a broad, submissive, background mysticism), and, on the other hand, another double layer from the angle of moral structure (individualism of a social, not metaphysical nature, and, as a background, "a piety, an ontological piety" by which it fits into the real). At the same time, he reformulated an older thought: is it not possible that "every metaphysician, *insofar as he is a metaphysician*, is a mystic?" (Băncilă, 2015, p. 345).

Therefore, concludes Băncilă, antinomies are fruitful and it is good that they are also illustrated by the Romanian space. However, he differs from C. Rădulescu-Motru in the way he conceives them: the latter "links contradictions, variations to philosophical thought itself and to the individuality of thinkers", whereas for Băncilă antinomies depend on ethnicity (see Băncilă, 2015, p. 328; for his former teacher, "ethnic vocation is a modifying factor").

11.4 Destiny, individualism and cosmic focus

Static and dynamic romanticism. By September 1943, Băncilă proposed to write three studies; the titles of the first two are already known ("The Romanian bivalence", "Transcendental Romanianism and Empirical Romanianism"), but not the title of the third: "Static Romanianism and Dynamic Romanianism".

In the latter, he would like to discuss: the preservation of traditional ethnic psychology and its correction "in order to be able to *enter history*, in the modern age"; he refers, for example, to the problem of Orthodoxy, whether it should be either corrected or more deeply understood; or he refers to Motru, Iorga, Mehedinți, who were attempting a "correction of the ethnic"; but above all he refers to Blaga, with his theory of withdrawal from history and major culture, the philosopher from Lancrăm being "the least tendentious, the least ideological and propagandistic", even if, together with Nae Ionescu, he had made important contributions in this field (he also gives Professor Ionescu credit for having "valorised Orthodoxy").

He again sketches an antinomy: while Iorga proposes *work*, Nichifor Crainic asks for heroism, *activism*, so that man is no longer *under the weather*. For this, it was also important to believe what the young Constantin Noica said in an essay: "What is eternal and what is historical in Romanian culture" (see *Pages on the Romanian Subculture*, 1944).

The fundamental idea for Băncilă was the following: *change* is necessary if Romanians want to live in the modern age. There had been so much debate about the relationship between the West and the East, but the transformation had to be made not as Eugen Lovinescu or Pompiliu Eliade wanted,[16] but as Nae Ionescu thought, i.e., without revolutionarism, but rather by *overcoming* and *fulfilling*.

*

In January 1945, Băncilă returned to the Romanian bivalence, giving some details about the idea of destiny, individualism and cosmic focus. The destiny of the people is seen as Blagian: cultural creation. What is important, however, is the *entelechy* "towards which a people gravitates and which is virtual and somehow permanent in it" (Băncilă, 2015, p. 342). It was the Romanians who defended Europe from the Turks, Tartars and Slavs, even though they are a defensive people, like the Spanish.

Our individualism seems to him to be a combination in which were layered features imprinted by the Dacians, Slavs, Levantines, French, "the German influence being at the *peaks*", an individualism that was an obstacle to national unity. But there is also Romanian individualism in the way intellectuals, not all of them, relate to each other. They criticize each other, but none of them quotes much from what the other has written. For example, the philosopher P. P. Negulescu refers to minor authors and ignores Motru, but the latter does the same. Even Maiorescu did not attach much importance to Conta, Xenopol or Iorga. The political man of the *Youth*, P.P. Carp, did not forgive the critical Olympian for having formed the government in 1912–1913, seeing in Maiorescu a "man without character", after considering him his model.

*

Băncilă writes about the Romanian *outbreaks* as early as 1940, when he observes that anarchic individualism (elsewhere he speaks of anarchic personalism)[17] and the imitation of Western forms have left their mark on linguistic expression. He finds it strange that the pronouns *I* and *he* appear in verbal expressions such as "*I* think that..." or "*he* shows that... (instead of "shows that'" (Băncilă, 2015, p. 315; it's a labile syntax, not at all redundant).

If we are talking about the use of language, i.e., pragmatics, we must also remember Iorga's observation about the way Romanians greet each other, inevitably asking: "how are you?" In this connection, Băncilă's remarks are approximate: the interrogation, borrowed from the Romans, does not at all express the fact that Romanians are workers. It is not what you work on that the questioners want to know, but "how you still spend your time", "how you still lead your life" (Băncilă, 2015, see pp. 350–351). And the answer proves this, for it doesn't tell you what they are working on, but specifies: "I'm sitting" (it's one variant, I believe, of many virtual ones). The conclusion, which seems one-sided, was: "To sit is (in this sense), for Romanians, to do", that is: it is "*contemplation, leisure, living life*" (to sit becomes the infinitive of to do!). These are antinomic statements of a negative note, which bears the title: "Deficit of will in Romanians". This does not mean that, in other situations, these same Romanians have not shown activism, a firm will: see the life of shepherds, monasteries, wars, political acts or the sphere of science.

Băncilă comments on linguistic errors on other occasions. He refers, for example, to the lack of correct grammatical accord that some cultured Romanians do not make, saying "they" "is", a tendency explained by the subconscious presence of the singular collective pronoun (!); the same would happen in constructions such as "the waters is poisoned"; or when talking about the Voivode, "they went to Ţarigrad"; in the latter, there is not only "the idea of politeness, but also the intuition of a rich, *plural* subjective". "The Romanian," concluded Băncilă, "works with categorical subjects"; he is "a historical, social, worldly personalist, but a resigned and ontological crusader" (Băncilă, 2015, see pp. 360–361). Here Băncilă overplays his hand, perhaps knowingly: the insinuation of the subconscious is false when we are dealing with an absence of grammatical correctness, of a sense of language, and the example of the Voivode indeed expresses, almost exclusively, the idea of respect, of politeness, being, it has been said, a *plural of majesty.*

He is also interested in whether the notion of *man of humanity* exists in the lexicon of other peoples, as it is different from *humanity* or *menschheit. Man of humanity:* "Some humble peasants from the Danube have thus created an idea that does not exist in the cultured languages." (Băncilă, 2015, p. 364)

*

Let's go back to the outbreak idea. In June 1944, Băncilă noted some approximations about *cosmic focus in the Romanians;* first, he noted that monism is expressed in forms similar to ancient hylozoism, the soul being imagined as a kind of steam. In Transnistria, there is a belief that sacrifice or prayer "go to heaven on the vapour of alms or by the rhythmic movement of the hand" (the idea belongs to Gh. Pavelescu, an anthropologist from Sibiu).

Romanians have, at the same time, a pantheistic intuition or state of mind of this kind, because "the peasant feels at home in nature, *trusts it* and is not afraid of death" (Băncilă, 2015, p. 335). But the dualism generated by Christianity is not as probable; the Romanians are the most ancient Christian people, after the Greeks, and they show a faithful knowledge of the *Bible*, even if they have not read it (our folklore is a fruitful combination of ancient mythology and Christianity).

The cosmic focus also obsesses Băncilă in his note of January 1945, when he takes up again the ideas that structure our *cosmicism,* adding the idea of freedom (the Romanian adopts free will in the social, economic and political spheres, whereas in ontology he is determinist and fatalistic) and the idea of death ("Coşbuc: there is light in the grave: what a difference from the *horror of the Westerners' pit!*"). It is a reconciliation of the Romanians with the cosmos and a kind of cancellation of death: "...with the Cosmos treading upon death!". In fact, thanks to his faith, the Romanian peasant is not afraid of death, because, whatever happens, everything happens *in Divinity.* Even the idea of sin is obsolete, "for all is God and in him is neither death nor sin" (Băncilă, 2015, p. 344).

Here Băncilă finds the explanation for the ease with which the hero of the tragic poem "Miorița" dies; it is not fatalism, passivity or cowardice, but a superior active behaviour, with an ethic similar to Stoic activism. A double focus is suggested, like two lenses; on the one hand, a "harmonious, cultured type of great goodness" (lyricism on a cosmic background); on the other, "great creative conflict and diversity" – the ideal being the congruence between lyricism-philosophy, on the fabric of *cosmic discretion*.

About holiness and longing. Another binomial specific to Romanians is the *doina – carol* one; the first is melancholic and refers to melancholy in this world, the second refers, most of the time, to the transcendent; it is a "melancholy through the idea of the Christian heaven", it has some melancholy in it, but it is "serene, definitive" (Băncilă, 2015, p. 313).

In fact, what the idea of sanctity meant to Romanians is learned from a note made in April 1944, where Băncilă laconically characterizes what is and what is not holy for Romanians, distinguishing our mentality from that of the West or the East. He elaborates on this reflection on 12 February 1958, when he dwells again on holiness in Romanians. The Romanian people, says Băncilă, are *hagiophagous*. It makes many saints, even if, in the calendar, there are not many Romanian saints (until Calinic). The justification is profound, beyond the fact that our people are "discreet, unselfconscious, *non-political*" (Băncilă, 2015, p. 378).

The Romanian "does not torment the flesh, the body", shows regret for the body ("God's building") and is aware that there is enough suffering in the world. According to Romanians, "the saint must wear his body, naturally, as God gave it to him, and not force nature".

And when the Romanian addresses a saint, he considers this to be "something serious, virile", he does not do it with "bourgeois, artificial, comfortable, egotistical emotional minorisms" (as in the West); he is not, therefore, sweet and does not express himself in approximate eroticisms. The Romanian does this above all because he does not find in the saint "a problematic personality, with a lucid and complicated internal life and a spiritualist pride" (Băncilă, 2015, p. 334).

On the other hand, the saint is the one from whom miracles are demanded, even if the peasant believes that he belongs to the ranks of the peasants, of the common people; the relationship of the Romanian with the saint is antinomic: on the one hand, he imbues him with a slightly distant, major seriousness; on the other, he perceives him as a close friend, a natural friend.

The saint has something *human* in him (just as heroes are portrayed), he performs miracles; he is not the wizard or Prometheus, but through him, the Absolute expresses itself.

In brief: *"In holiness and saints, the Romanian people see the expression of the divinity of reality itself. Saints are only its trumpets, its flashes, like fires that sometimes come out of the ground"* (Băncilă, 2015, p. 379).

Here can be discovered, says Băncilă, the attitude of a patriarchal people, in which the natural and the supernatural are mixed; thus, it is significant how the Mother of God is imagined – "as the *mother* and as the begetter of God", far from the Western image of "*Madonna*, a beautiful mother, in whose arms the Saviour is more like a trinket somewhat foreign to her, a prestigious doll".

*

Băncilă was also trying to discover the ontological code of longing (Blaga himself had a paragraph on this subject in *The Mioritic space*, 1936). He starts from the premise that Romanians have a sense of measure, are balanced – as expressed in our art, politics, literature or morality. And since he was aiming for a duality, he uses lyricism as a polar term (Romanian literature is lyric-didactic), which, "placed in the mould of balance, of measure, gives a change"; such a change is nothing other than *longing*: "It's like a wisp of smoke, coming out of the combustion of lyricism into the furnace of equilibrium" (Băncilă, 2015, p. 329).

Longing is a special construct which, it seems, is not found in the lexicon of other peoples (Noica once proposed that this term be included in a UNESCO dictionary). In general, man has in him something nostalgic or bohemian, but such nostalgia is also, with us, more polite and disciplined. And yet, Băncilă believes he has found a counterpart of longing: in the Swedish word *loengtan*, for which he refers us to the preface of a book: *Le merveilleux voyage*, by Nils Holgersson.[18]

Traces of anarchic personalism. Another antinomy of the Romanian space: in spite of the fact that they prove, as a people, a "geographic, linguistic, soul unity", the Romanians, paradoxically, "quarrel among themselves, have anarchic personalism" (Băncilă, see pp. 324–326). On the other hand, Băncilă states that "Romanians despise Gypsies (see all Romanian folklore), yet there is a lot of "Gypsyism" in Romanian psychology: lack of method, improvisation, unpredictability, swearing, sensualism, lack of social spirit, etc.".

Contempt for Gypsies can have a *pedagogical purpose* if it means disowning what is Gypsy in these people, or it can be a consequence of: "Romanian aristocratic aestheticism; or Romanian parvenitism; or the basic moral health of the Romanian (a strait-laced village householder could only have contempt for Gypsies).

Or all of them?"

Over time, Băncilă's meditation on this ethnicity will be somewhat attenuated: "I pity them [the Gypsies], but they really spoil my appetite (they have spoiled some of Romanian musical folklore too)." (Băncilă, 2015, p. 411) The focus was on lute music, with Gypsy orchestras being sent across Romania's political borders. However, Băncilă also had in mind the multiplication of Gypsies, "like microbes or bacteria", so he naturally believed that their women should be allowed to have free abortions, otherwise our country risked becoming a Gypsy one ("There's a big problem here – it's tragic!").

It would be rash to think that this is laden with subterranean ideological or political overtones, but there is too much haste towards generalization on Băncilă's part (the accidental takes the place of the essential), not to mention the metaphorical over-emphasis of allusive meanings. Băncilă supposes that the depreciative meaning might come from the *slave* status that the Gypsies had in our country, a status that was inevitably despised.

Besides, Băncilă is no exception, since neither Iorga, Crainic, Motru or Drăghicescu would have adequately captured the particular, often constructing formulas that were too general, whereas Lucian Blaga or Nae Ionescu gave something special, as Băncilă himself says.

11.5 Romanian Mission

Some prejudices. Allusions to some inferiority complexes can be found in other entries, as well as in many notes on the Romanian mission, in which Băncilă feels challenged – and irritated – by various prejudices of our collective mentality. In March 1940, he says categorically: "Let's get it out of our heads that we're an unimportant people!" (Băncilă, 2015, p. 310)

And he recalls the words of Nae Ionescu in an article entitled "*The Second Nation of Europe*" (*Word*, 1938, April 9), where he says that, despite the fact that we are a nation of 20 million inhabitants, we still have the humble reflexes typical of a small Romania. Or Gh. Brătianu, in a conference held at Dalles (March 1940), invoked the opinion of a foreigner, who wondered that Romanians still have a *Montenegrin* conscience.

Băncilă's reply is prompt: "Come on! We're not a small country anymore." but it's strange that we show either "gratuitous hyperbolic confidence or humility"; we show "*servility* to strangers": "we bow before anything *made* abroad". The phenomenon was evident in the capital, where the allogeneic dictated: "Oh, *this international of heitmatologists!*"[19] (Băncilă, 2015, p. 311; my emphasis)

It was the same with self-denigration. Those who went to Bulgaria, Serbia or Albania, on their return said in unison that Romania was 40–60 years behind them. They have roads, dairy industry, farms, there is no stealing, there is honesty. Romanians, on the other hand, are: "lazy, thieving and lacking method", even if they are intelligent, as the Bulgarians think we are. Băncilă was astonished to hear even Victor Rădulescu-Pogoneanu[20] or Simion Mehedinți criticising us:[21] "You wonder: how can they sleep peacefully afterwards? But they have no problem, they sleep and digest peacefully."

Therefore, an essential shortcoming of ours, also noted by C. Rădulescu-Motru, is the absence of a method. The Romanian oscillates between being complex and being obliterated: "Either he is interesting, like a jinx between two continents, or he is like an obliterated coin." (Băncilă, 2015, see pp. 313–314) And in our geographical situation the greater misfortune is indicated, even if there may also be advantages arising from this fact: the possibility of a balancing policy, but also a certain psychological complexity, the latter evident in the stylistic mark of folklore. And our geographical position meant that in 1940 Romania was surrounded by states with imperialist tendencies (Russia, Germany). Our misfortune, says Băncilă, is to "come into the world when Europe is overpopulated with people and civilization".

*

If we the Romanian mission is invoked, various stupid formulas are rejected out of hand: that, intellectually speaking, the *cell* of the Romanian does not resist, as Maiorescu believed; or "slowly, the nation is melting"; or that, voluntarily, the Romanian people is tired of two millennia of history, which has been against it; or that, from a spiritual point of view, it is sceptical, irreligious; finally, from a moral point of view, it is individualistic, boorish. Băncilă is outraged at the attitude of some who see Romanians as individuals "full of vices, wretched servitudes, loaded inheritances, slave psychology" (Băncilă, 2015, p. 320).

It admits some of them, but does not develop a critique of them. It even aims to combat what "Ralea, Suchianu (the sluts) say. They look in the mirror and say what they see". He refers to Camil Petrescu, *Theses and... prostheses*, and to Mircea Eliade's article "Ceasing to be a Romanian", as he (positively) reminds us of Nae Ionescu and P. Marcu-Balş (alias Petre Pandrea), regarding the religiosity of the Romanian.

This also seems wrong to him: "Let the Germans come and discipline us!" On the one hand, there is a surface and temporary phenomenon: you can only be disciplined in the presence of the stranger; on the other hand, the strangers themselves become corrupt: "the Germans who asked for a ticket in 1918, at Cazașu; or the French in Moldavia, 1917–1918; or how, after a while, even the Germans from Burdujeni no longer asked for a train ticket after 1918, but asked for money" (Băncilă, 2015, p. 316). And something else happens: the new skills can quickly be suspended after the foreigner leaves, and the old habits return (the example of the people of Transylvania and Bukovina is given, but after 1918).

Another bias that Romanians believe will save them: the remedy brought by the time factor in a few years; or, on the contrary: "even in 100–200 years we won't be nice".

And all our improvement as a nation came from education or organization, except that Nicolae Iorga blamed the dysfunctionality of the system. The reality, says Băncilă, was somewhat different: "the boss has to do everything", because there are no trustworthy people: "You have to follow the tail of every firefly! Whereas in Germany, if the boss presses the button, everything is executed" (Băncilă, 2015, p. 322).

If we speak of our forms of salvation, perhaps the most important of them is monarchism, by which we can annihilate anarchic personalism. Through such a structure, we are, says Băncilă, unique in the South-East Europe, even if the Romanian people are personalistic, as the struggle for political power has proved.

However, he criticises the 1848 idea of a foreign ruler. The ruler has a dual nature for the Romanians: half god, half man, and the Transylvanians confirmed a great faith in the emperor, even though this belief was speculated. And the attitude of Carol II, a king who enjoyed the support of intellectuals (Blaga, Nae Ionescu, N. Crainic), was also an abuse of our idealistic convictions.

Băncilă makes an analogy between the kings and "des demi-dieux", the political leaders of the Homeric Greeks, but their background of divinity is different: it is not "the capricious, almost morally lawless, godlike divine", but "the Christian, moral, ontological, luminous, necessary, universal divine". In other words, the Ruler of the Romanian space: "was the metaphysical-historical *Dominus*, a kind of political vicar of God and Christian hero, a wonderful outlaw, a face of virile light, finally: the Voivode!" (Băncilă, 2015, see pp. 363–364).

The Romanians were also saved by Orthodoxy, which would not have happened if they had been Catholics or Protestants. Romania would not have been able to take refuge in the transcendent, despite a Western discipline or personal conscience, or even anarchy. It is true that Blaga spoke of retreating from history in the medieval period, a strategy that was not at all fruitful for the Romanians; for Băncilă, it was "a defensive means of salvation". It was the Romanians' religiosity that made them hope for an immanent justice, a "metaphysical heaven".

The resistance of Romanianism also came from the much-discussed patience and hope, our basic, organic, natural traits: "And the Romanian says to himself: *zam zi avăr*, but not demonically, presumptuously or sceptically, like the Jew, but because the anonymous contemplation of the world has taught him that all phenomenality passes..." (Băncilă, 2015, p. 351)

Patience and hope can be based on a kind of melancholic optimism in Romanians: they believe more in *metaphysical justice* than in concrete-historical *justice*. A scepticism that turns into metaphysical dogmatism, into metaphysical faith: "And the greater the historical injustice, the more the Romanian takes refuge in metaphysical justice and *sublimates* it" (Băncilă, 2015, p. 357). This may also be the reason why the Romanian soul has a kind of drainage, a draining of hostile energy, which makes the Romanian serene.

*

In the collective mind of Romanians, there are also implicit forms of salvation: the phrase "this too shall pass", by which the ephemerality of any political regime is admitted, however mystical it may be; "satirical humour", a substitute for revolutionaryism, a means of persiflage against the *invaders*, the oppressors (Băncilă refers, cryptically, to the multitude of jokes made at the expense of King Carol II[22] – "two sticks", Ion Antonescu – "the red dog" or the totalitarian regime – "Beelzebub"); "conformity or historical disguise", positive masks which also include apomorphisms: enthusiastic licentiousness and dryness, opportunistic and frivolous attitudes; therapy through "forgetting and forgiveness", hypostases that express the Romanian soul – without hatred, devoid of rancour, not at all prone to revenge (the Transylvanian, says Băncilă, "remembers", even if not much); finally, the prudence of the Romanian, which makes him avoid extremism, fanaticism.

Apart from some historically justified emphases, Băncilă judged the allogenic elements in a balanced way. Made up of foreigners, the *superimposed layer of* which Eminescu spoke was a generator of evil; but, to be fair, a society or a people "has, up to a point, the leadership it deserves"; and, in our country, the ruling class included "sons of peasants, many shepherds, politicians with 100% Romanian blood" (Băncilă, 2015, p. 317); so that innumerable features or shortcomings of the peasant spirit were refined and expressed in the psychology characteristic of the ruling structure.

Osmotic knowledge: supporting points. It isn't possible to speak of the Romanian mission if the fate of the Romanian peasant is not accounted for: his economic and cultural uplift. Only, according to one prejudice, the peasants may be good, but the rulers are incompetent, even though "even the peasants give faults to the ruling class: see how the former peasants behave when they reach the top" (Băncilă, 2015, p. 322). Equally necessary, however, was the development of a native bourgeoisie, a theme that would have made it easier for Băncilă to "move on to the chapter on the Jews" (Feb 1941).

If the notes on the Transylvanian spirit were of differential ethnic psychology, those on the Romanian existence are mainly on the psychology of the Romanian in general, with emphasis on the structure of the peasant. Speaking of *osmotic knowledge*, for example, he also starts from the peasant state, from the peasant (he extends the thesis to the level of any peasant –!), from the fact that he is at peace with life, fate, nature. The Romanian peasant is "ontological, communitarian", he is full of vitality, the world in which he lives and which he feels with his whole being is one in which there is an order, a world with a clear purpose which offers him the solution to "*ontological framing*". Here is an empirical datum, to which, for his metaphysics, Băncilă adds an aprioric factor: the datum of consciousness (these are the "two spiritual soles" specific to his metaphysics).

And there is another dimension of the peasant, one that should not be eluded: his devotion when it comes to defending the Romanian nation. He went to war in 1877 without being called up, and in 1939 the military courts were full of peasants whom the officers could hardly persuade to go home, because there was no mobilization yet; the same thing happened in Crimea, where most Romanian soldiers were peasants.

From the equation of such osmotic knowledge, *the intellectual* is not excluded, even if he is not as vital as the peasant and lacks the awareness of a critical communitarianism. Băncilă points the way for the intellectual to acquire in his soul a kind of metaphysical luminosity, a sufficient reason in spiritual terms.

The structure of the Romanian includes *etatism*, a trait with a harmful charge. The Romanian wants to occupy positions in the state, and this is because he lacks the spirit of initiative, he is interested in a modest but secure income, if possible guaranteed. And he has two or three other traits in this respect: he is a shepherd, he despises business and is, paradoxically, Asiatic; that is, he has "the mentality of *the enemy state*" (Băncilă, 2015, p. 321), which is hostile to society (quoting a line by the writer N. Crevedia: "It is not a sin to steal from the thieving state!") Being part of the state, even "the last Romanian *scribbler* treats you badly, despises you", which induces hostility in his relationship with his fellow men.

Relationship with the stranger. Băncilă's diatribe returns to the relationship between Romanians and foreigners. Foreigners have been denationalised over the years, they feel comfortable in our country, because "they no longer have to be serious and morose. They can be natural, party animals, banterers, comfortable, inconsistent, erotic, slightly sceptical" (Băncilă, 2015, p. 320). Such a Romanian attitude, favourable to the arrival of foreigners, is called by Băncilă *sympathetic,* amiable, epicurean, sceptical sectarianism, a *factor of... denationalisation* (with the French, the Hungarians or the Russians, things are exactly the opposite).

This is not a favourable factor for creating a major culture. Moreover, as a nation, Băncilă doubts our major sense, drawing a somewhat hasty conclusion: because we, he says, have the diminutive *the little Romanian,* a lexical construction that might not be found in Germans, French, English or Russian (however, that Germans have a kind of diminutive, *der deutsche Michel,* and the French have *le petit français,* phrases with a depreciative semantic value).

According to the term has the meaning of "*sympathetic Romanian*" (Scriban, 1939, p. 1136), while others use it to express either feelings of annoyance (see also the poem "The little Romanian") or – in the jargon of the day – accents of some contempt. And in the county of Sălaj there is, today, a commune with the name "Little Romanians" (documented in 1310). Lexically speaking, the meaning of the term was overrated by Băncilă, as it is not the facade of any characterological record.

Negative ethnic personalism. In August 1977, Băncilă countered that the ideas of *sense* and *cosmicism* expresses our philosophical Hellenism and Byzantinism. Romania has particularly valued social and political law, while the Hellenes have prevailed on cosmic and metaphysical law. With the sense of *moral-cosmo-metaphysical reason,* taken from the Christian vision of Byzantium, the idea of sense (from *nomos*) seems to be singular and specific to the Romanian space.

Vasile Băncilă, on the other hand, observed a gap between the mission of the Romanians and the spirit of the historical time. Serious phenomena were occurring, especially when the ethnic was diminished, dissolved by technical progress: "Ethnic personalities (nations, peoples) are today washed away by modern civilisation." (Băncilă, 2015, p. 322)

Conclusion: Romanians seem to have had a childhood that has been prolonged, because they should have grown up long ago. It was time, says Băncilă, for Romanians to really create their own state (hence *our polity*), and this precisely "when the time came for the big empires" (he doesn't tell us which rapacious states he is referring to).

He repeats, from time to time, the inventory of defects and qualities found in Romanians. He also adds new ones, as he does in a 1941 reflection; faults: "inability to keep secrets, luxury, intrigue, sycophancy, diphonia, trust in strangers, alcoholism, swearing, blasphemy, lack of strong religiosity", traits which, the thinker wonders, are somehow related to primitive populations! Weak religious faith does not facilitate the emergence of *sects*; perhaps the lack of a vigorous culture would, through ignorance, fertilize their existence.

And new qualities: "aesthetic sense, lively intelligence, open-mindedness, hospitality, sense of measure, kindness, humanity, talent for disguise in the face of history, power of hope, serenity in the face of death, love of the earth, a certain naivety, credulity, which goes hand in hand with scepticism, distrust" (Băncilă, 2015, p. 325).

To the inventory of faults (or a kind of skilful "adaptation to the environment"?) I have made so far, I will add again the *opportunism* of some personalities, a trait that Vasile Băncilă noticed in C. Rădulescu-Motru, Victor Eftimiu or Mihai Ralea: Germanophiles in 1916–1918, Anglophiles by 1942. Or a profoundly anti-social tolerance: "The citizen is sick in Romania...", he is a "good-hearted individualist", but does not attach any importance to the social interest.

Don't forget, among the negative Romanian traits, *arrivism* (is it only Romanian!). What are the ways in which the exercise of *parvenus* is carried out in our country? For this, the Romanian, and not just any Romanian, joins Freemasonry or Communism; practices an abject politicism; rummages through his biography to find a Jewish ancestor, if he does not have the option of marrying a Jewess (marriage for the sake of *relationships* is a goal); or "sends his wife to sleep with potentates, so they can make him a minister or something else" (Băncilă, 2015, p. 352); or is capable of betraying God, also in order to get ahead. The motto of the Romanian upstart is in the altered meaning of the French expression: "*Paris vaut bien une messe*" ("Paris is well worth a Mass"), words attributed to Herrich IV, who, in order to gain the throne of France (1593), switched from Protestantism to Catholicism.

*

In 1943, Băncilă recomposes and expands another Romanian mission plan, in three parts. In the first, the emphasis is on the idea of ethnic destiny and the originality of culture; in the second part, some new ideas: *a people on the edge of the Slavic invasion* and a function that Romania had in Europe: to be against Bolshevism. But here too he revives old ideas and sets some methodological milestones: the psychology of the Romanian people situated between social, historical and ethnic essence.

The last part of the plan is reserved for applications, but without telling us what they would be, he only makes some clarifications: the demarcation between Levantines, Westernism and modern individualism is risky; he then wonders whether ethnic creation is growing old and whether better conditions should not be created: he refers to Eminescu, Blaga ("the ethnic works unconsciously") and Nae Ionescu (he too was "against Brownism").

As he goes deeper into the Romanian nature, Băncilă discovers other habits. The Romanian ego is in an unstable balance, "as if it were not bounded by a *psychological tegument*": "now it is compressed to the point of an ethics of decency (or humility), now it expands pathologically" and takes revenge on the past (Băncilă, 2015, p. 374; the example of those who become ministers is given). Could it be the structure of that ethnographic self?

At the same time, the folds of a negative personalism are revealed to him, through two national defects: ethnic masochism and mutual envy. While in the English individualism, the individual wants to live for himself (liberal attitude), rejecting the favours of the state or the collective, in the Romanians things are exactly the opposite: the state, the nation and everyone else should take care of each individual Romanian. An attitude that is not at all calm, but aggressive: "And if it doesn't, I'm kicking the can down the road! I mock the nation, I mock the world, and I stand by, lest someone else rise above me." (Băncilă, 2015, p. 375)

The anarchic personalism, always reiterated, should not be exaggerated; it is also found in other peoples, even if it is a bit more pronounced in Romanians. In our case, Romania has a certain infantilism because it is a young nation, the social and cultural environment puts pressure on the individual, the man of culture *goes mad*, and the Romanian, as I have shown, kicks the can down the road.

Opaque to Heidegger. The question has been asked, not only rhetorically and not just once, whether Vasile Băncilă's meditations on Romanian existence or *being* can be related, even sequentially, to Heidegger's metaphysical discourse in *Being and Time* (1927). There are only faint signs in the philosopher's notes that he had read the German thinker, whose spiritual destiny was often intertwined with that of Romanian intellectuals who had listened to his lectures at the University of Freiburg, or who were, for a time, his doctoral students (Dumitru Cristian Amzăr, Nicolae Balcă, Walter Biemel, Virgil Bogdan, Alexandru Dragomir). Heidegger was well received in Romania and even translated in fragments during the interwar period (Walter Biemel and Alexandru Dragomir translated, in the fifth decade of the twentieth century, *What is metaphysics*, a text that appeared in the magazine *Notebooks of longing* of the Romanian diaspora).

Vasile Băncilă's reaction is categorical and partisan: "In Romania, a philosophy like Heidegger's etc. could never have appeared." (Băncilă, 2015, see pp. 372–373) I would not insist on this statement, but I believe that the thinker Băncilă superficially expunges the fundamental Heideggerian ontology, which meant, particularly through *Sein und Zeit* but also through *Kant and the Problem of Metaphysics* (1929), a break with ontological thought since Plato. The German philosopher resignified the question of being. Man, in Heidegger's view, has the certainty of an inexorable death.

However, Băncilă reduced most of the mechanism of Heidegger's existentialist thought to that *Sein-zum-Tode*, translated by him as "the road to death", with which he identified human life. In Romania, he says, there is no such thing as in Western individualism. He does not find the desperate pathos of existentialism in Romania, because: "Romanians have osmosis with ontological reality and are well trapped in ontic, cosmic alveoli. For Romanians, ontic reality is not the *studina*[23] of man, but it is *light. The world is lumen.*" (Băncilă, 2015, p. 372)

If Băncilă had had the patience to read Heidegger in depth, but especially had he had access to the original texts, he would have found many and increasing confluences between two apparently different views of being. Alongside *Being and Time* (and also *Time and Being*), texts such as Letter on "Humanism" (1946) and Phenomenology and Theology (1927) would have shed some light on the problem of the transcendent, the sacred, "Christhood", the positivism of theology, the way Heidegger thought of man as "shepherd of being", the relationship between being and God, but also the role of language; language being, as Hölderlin says, when analysed by the German philosopher, "the most dangerous of things" (Heidegger, 1982, see pp. 192–266).

*

The Christian thinker Băncilă acknowledges that the true Romanian is not afraid of death, because he has the feeling of being in brotherhood with the cosmos, or that he is part of an ontological community. After all, does this not mean that life, for the Romanian, can (also) be a *road to death*! It is true that, for Băncilă's ethnic-spiritualist metaphysics, life represents "the road *to the glorification of the ontic Absolute* and the *journey towards the last great meaning, towards the confluence with the Absolute* (this is death for the Romanian!)" (Băncilă, 2015, p. 373).

It should be clear by now how Băncilă neutrally quoted the Heideggerian *Dasein* as an equivalent of *being* or *beingness*, but he did not have the reservations that he later formulated as an undifferentiated block towards existentialism (Heidegger does not mean Sartre, nor vice versa). Unwittingly, through his reflections on Romanian existence, on a spiritualist ontology, Băncilă is part of the interwar Romanian existentialism, a Christian, ethnic-spiritualist existentialism.

Like Heidegger in the German space, he also wonders about the meaning of (Romanian) existence, somehow fallen into oblivion or ignorance. Băncilă also speaks, in a way, of the *authenticity* of the Romanian, the one who is part of an ontological community and whom he wants to remove from the state of untruth, of *inauthenticity*. The authenticity of being has, moreover, been a concern of philosophers since antiquity. Parmenides wondered whether "it is the same to think as to be". It is the intuition of a supposed identity that has challenged, over time, much of the history of universal philosophy.

Beyond some uncertainties, inadequacies or hesitations, one thing is certain: *temporality* remains, even for Băncilă, the horizon of his syllogisms about the *Romanian dimension of existence*, to mention again Mircea Vulcănescu. The Romanian is always perceived, as Băncilă himself says, in endosmosis with the *ontic alveoli*, in the horizon of time (he is a wanderer in time, as he says) and of space (where he is autochthonous), that is to say: of the *land he inhabits*. It is precisely by existing in such a framework that the Romanian has "ontological confidence" in the world, a world in which he seeks and finds his place. And *"the journey towards the last great meaning, towards the confluence with the Absolute"* means the beginning of eternity, where time is suspended, because everything being will be an uninterrupted day. The threshold of salvation is thus reached (Băncilă knew, at least from Nae Ionescu, what the relationship between Faust and Mephisto meant).

The truces of history. In a note of 30 April 1952, thinking of the duality that controls the psychology of the Romanians, Băncilă invokes, above all, the *need for celebration*, events of this kind being *"trêves de l'histoire"*, i.e. truces of history, through which time, generously, gives space the opportunity to display its beauty. With the celebrations, history is annulled and the reign of the transcendent is established, time is somewhat bracketed, just as the Greeks established limits, and this in order to tame or overcome the infinite.

Through our organic Christianity, time or long duration indicates that life is mostly pain (Schopenhauerian mark), as it is history in motion, flowing; while space accustoms Romanians to the idea of the existence of Paradise. So it is time, not space, that is most painful. The destiny of Romanians, observes Băncilă, "is a discreet lament about the victimisation of time, of history, and a *naive puzzlement* that history is bad, because the Romanian sees that life could be beautiful, because space is wonderful".

A Heracliteism specific to the Romanian space is thus identified (because God is eternal), not of a metaphysical nature but of a historical, temporal one. A historical *panta rhei*, a sense of the ephemerality of worldly existence. This is where the spirit of improvisation, the lack of the monumental, the skill in miniature art, the privilege of *carpe diem* (live the moment! "Romanian eudemonism"), or the spirit of "contemplation of essences" ("Romanian asceticism") are all sufficient.

Băncilă also often speaks of *Romanian* materialism, a deeper one, beyond the surface, specific to the allogenous propaganda or *to the country's intelligentsia*. While serious materialism is that of the Romanian who "sees in nature, in matter, something profoundly quasi-mystical, a principle of life, almost a *Logos*" (Băncilă, 2015, p. 408). It's an intuition that, in the end, is no longer materialism, but something else.

*

The Romanian has a melancholic nature, which is not a minor trait, because it is "*a spiritual result of metaphysics* and a supreme grace of the Romanian: (constitutional) sadness, but against a background of (ethical) optimism"; being melancholic, he "can be neither tragic nor *drunk-optimistic*", a solution to the way historical evil relates to the beauty of the world. Here, in melancholy, we again find an antinomic construction: positive space and negative time, one that gives unity to the Romanian soul. Those who create materialism, says Băncilă, only value space, which is spiritually charged. The reality is different: "Romanians have neither the telluric materialism, nor the exaggerated mysticism of the Polish or even Lutheran type. The Romanian has geometry, discretion, grace." (Băncilă, 2015, p. 403)

Romanian melancholy is an important semantic core for the philosophy of our space and time. Suggestive, in this sense, is "Miorița", a creation which, beyond its symbolism, explains Romanian psychology, "exalts the beauty and joie de vivre of the Romanian space, but laments the pain of Romanian time (history)" (Băncilă, 2015, see pp. 405–406); Romanians have found an ingenious way to resolve the space-time contradiction: the first is optimistic, the other pessimistic. And between them "a mutual translation, a rapprochement, a spiritual intimation has taken place, and a sublime and discreet synthesis has resulted, in which optimism includes pessimistic nuances and pessimism, optimistic nuances, all in a fusion of great and complex fluidity".

The fusion of space-time gave rise to something essential, a *Weltanschauung*, a worldview whose virtual alternatives would have been twofold: either categorical optimism or pessimism, or an eclectic, dual variant; one or the other. The optimal hypothesis, however, was that specific synthesis. The Romanians experienced both time and space, the latter likened by the Christian Băncilă to the Garden of the Mother of God. And in terms of content, *the* Romanian *Weltanschauung* "was formed by the Latinization and Christianization of the Dacians, with some later penetrations of Byzantine metaphysics (and with some Slavic emollients, and some Turkish and Hungarian splinters in the language)" (Băncilă, 2015, p. 427).

It is essential, however, that the tragic is missing in the Romanians (as well as political extremism), as the key of our space could not produce such a thing (subjective assumptions are debatable, of course). Even the tragedy of Vasile Pârvan "is disciplined by the classics themselves, has nothing of the likes of Sartre, Heidegger, Camus, Kafka, Beckett – and other denationalised or disaffected talent" (Băncilă, 2015, p. 412; a note with a hint of rancour).

*

Băncilă's notes are often intensely expressive, sometimes even unintentionally so as well as sarcastic. The Romanian melancholy gives him a lot of semantic energy, especially when he thinks about the organic specificity of the space: the Danube is a kind of foundation, the *cosmic sole*, the Carpathians represent the *side*, the rivers – *the poems*, the plains – *the lungs*, and the hills mean *congratulations or smiles*.

Emphasizing his autochthonous style and thus exaggerating somewhat, it seems to Băncilă that the Romanian space has its own self and that nowhere else in the world is it so well-organized that it resembles a breathing being (November 1971, Băncilă, 2015, see p. 406). Băncilă sees here the reason why *Dacia's being* would have imposed itself even from antiquity.

The Romanian space is so wonderful that our geography is superior to the art that wants to express its greatness. Life beats art, as a slogan would say. Even Grigorescu's painting[24] does not achieve such an artistic performance. Perhaps in literature or music the Bărăgan (Odobescu) could be sublimated differently, or the Brăila Lake (Panait Istrati), or the sea (Eminescu). And the poet Goga, in some of his verses, wonderfully captured *the opposition* between "the beauty and euphoria given by the specific Romanian (Mioritic) character, but [also] the grief given by the history through which we have passed" (Băncilă, 2015, p. 409).

Therefore, Romanian melancholy is also an antinomic structure: "Good country, bad haggling..." (Sept. 1974, Băncilă, 2015, p. 413). Romania has been, so many times, in the path of all evils, like the apple on the side of the road: barbarian invasions, *those on the other side*, the Communists, the Gypsies, the transactions between the potentates of Europe (Napoleon and the Tsar, Churchill and Stalin), the Turks who separated us from Latinity and the Western world, the evil and fanatical Boyarism, the *dynastic* landlords. Romania's destiny, concluded Băncilă, is "a *resigned interrogation*. An affective lucidity, a luminous affectivity" (Băncilă, 2015, p. 413).

11.6 The unity of "a collective martyrdom"

A history of the Voivodeship. Perhaps in Eminescu there is a higher, more refined and more passionate eulogy of the Romanian peasant, of the Romanian people, than that of Vasile Băncilă. For him, our people: "has been, through the ages, and almost since its formation, like a tree laden with caterpillars. And yet all the rows of caterpillars have died, and our people live"; and it does so "as a collective martyr, permanently crucified. History, for us, has been a cross with a thousand arms and on each, a crucifixion stake.

But also with a thousand rays of light between them" (Băncilă, 2015, p. 403).

A tense area, not once permeated by masochism and arrivism, in which Penes the Turkey remained a platoon leader all his life, instead of being made a general ("This is what the Communists would have done", Băncilă, 2015, p. 402). A destiny unfolding between two columns: Trajan's Column and Brâncuși's Infinite Column[25], in which the former categorically consecrates a past and a present while the latter opens the way to the future, or, as he noted in the last months of his life, one is the *infinity of the past*, the other the *infinity of the future*.

In the work of art of the genius from Hobița Gorjului, Băncilă saw a kind of metaphysical rocket, one that has infinitely many steps, an organic link between the world of the empirical and that of the absolute, between the sensitive and the Transcendent. Through Brâncuși, the Romanians "gained the leverage to heaven" (Băncilă, 2015, p. 405), and through his ethnic vision, he became, alongside Eminescu, the greatest *Romanian*, and at the same time, an *universal spirit.*

*

Among Vasile Băncilă's notes, there are a few that can be coagulated under a view of the history of Romanians, as he himself noted in September 1954, a *Voivodal history*, according to the formulation of December 1964 or of 18 October 1965. He even wanted to write books with this title. He makes extremely interesting historical judgements and assumptions. He considers, for example, that Emperor Aurelian did the wrong thing when he withdrew the administration from Dacia Felix, particularly the political elements of the society. Some Roman political forms were retained, it is true, but it would have been different if they had remained in place.

At the same time, he notes the vitality of the Romanian nation and the defensive political instinct it had in the Middle Ages, when it *went from history to prehistory* (that was when the "thousand-year *septicaemia*" occurred: Băncilă, 2015, p. 365). He notes that our political element ran from the mountains to the highlands and that a union between Wallachia and Moldova would have created a very strong country, one that would have stood up well to its neighbours and "would have grown larger with time" (Băncilă, 2015, p. 368).

It is a historical fatality that developed in the three countries: Wallachia, Moldavia, Transylvania, a historical state through which subterranean strong links were formed thanks to religion, folklore and transhumance. The Romanians, says Băncilă, confirm a not negligible psychological unity, even if, anthropologically speaking, they are relatively different. Moreover, they have fought "not only with arms, but also with spirit, to defend themselves against the Röslerian theory, as far as the nation is concerned, and against the Calvinist and Papist attacks, as far as faith, religion, is concerned" (Băncilă, 2015, p. 369).

A year later, in April 1955, Băncilă identified, at that historical moment, the presence of a *feeling of agony* (which was lacking among the peasants), most of which was felt by the Bessarabians. A historical restlessness not found, in its defeatist-spectacular form, in the Germans, Russians or Jews, peoples who did not reach a state of despair when they went through difficult times.

Thus, besides many qualities, Băncilă noted not only the shady face of the Romanians or reasons for division, but also harmonious bonds between them. He is attentive to what the unification of the Romanian people meant over the centuries, as it was achieved through transhumance or rafting, through the great trade routes that crossed the Romanian principalities, through churches and ritual or prayer books, through preachers, through the movement of human groups from one part to another (small colonies, such as that of the Transylvanians settled in the Bărăgan), through the so-called *wanderings*.

Băncilă also observed a somewhat unusual feature, citing the book of a German (Ernst Gamillscheg, *Romania Germanica*, 3 vols., 1934–1936), namely that the Romanian language functioned as an international language for the Slavs in our principalities, just as the Germans in the Transylvanian area did with the Romanian language; moreover, the Romanian language also had the status of an international idiom for the Balkan Peninsula.

This was the starting point of Băncilă's thought in November 1953, when he assumed that this international status, albeit ephemeral, of the Romanian language was due to a kind of *logicism*, clarity and grace that our idiom possesses, traits that coexist with a "metaphysical intuitionism, with a subtle ontological skill" (Băncilă, 2015, p. 364).

The Romanian people: *curriculum vitae.* Reflection on the history of Romanian time and space is, with few exceptions, a constant in Vasile Băncilă's thought. Since 1955, he has been constantly returning to his notes, which he calls, in a sort of personification, *the autobiography of the Romanian people.* Before looking at the episodes that record statements from this *curriculum vitae*, let us stop at a finished text such as the one on "The Miracle of Romanian Unity" (31 January 1971, Băncilă, 2015, see pp. 270–273), in its own way a kind of autobiography of our solidarity as a nation.

These are lines that summarize the essential determinations revealed by the history of the Romanians, in which they have shown unity of language and culture, plus the desire to be together. It is not a question of unity or an absolute identity ("nor would this be good"), but of a historical reality in which an ethnic community, individualistic in structure, has always had the will to create a *unitary state.*

It is a kind of Greek miracle and a historical enigma for a people who have not had the "taste of local, provincial führerism" politically. The explanation of the enigma is relatively simple: the imposition everywhere, from top to bottom, of the Latin language, which has been preserved in its popular form with the syntax we still inherit today. Here he identifies the Latin myth that subsists through the consciousness of Latinity.

Temporally speaking, our unity is a gift that the Roman administration and civilization gave us first, through the Latin language, just as the same unity is also a Dacian gift. This is the Dacian myth, illustrated by Lucian Blaga in a significant essay: "Revolt of our non-Latin background" (*Thought*, 15 September 1921), but to which Vasile Pârvan, Nae Ionescu, Motru also contributed. A unity to which are added the influences coming from the migrating or immigrating peoples, accidents that, with time, have disappeared.

But the Latin dimension is fundamental: "We are not a bastard son of Latinity (or branch), as Mussolini said, probably at the suggestion of the Hungarians; the Romanian language is the most Latin of the non-Roman languages (the Russians also recognized it)." (Băncilă, 2015, p. 418)

And those who moved the process of our ethnogenesis after the arrival of the Slavs (see the Communist historian Mihail Roller) "eat borscht – meaning they tell lies", falsify our being, amputate our history by several hundred years. If we have Romanised the Slavs, it is a sure sign that, at that time, there was a definite and powerful ethnic group, and a large one at that; and this in the absence of structures such as the state, the administration, the school, the army – it was, says Iorga admirably, the period of *stateless villages*. Our ethnogenesis represents Thracian Dacia, says Băncilă conclusively. And what is needed is the *myth of Romanianism:* "We are not xenophobes or anti-Semites, but we must be *phyllo-Semites.*" (Băncilă, 2015, p. 432)

Among the priority occupations of the Romanians, shepherding was a basic one, which is why the phenomenon of transhumance transformed the shepherds into the *bearers of Romanian unity*. Unlike other ethnic areas, our transhumance was, due to geography, a large-scale one and supported by a natural discipline, besides being a real anthropological phenomenon. Băncilă does not hesitate to invoke folklore which: "is full of echoes of the idyll between village girls, sibyls, and traveling demigods, fed on sweet milk and lamb" (Băncilă, 2015, p. 272).

The French influence in the nineteenth century *perfected* the Latin foundation of our language and culture, being a kind of "*purifier* in polluted water: in a short time, it drove out a lot of Slavisms, Turkisms, Hungarianisms, etc.". We were also lucky in this respect with the boyars, otherwise we would not have been able to hire French teachers, or to buy French books. Add to this the beneficial efforts of the French Mission (1916–1918), the French teachers (1918–1940), even Napoleon III and his wife.

*

Similar to the transhumance in terms of influence was the religious phenomenon, especially through the books spread to all Romanians. Orthodoxy has united us and has also made us preserve and deepen our connection with the Cosmos and nature.

To all this, also with a unifying effect, Băncilă added "the arrival of 200 students from Transylvania, in 1919, at the University of Bucharest (and intellectuals from Wallachia who went to Transylvania). The Saintly Voivodes hostel was a *laboratory of unification*, of perfecting this unification, a cultural-ethnic 'osmosis'" (Băncilă, 2015, p. 273). Together with the train that brought them to and from Transylvania, these dormitories represented "the last ring that contributed to the shaping of Romanian unity".

These are determinations of our ethnicity that obsess Băncilă, hence their repetition in various historical moments (see, for example, the summaries in the notes "What kept us Romanians" and "The Romanian Miracle"; Băncilă, 2015, see pp. 425–426). This does not prevent Băncilă from overlooking an important contradiction in Romanian history: those who supported modern nationalism (Iorga, Nae Ionescu, Crainic, etc.) had the same ideas, only they quarrelled terribly among themselves; philosophers and literary critics (Pârvan, Densușianu, etc.) had the same ideas, only that they too quarrelled terribly among themselves, "made little churches, poured out their (sometimes thin) venom", even "the gentle Motru jumped on Blaga" (and vice versa, proof: the pamphlets in *Saeculum*, 1943); even the diaspora was divided by quarrels.

Compared to families, peoples are a kind of orphans, growing up alone (*Self-made ethnos*), without knowing their parents and without anyone telling them where they come from and what their history is. Except in the patriarchal phase, when their development is helped by religion, by God, aspects which have an idyllic character. And when there is no science of history, all kinds of legends are created at once.

*

In 1960, invoking an argument from the Apostle Paul, he wondered whether the Hellenists were those Thracians whom he does not cite in his *Epistle to the Colossians*: "Where there is no longer Hellene and Jew, circumcised and uncircumcised, barbarian, Scythian, slave or free, but all, and in all Christ". Instead, he mentions the Scythians and not the Thracians, because, says Băncilă, they "were not considered foreigners, but as a kind of kinsmen of the Greeks"; he mentions them as "very different, precisely to show that the Christian religion makes no distinction between them" (Băncilă, 2015, p. 383).

And in December 1974, Băncilă was overcome with discontent, because the Romanian nation had not yet fully realised itself. For this, a few more Eminescu, Blaga, Nae Ionescu, Iorga, Pârvan, Enescu, Brâncuși, Grigorescu, Anghel would have to appear. To which were added two *collective suicides*:

mass abortions, which reduced the country's population, and those who chose to go *abroad*, to the West, a sort of "*second abandonment of Dacia* (after the Aurelian one)", the flight of Romanian citizens across the borders. Losses that amplified the disaster of 1916–1918, or that of 1941–1945.

*

Throughout their troubled history, the Romanians have not once stood on the edge of tragedy or the precipice. We were, as Simion Mehedinți said, an *autarchic country*, but, paradoxically, we were at the mercy of foreigners, those who gorged themselves on our wealth and beauty ("rich country, poor people"). The historical past was hard, with its bullies, with three greedy empires: Austro-Hungary, the Slavs, the Turks. Hence Băncilă's Christian thought, imploring the divine: "Keep us, O Lord, from water, from fire, from the coming of other nations upon us..." (Băncilă, 2015, p. 417)

And these aspects characterize a people made up largely of peasants, a conservative community that did not make revolutions, triggered mainly by the middle classes, the bourgeoisie or the proletarians (this is why "Communism was so keen to proletarianize the world"; idem, 2015, see pp. 428–429).

The representation of society, for the peasants, is a kind of cosmic stratification, and the uprisings they participated in have something of an apocalyptic nature. True, they were also in revolutions or wars, but they went there with "*metaphysical* conviction"; "socially, the Romanians made uprisings; nationally, they made revolutions".

In the summer of the same year, 1978, Băncilă observed the unprecedented appearance in the history of Romanians of two phenomena: the agonizing feeling, as a nation, when some patriots thought of the country like the French: "si la France périt..." ("if France were to perish"); then, taking up an older thought, the feeling of departure, which called into question our millennial autochthonism; to which he added another aspect, also noted in another context: by reducing the birth rate, the Romanians are doing nothing but implicitly committing suicide as a nation.

Most of Băncilă's notes on our history can be placed under a reflection on the importance of historical memory in the formation of the Romanian nation, written shortly before he began his eternity: "National memories are the memories of your larger-than-life person: your historical self, as the images *of space* are of your larger self: the ethnic man has a personal self and a geographic-historical self: together they represent your destiny." (Băncilă, 2015, p. 435)

*

Vasile Băncilă meditated on the Romanian destiny with a certain tension in a text somewhat unique (1 July 1974), composed of six parts (see Băncilă, 2015, pp. 294–303). A nation, he says, "must *think about* their *destiny* and give themselves an ideal, a purpose, a mission of spirit (not of shoulders, etc.)" (Băncilă, 2015, p. 294). Initially, it synthesizes the interpretations that have been given to the destiny or the role of our people. Romania has been a bulwark for the West against the invasion of barbarians, particularly the Asians: "We have bled for ourselves, but also for the Westerners – and for our Christian law (Christianity gave us our law in the fight against the Crescent. It was the *ethic of our ethnic and militant conscience*, culminating in Brâncoveanu and Stephen the Great)." (Băncilă, 2015, see pp. 294–296)

Romania has also been given another role: that of spiritual filter. For a millennium, "we have been purifying the exotic peoples or individuals – *the asymmetric ones* – who have come and isolated themselves among us, causing smaller or larger septicaemias". Our ethnic pattern has always been altered by the misfortunes caused by Jews, Gypsies, Slavs, Mongols, Turks, Greeks (with the last ones, structurally related). Moral corruption, harm to culture and language, "hybrid types, intelligent bitches" (*à la* Ralea), "the destruction of some Romanians, so much boorishness towards them: that Ivașcu".

A third perspective on our role: we have given the world a synthetic (not eclectic!) culture, a "*cardinalization* of the culture of the spirit, but in Greco-Roman symmetry and the Getic-Christian transfiguration"; the synthetic spirit we also discover in Orthodoxy; Romanian culture "it is not extremist, like the Russian one, with dramatic one-sidedness (*did Legionarism have something non-Russian?*), it has no prozaisms or Bulgarian tropisms".

Băncilă wonders which of these interpretations to adhere to. The first becomes redundant, because the question of defending the West has become superfluous (the studies of Henri Massis, *Defence of the West*, 1926, and Julien Benda, *The Betrayal of the Scholars*, 1927, were no longer relevant). The same cannot be said of the second role, for there was a pressing "problem of removing *the soul residues* and moral *pollutions* produced by asymmetries of all kinds over decades (and hundreds) of years".

This expressed a maximum intransigence towards the *ausländers*: Bulgarians, Hungarians and especially Jews (many worked in culture, but they should also be involved in other things, including agriculture). Without being xenophobic, but fearing the danger of Jewry, Băncilă's attitude is radically partisan, even if it can be said to be *fair* and *dignified*: "Let the Jewified, opportunist, mangy lechers be stigmatized: let it be known that one cannot [make] a career through them." (Băncilă, 2015, p. 297)

Nor does he forget the Gypsies, anathematized until then. On seeing our orchestras, some Westerners, says Băncilă, would ask if Romanians are black. He is worried about the danger of Gypsies, he thinks it wouldn't have been bad if the Gypsies had stayed in Transnistria, taken there by Antonescu. But he thinks there exists a solution that can save them: to re-educate them, to straighten them out, to save both them and us.

*

Finally, the role of the Romanian people remained predominantly cultural, in other words: "*what kind of culture* and its degree *of intensity,* or emphasis of culture in destiny" (Băncilă, 2015, p. 297). Here he invokes that doubled polarity: the first represented by the rationalist (intellectualist) pole and the mystical (abyssal-sidereal) pole; the other, organically linked to the first, the individual and the communitarian pole.

Through the lucidity and lyricism of knowledge specific to us, Băncilă notes the presence of lyrical poetry, the skill for essays, advocacy, journalism, mathematics, philosophy (without being a systemic one –!) or positive research (he does not insist on the particular stamp that would differentiate us from other cultural spaces). As for mysticism, particularly that of the peasant, it is "balanced, serene, of a Christian temple and in *osmosis with nature,* with the Cosmos", expressing "an ontological vision: it is a Greco-Latin mysticism, Thracian (Getic), Christian in fulfilment".

The features of mysticism are those that also give the foundations of our culture and spirituality, where we find a differentiated optimism, often melancholic, but without having an existentialist tragism. He sees in Tudor Arghezi[26] a creator who "is not altogether Romanian, because of his impurity and his grumbling, dramatic, hoarse doubts", as Cioran's existentialism "is certainly not Romanian", and this is because Romanians do not have metaphysical despair in their blood, as Germans or Slavs may have. It is the Romanian balance that dominates: in music, in sculpture, in the Orthodox faith, the latter being "*a model of reason and mystical spirit: Platonism in Christianity*".

Beyond this gnostic bipolarity (rationalism-mysticism), Băncilă identifies another one: ontological or moral, expressed through the individual and community poles (which I have already referred to in another context). He takes up his earlier notes on the family community, the village, the nation, the ontological community (its modes: monism, pantheism, Christian dualism).

Vasile Băncilă concludes, in the last instance, that such a bent spiritual bipolarity that characterizes our ethnicity is "like a lens with two foci", "something very complex and alive, a dynamic 'dialectic', producing cultural creations in a varied and harmonious way" (Băncilă, 2015, p. 302; he praises Ion Heliade Rădulescu's[27] work *The Balance between Antitheses*, a document to study for the harmony of the two foci).

He agrees with various perspectives, but with a single and fundamental condition: that no fatal dissociations take place, because such operations are not Romanian. And he lists, slightly caustically, what we don't need in the crucible of our culture: "Voltairian indifferentism in religion"; "stifling Slavic culture, with dark mysticism, with quasi-pathological hallucinations"; "Semitic culture: Gherea etc. have falsified, in part, Romanian culture. What do we have in common with the Fundoianu fauna, to say that... we can no longer do without *Fundoieni, Blecheri, Călugări, Breslași* etc.? who eat away at the harmony of Romanian culture!" (Băncilă, 2015, p. 302; we do not at all subscribe to his obtuse opinions, on the contrary).

Reservations are also expressed towards Communist materialism, towards Conta (a law professor who wanted to create a philosophical system; moreover, the relationship of his thought to positivism and empiricism needs to be reviewed), again towards Cioran ("with his macabre, desperate spiritualism").

*

For the Romanian spirit, the supreme value is represented by: "a Beauty in which the moral, the religious, the social are integrated; in this sense, God is Beauty itself, absolute Beauty" (Băncilă, 2015, p. 303). We cannot have allogenous guardian spirits in the Romanian space: "such as Voltaire, A. France, Mordechai..." (Mordechai: Karl Marx). He admits, it is true, cultural links with everyone, but we must make the most of our *native heritage* (he quotes a line from Iorga: to be everywhere, you have to be from somewhere).

From such a deep approach to our ethnic background, another example focused on researching "The idea of health and folk medicine in Romania" (see Băncilă, 2015, pp. 274–293).[28] The main character of this conference was the traditional peasant of the Wallachian plains, but, through the rustic mentality it explored, the Romanian people themselves were largely targeted.

He admirably analyses the Romanian's way of working, his diet (with a fruitful form of peasant alcoholism: wine as a *sign of life*, the one that gives man strength), clothing, the idea of cleanliness, the experience of holidays, the phenomenon of illness and how to get well (with an excursion into the relationship between religion and magic), the medical and extra-medical value of folk medicine, the ethnic dimension of the latter.

At the end of the text, he made a number of urgent demands: the collection of all medical folklore (he welcomed the Chinese government's gesture to set up a Faculty of Folk Medicine), and the scientific exploitation of all folk medicines and directions. We must not destroy anything, Vasile Băncilă urged, but everything must be collected and put in order; even if all the folk material will be ineffective for human health, it remains valuable for the theory of our culture, as a kind of philosophy lesson.

A wave of regret, of melancholy crept into Vasile Băncilă's imperial peasant meditation: "Medical folklore, as a living function, disappears, because the peasant disappears"; but mankind must not suffer from amnesia: "The values of the past form the consistency of the self. The earth will remain our foundation", because, according to Christian theology, "even Paradise is a kind of transfigured earth".

The last thought of the septuagenarian Vasile Băncilă's conference was like the arch of a circle opening towards Heaven: "I'm interested in what's on the moon, in the sun, in the stars. But I am just as interested in the stars that burn in the Romanian soul" (Băncilă, 2015, p. 293).

Notes

[1] Until Băncilă's conference, several authors had tried to understand the Romanian people: Drăghicescu, D. (1907). *From the psychology of the Romanian people*; Rădulescu-Motru, C. (1910). *The soul of our people. Good qualities and defects*; (1932). *Vocation, decisive factor in the culture of peoples*; (1936). *Romanianism, catechism of a new spirituality*; (1942). *Romanian ethnic*; Ralea, M. (1927). *The Romanian phenomenon*, to which we could add the metaphysical-cultural vision of some of Lucian Blaga's works.

[2] The "Old Kingdom" is the *Kingdom of Romania* before 1918, made up of the territories of *Moldova* and *Herța Land* (excluding *Bukovina* and *Bessarabia*), *Wallachia, Oltenia* and *Dobrogea*, including the *Cadrilater* (i.e., Southern Dobrogea). The inhabitants of this Romanian land were called *Wallachians*.

[3] In 1962, Băncilă exclaims imperatively: *the time of the Transylvanian school has come*; he firmly believes that we need to make the most of our Latinity if we are not to perish: "Language is now becoming the most important ethnic factor"; we should *also Romanianize the stones*; he notes that "the people have begun to speak the cultured language", that they are "more Latinized and more Frenchified than the intellectuals" (see Băncilă, 2015, p. 387).

[4] Iancu, A. (1824–1872). Revolutionary with an important role in the Transylvanian revolt of 1848, Romanian lawyer from Transylvania.

[5] The three are prominent representatives of a phenomenon called the *Transylvanian School*, which aimed at the cultural and social-political emancipation of the Romanians in Transylvania.

[6] In 1784, there was a revolt of the Transylvanian serf peasants that has remained in Romanian history as the *Horia, Cloşca and Crişan Revolt*. They demanded the removal of the feudal constraints to which the rural population of this part of Romania was subjected.

[7] Şaguna, A. (1809-1873). Orthodox Metropolitan of Transylvania, militant for the rights of the Orthodox Romanians in this national territory.

[8] Diaconovici Loga, C. (1770–1850). Romanian educator, teacher and writer. Among his writings: *Calligraphic Characters for the People's Schools* (1813), *Instruction for Romanian Schools in Banat* (1815), *Grammar for the Instruction of Young People* (1822), *The Life of our Lord Jesus Christ, the Saviour of the World, with 12 illustrations* (1831).

[9] Puşcariu, S. (1877–1948). Romanian publicist, philologist, Right-wing ideological professor, linguist. Among his writings: *Istro-Romanian studies* (3 vols, 1906–1929), *History of Romanian literature. Ancient times* (1921), *Romanian language*, vol. I, *General overview* (1940), *Mounted on two centuries* (1968), *Research and studies* (1974).

[10] Maniu, I. (1873–1953). Romanian politician, president of the National Peasant Party; see Băncilă, V. (2015). *Works*, vol. X, quoted edition, pp. 247–255.

[11] Cantacuzino, Ş. (1640–1688). Ruler of Wallachia (1678–1688).

[12] Brâncoveanu, C. (1654–1714). Ruler of Wallachia (1688–1714).

[13] The Brave, Michael (1558–1601). Ruler of Wallachia (1593–1600).

[14] See Ionescu, N. (2003). *Theology. Integral religious publishings*, edited by Dora Mezdrea. Sibiu: Deisis Publishing House.

[15] Cârţan, G. (1849–1911). Known as Badea Cârţan, was a Romanian peasant who fought for the independence of the Romanians in Transylvania; he distributed Romanian books, smuggled from Romania, to the villages. He travelled on foot to Rome because he wanted to see Trajan's Column and other testimonies to the Latin origins of the Romanian people.

[16] Eliade, P. (1869–1914). Romanian professor and literary historian. Among his writings: *De l'influence française sur l'esprit public en Roumanie. Les origines: Étude sur l'état de la société roumaine à l'époque des règnes phanariotes* (1898), *La Fontaine's Philosophy* (1901), *Grigore Alexandrescu and his French teachers* (1904), *Histoire de l'esprit public en Roumanie au dix-neuvième siècle* (2 vols., 1905, 1914).

[17] Băncilă wanted to apply to Romanian society an idea from a statement by Pamfil Şeicaru (July 1940): "In a country where everyone wants to dictate, the foreigner dictates" (Băncilă, 2015, p. 315).

[18] Could it be Swedish writer Selma Lagerlöf's *Wonderful journey across Sweden*? A book in two volumes (1906–1907).

[19] Allusion to a song from Transylvania: "Siebenbürgen susse heimat – Sibiu, sweet motherland".

[20] Rădulescu-Pogoneanu, V. (1910–1962). Romanian diplomat, anti-Communist.

[21] Mehedinţi, S. (1868–1962). Romanian geographer and geopolitician. Among his writings: *Die Kartographische Induktion* (1900), *Introduction to the Study of Geography* (1904), *Die rumänische Steppe* (1904), *To the New Generation* (1912), *The Political Man* (1915), *Titu Maiorescu* (1925).

[22] Carol II (1893–1953). King of Romania (1930–1940).

[23] The term is a toponym used especially in the mountain area: it means *cold* (*water*).

[24] Grigorescu, N. (1838–1907). The first founder of modern Romanian painting. He excelled in religious themes, landscapes, portraits and nudes.

[25] Brâncuși, C. (1876–1957). Romanian sculptor with a fundamental contribution to the renewal of artistic language and plastic vision in contemporary sculpture. Among his works: *Laocoon's Head* (1900), *Child* and *Child's Head* (1906), *The Kiss* (first version, 1907), *Two Caryatids* and *Prodigal Son* (1915). The ensemble from Tîrgu-Jiu: *The Gate of the Kiss, The Table of Silence and The Column of Endless (Gratitude)* was "rediscovered" in 1964 by the culturologists of the totalitarian regime in Romania.

[26] Arghezi, T. (1880–1967). The pseudonym of Ion Nae Theodorescu, an original writer with a strong pamphlet and polemic, an author who marked another era of Romanian literature after Mihai Eminescu. Among his writings: *Appropriate Words* (1927), *Wooden Icon* (1929), *Flowers of Mold* (1931), *The Eyes of the Mother of God* (1934), *The Cemetery of the Annunciation* (1934), *Song of Man* (1955), *With my cane, walking through Bucharest* (1968).

[27] See Heliade Rădulescu, I. (1976). *Equilibrium between antitheses*, 2 vol., Bucharest: Minerva Publishing House.

[28] The original form was that of a lecture that Băncilă gave on June 18, 1973 at the Union of Medical Studies Societies; it was then included in the volume, but also circulated in the form of an extract with the title: "The idea of health and popular medicine among the Romanian peasant of yesterday".

Epilogue

Springing from both ethnic and spiritual factors of the Romanian cultural space, Vasile Băncilă's metaphysics awaits its exegetes in order to be (re)evaluated and restored to its legitimate rights. Forbidden by the totalitarian regime for ideological reasons, its author was unjustly marginalized as a philosopher, given freedom of expression in small spoonfuls, only a few times. However, the climate opened up by the post-Communist period has allowed half of Băncilă's work, estimated by the publisher Dora Mezdrea at around 32 volumes, to be put into circulation.

The interpretations that have been made and will continue to be made in the margins of his philosophical work will explore, I am sure, the surfaces and depths of his writings and will decant the value and originality of Băncilă's ideas, of what he left us through his texts, and not – as he playfully says somewhere – through the grid of what he could have given us.

We will thus see the national imprint of his projects, but also the way in which they synchronize with the atmosphere of Western thought. Finally, we are interested in the coefficient of novelty that his metaphysical discourse brings, both in terms of local philosophy and – if necessary – in terms of universal philosophy. In any case, the author must be given a place in the table of values of the history of Romanian philosophy, a place unquestionably claimed by the existence of a *work* in the framework of which we have the projection, admittedly unfinished, of a possible *system of philosophy*.

*

The question of how original Vasile Băncilă was in his ethno-spiritualist metaphysics remains open. With a certain exigency and without taking into account his published and unpublished texts, we could repeat here, about part of his work, what he himself once said about Arthur Schopenhauer, on whose writings he wanted to write his doctorate: "an impressive conglomeration of adverse virtualities; and his philosophy, for those who observe carefully, is a real explosion of disparate tendencies in potentiality". This is particularly true of the crates of files left by Băncilă to posterity. But our quotation also suggests something else: stylistically speaking, much of Vasile Băncilă's writing can be identified with Schopenhauer's, to the extent that he combines the literary or lyrical with the philosophical. The same stylistic binomial: literary art-philosophy also shows us that the thinker Vasile Băncilă is somehow repeating Blagas lesson in the first place; but he is also not far from Constantin Noica's utterance or the syllogisms constructed by Mircea Vulcănescu and Cioran.

Of these stylistic marks, the Blagian one has undisputed primacy. Giving a profound exegesis of Blaga's work (see *Blaga, Romanian energy*, 1938), the stylist Vasile Băncilă has contaminated himself with a kind of literaturisation of philosophy, with a somewhat hermaphroditic discourse, as Băncilă himself would say. Moreover, we see that he either expresses his adherence to Blaga's ideas or subtly increases them, except when he departs from them categorically, especially on the questions of *salvation*, religion, Blaga's relationship with God.

*

I received the metaphysician Vasile Băncilă *sine ira et studio*. However, I did not hide the shortcomings and shades of his reflection, the resentments expressed towards various thinkers, the xenophobic accents directed towards Jews and, partly, towards Gypsies. I have approached him in the same way that he himself has treated others – without mincing his words, events and attitudes.

Receiving a philosophical system, Băncilă says at one point that: "you occasionally get to places where the argumentation becomes worryingly sparse and you see the author instinctively resort to paralogisms or, in the rarer case, when he is aware of what is happening, sophisms". It is an approximation that can, unfortunately, also be self-referential, and I have used it sparingly in our exegetical approach.

*

Let's not easily overlook the philosopher's critical reaction to the hell set up by the Communist regime. As we have already seen, we find harsh judgments against Romanian national-Communism in the writings he left to posterity. In particular, he sanctions the human tragedy that it brought about in Romania, a country that had become, under the dictatorship, a desolate place in terms of the soul, or rather, a desert of the soul. A desert that changed even the meaning of his metaphysical meditation, as he said in a confession made in 1962, somewhat at the beginning of the totalitarian hell: "my philosophy fights against the decline of the spirit: today, the values I believe in, the classical values of man, are in decline, in danger of death; so my philosophy *today* is an *agonistic* philosophy: it fights death".

Only to talk about the birth, a decade and a half later (in 1976): "of new man, the laboratory and plank demiurge, the human termite armed with 'science'", the "original" product of a miserable *industrial and political romanticism*.

Schopenhauerianly speaking, such a form of philosophical reflection was in subtle and full accord with Vasile Băncilă's temperament.

And one more insurmountable thing. Towards the twilight of his life, the thinker made a sort of nomenclature of the meanings of philosophy, over 20 of them. They were actually stylistic nuances, temperamental-cognitive receptions, just as facts happen inside consumer aesthetic when decoding a literary work. The last of these senses accorded to philosophy is formidably significant.

Both the most rational and the most irrational of the disciplines of the spirit, philosophy was, says the octogenarian Vasile Băncilă at "a very old age", "a profession of faith or generalized (determined) perplexity; in very rare cases, a *sanctity* (if philosophy helps). Compared to the dog, which hides its provisions in the ground and forgets them there (rotting)".

That philosophy was, for Vasile Băncilă a noble aid for his long intellectual exercise is a fact. We are not so sure, however, whether he reached the threshold of sanctity through the philosophy that he constructed as a potential *system*. We fear not, apart from a kind of sanctity of his literary-philosophical imagination, a stylistic piety towards words, concepts or metaphors. It is also the reason why the *provisions* he left us do not deteriorate, but, on the contrary, are a model of exceptional spiritual nourishment for the philosophy of the Romanian space.

Vasile Băncilă was and remains a *spiritualist* philosopher, with a completely open belief in the Absolute, in the Great One, in God. He has always been so because of his temperament and convictions, and the obtuseness and utopia of Communism led him to reach the Logos as soon as possible and, due to the cultural insufficiency of this oligarchic and inhuman system, to believe "in spirit as the ultimate ontic factor for the salvation of man". He is a spiritualist who makes almost excessive use of *antinomy* (which, he believes, Kant would not have understood), a legitimate strategy in the sphere of metaphysics (but also of religion), for otherwise "it would be to *impoverish* the Real, to understand it unilaterally". A Real whose essences are equally abstract and plastic, in the manner of the art of Brâncuși.

*

So: *Make way!* – so would sound the command of the metaphysician, ethicist and moralist[1] Vasile Băncilă, a command not at all pathetic or indulgent, but uttered in a clamorous tone; as an argument for such an imperative, coming from the best of all possible worlds, he points with his finger, as I have shown, to the edited and unpublished printed essays, along with the dozens of stacks of his manuscripts, many of them in the form of thematically titled worksheets.

The hundreds and thousands of Vasile Băncilă's worksheets are, basically, the pages of an interesting *atypical metaphysical diary*, certainly one of ideas, in which the author expounds concepts, his own syllogisms, or fragmentarily enters into a dialogue on various topics with philosophers of all calibres and from all times, including philosophers considered "anonymous". A *diary-deposition* that should give food for thought to those interested in the Mendeleev table of values of Romanian philosophy.

Notes

[1] For the last two hypostases of the work, see Stroe, C. (2021). *The ethical-moral dimension of Vasile Băncilă's philosophical system. The role of morals and the constellation of morality in his ethical conception.* Brăila: Istros Publishing House of the "Carol I" Museum of Brăila.

Bibliography

Băncilă, I. (2000a). *Arch over times.* Brăila Museum: Istros Publishing House.

Băncilă, V. (2003). *Works,* vol. I. Brăila Museum: Istros Publishing House.

Băncilă, V. (2004). *Works,* vol. II. Brăila Museum: Istros Publishing House.

Băncilă, V. (2007). *Works,* vol. V. Brăila Museum: Istros Publishing House.

Băncilă, V. (2008). *Works,* vol. VI. Brăila Museum, Istros Publishing House.

Băncilă, V. (2009). *Works,* vol. VII. Brăila Museum: Istros Publishing House.

Băncilă, V. (2015). *Works,* vol. X. "Carol I" Museum of Brăila: Istros Publishing House.

Bădescu, I. (1994). *Eminescu's sociology.* Constanța: Porto-Franco Publishing House.

Cioran, E. (1995). *Letters to the folks back home.* Bucharest: Humanitas Publishing House.

Dungaciu, D. (2011). *The Interwar Elite. Romanian Sociology in the European Context.* Bucharest: Small Wallachia Publishing House.

Heidegger, M. (1982). *The Origin of the Work of Art.* Bucharest: Univers Publishing House.

Ghișe, D., Gogoneață, N., coord. (1980). *History of Romanian Philosophy,* vol. II (1900–1944, part I). Bucharest: Publishing House of the Academy of the Socialist Republic of Romania.

Ionescu, N. (1990). *The Weatherwane.* Bucharest: The "Weatherwane" Publishing House.

Maiorescu, T. (1980). *Philosophical Exposes.* Craiova: Romanian Writing Publishing House.

Mihăilescu, D. C., "Recovering archeology", 2020, *Horizon,* no. 10.

Noica, C. (1992). *Sunday Essays.* Bucharest: Humanitas Publishing House.

Pătrășcanu, L. (1946). *Currents and trends in Romanian philosophy.* Bucharest: Socec Publishing House.

Petrovici, I., 1937, *Journal of Philosophy.* XXII, no. 4, Oct. –Dec.

Popa, V. (2006). *Vasile Băncilă. The man and the philosopher.* Brăila Museum, Brăila: Istros Publishing House.

Scriban, A. (1939). *Dictionary of the Romanian language.* Iași: "Good Press" Institut of Graphic Arts Publishing.

Vlăduțescu, Gh. (2002). *Unconventionally, about Romanian philosophy* (2002). Bucharest: Paideia Publishing House.

Vulcănescu, M. (1990). *Nae Ionescu. As I knew him.* Bucharest: Humanitas Publishing House

Further Reading

Băncilă, V. (1993). *Aphorisms and para-aphorisms*. vol. I. Timişoara: Marineasa Publishing House.

Băncilă, V. (1995). *Lucian Blaga, Romanian energy*. Timişoara: Marineasa Publishing House.

Băncilă, V. (1996). *The religious initiation of the child*. Bucharest: Anastasia Publishing House.

Băncilă, V. (1997). *Philosophy of ages*. Bucharest: Anastasia Publishing House.

Băncilă, V. (1999). *Small testaments*, vol. I–II. Bucharest: Eminescu Publishing House.

Băncilă, V. (2000). *The space of the Bărăgan Plains*. Bucharest: Museum of Romanian Literature Publishing House; Museum of Brăila: Istros Publishing House.

Băncilă, V. – Blaga, L. (2001). *Correspondence*. Bucharest: Museum of Romanian Literature, Museum of Brăila: Istros Publishing House.

Băncilă, V. (2006a). *Works*, vol. III. Brăila Museum: Istros Publishing House.

Băncilă, V. (2006b). *Works*, vol. IV. Brăila Museum: Istros Publishing House.

Băncilă, V. (2016). *Works*, vol. XII. "Carol I" Museum of Brăila: Istros Publishing House.

Constantinescu, P. (1967). *Works*, vol. 2, Bucharest: Eminescu Publishing House.

Dungaciu, D. (2011). *The Interwar Elite. Romanian Sociology in the European Context* (Contributions to a Sociology of Sociology). Bucharest: Small Wallachia Publishing House.

Heliade Rădukescu, I. (1976). *Equilibrium between anthiteses*. Bucharest: Minerva Publishing House.

Ionescu, N. (1996). *Course on the history of metaphysics*. Bucharest: Anastasia Publishing House.

Ionescu, N. (2003). *Theology. Integral religious publishings*, edited by Dora Mezdrea. Sibiu: Deisis Publishing House.

Rădulescu-Motru, C. (1984). *Energetic personalism and other writings*, Study, anthology and notes by Gh. Al. Cazan, text established by Gheorghe Pienescu. Bucharest: Eminescu Publishing House.

Stroe, C. (2021). *The ethical-moral dimension of Vasile Băncilă's philosophical system. The role of morals and the constellation of morality in his ethical conception*. The "Carol I" Museum of Brăila: Istros Publishing House of Brăila.

Author's bio

Ion Dur - university studies in Bucharest, Romania, Faculty of Philosophy. Ph. D. in Philosophy from the University of Bucharest. Ph.D. Scientific advisor at the Technical University of Cluj-Napoca, University Centre North of Baia Mare, Faculty of Letters: B.A. in philosophy. Professor at the "Lucian Blaga University of Sibiu, Dean at the Faculty of Journalism of the same institution. As editor-in-chief, he coordinated the *Saeculum* Magazine (new series) for twenty years and is now its director of the new series. Member of the Writers' Union of Romania, with seven prizes awarded by its Sibiu subsidiary. He obtained the Mircea Florian award for Philosophy of the Romanian Academy.

He has published essays, chronicles, studies and articles on philosophy, literature, aesthetics, literary criticism, media criticism in several Romanian and international cultural publications; collaborated with the Romanian Radio Broadcasting Services, on public and private television; was a participant and organizer at/of national and international symposiums.

He has written over twenty books of philosophical essays and monographs (Cioran, Constantin Noica, Vasile Băncilă, Horia Stamatu, Nae Ionescu) and translated in collaboration two works by Hannah Arendt: *The Origins of Totalitarianism* (with Mircea Ivănescu; 1994, Bucharest Humanitas Publishing House) and *Crises of the Republic* (with D.-I. Cenuşer; 1999, Bucharest: Humanitas Publishing House).

Index

Lightning Source UK Ltd.
Milton Keynes UK
UKHW021958051022
410003UK00008B/425/J